MAN MADE

MAN MADE

A Stupid Quest for Masculinity

JOEL STEIN

GRAND CENTRAL
PUBLISHING

NEW YORK   BOSTON

Grand Central Publishing
Hachette Book Group
237 Park Avenue
New York, NY 10017

www.HachetteBookGroup.com

Printed in the United States of America

RRD-C

First Edition: May 2012
10 9 8 7 6 5 4 3 2 1

Grand Central Publishing is a division of Hachette Book Group, Inc.
The Grand Central Publishing name and logo is a trademark of Hachette Book Group, Inc.

The Hachette Speakers Bureau provides a wide range of authors for speaking events. To find out more, go to www.hachettespeakersbureau.com or call (866) 376-6591.

The publisher is not responsible for websites (or their content) that are not owned by the publisher.
[That might seem obvious. But our lawyer thinks it is not.]

Library of Congress Cataloging-in-Publication Data
Stein, Joel.
    Man made : a stupid quest for masculinity / Joel Stein.—1st ed.
       p. cm.
    ISBN 978-0-446-57312-2 (regular edition : alk. paper)
    1. Masculinity—Humor.   2. Fatherhood—Humor.   I. Title.
PN6231.M45S76 2012
818'.607—dc23

                                              2012001146

INTRODUCTION

This is not how a man feels.

I should be lighting a cigar, high-fiving the doctor, and grabbing my genitals to celebrate that my sperm are manly, even for sperm. But when I look at the tiny splotch of Doppler weather pattern on the screen and Cassandra's obstetrician says it means we're probably having a boy, I do not do any of these things. Instead, I have my first panic attack—my hearing and vision receding, my heart pumping as if I were doing something manly that makes your heart pump. Which I am not. I am merely picturing having to go camping and fix a car and use a hammer and throw a football and watch professionals throw footballs and figure out whether to be sad or happy about the results of said football throwing.

So I hope the doctor is wrong. No man has ever stared so hard at a screen and hoped a blur was a vagina since they eliminated those 1980s cable boxes where you could press two buttons at once and get scrambled porn.

"A boy. That's great," I say.

"You wanted a girl, didn't you?" Cassandra says.

Until now, I thought I didn't care. Apparently I care so much that I said "that's great" in a deflated tone that people never use when they are told a child's gender, despite the fact that there's nowhere to take that conversation. Yet somehow everyone else can manufacture excitement, as if they're thinking: *A boy! That's great! It's one of the two major genders!* It's not as if we live in China, where they can continue, *A boy! That's great! Now we don't have to abandon it on the top of a mountain!*

"On some level I suspected you didn't want a boy," Cassandra says. "But you're not one of those touchy-feely yoga guys who really get women. So in that sense, I thought you would love a boy. It's not like you're sensitive to the needs of women."

I've had one minute to deal with my insecurities about my masculinity when I find out I'm also inadequate in bed. I hope that, within the seven months before the baby is due, Cassandra is able to generate more sensitive, maternal feelings. Towards me.

At home Cassandra mocks my freak-out. She argues that while I may not be tough enough to hang out with men, I can probably gin up enough testosterone to keep up with a small boy. "Especially the boy we'll have. If he turned out to be a jock, I'd say, 'What genes are those?'" She said. The only thing worse than having your masculinity questioned by your pregnant wife is having your paternity questioned by your pregnant wife.

She's not wrong, though. I don't think of myself as a man so much as a person who happens to have a penis. If I got dropped on an island inhabited by a less technologically advanced society, I'd be killed immediately for being useless. Though the one time I actually was dropped on an island inhabited by a less technologically advanced society I was greeted with chilled scented towels and grilled lobster tails. This was on my honeymoon. An hour later, I called the front desk because there was a lizard in our room.

But I've never suffered for my lack of manliness. I've always had girlfriends. I have plenty of guy friends. I've had great jobs. My wife, Cassandra, has never complained about my wimpiness.

In fact, she's so disgusted by sports and fraternities that she slept with at least one guy who turned out to be gay. I am unable to get a firm count on gay ex-boyfriends because Cassandra had a much more sexually active college social life than I did. And post-college. "Basically everyone I slept with is probably gay according to *somebody*," Cassandra says. "Not the cocaine dealer guy, though. He was definitely not gay. The army guy, he wasn't gay." I end this conversation before she starts telling me about *Apollo 13* astronauts and rodeo clowns.

I get along great with my dad, even though he's not at all girlie. He grew up in the Bronx, has scars on his hands from childhood fights, played high school basketball, boxed, fixed his own cars, and was in the army. He has read even more books about World War II than your dad. But it didn't bother him that I didn't want him to teach me any man skills.

I never minded being unmanly. Until right now. Because Cassandra is wrong: I can't hold my own with even a small, non-jock boy. Because I have no experience. I was even worse at being a boy than I am at being a man. Almost all of my friends in elementary school were girls. I owned no Matchbox cars, no dirt bikes, no nunchucks. I never climbed a tree, built a fort, or broke a bone. I had an Easy-Bake Oven, a glass animal collection, sticker albums, a stack of LPs of nothing but show tunes, and a love for making stained-glass window ornaments. I'm not equipped to raise a boy. I'm equipped to raise a disappointed contestant on *Antiques Roadshow*.

I'm still pretty freaked out two weeks later, when Cassandra and I go to a specialist with an impressive, 3-D sonogram that is so detailed, I cannot believe anti-abortion activists haven't purchased every one of these machines. This doctor, who mentored our obstetrician, says he's pretty sure our fetus is a girl fetus. I feel an incredible relief. But when we walk out of the building and I turn to Cassandra to talk about buying girl clothes and picking out a girl name, she hugs me tight and cries.

"If I put on makeup in front of her, I'll worry that will make her think looks matter too much. Everything is loaded. I don't have a career, so I'm a poor role model. I'm a mess, my life is a mess, women are a mess. She's going to be an anorexic, slutty emotional basket case. That's what all women are," she says. I hold Cassandra while she sobs. Then she adds: "The other reason I didn't want it to be a girl is that we both have big noses." For eleven years Cassandra has been lying and telling me how nice she thinks my nose is. We now have only six months for those sensitive, maternal feelings to emerge.

But that 3-D sonogram is wrong, as the genetics results from the amniocentesis prove. The blur from the first ultrasound was indeed a penis. And, as Cassandra's obstetrician keeps uncomfortably pointing out at every sonogram, a large penis. She indicates this with a crude drawing of a penis and testicles and the word wow in the white spaces on the photo-booth strip of black-and-whites of a second-trimester, spread-eagled fetus. This Princeton-educated doctor tells us that our son's prenatal penis is so huge, if he does poorly in school he can always "work in the Valley," by which she means "perform in hard-core pornography." I believe this is her way of telling me that this kid is already doing better as a man than I am. Or maybe it is her way of telling me that we should find another doctor.

That night I put on *Free to Be You and Me*, the soundtrack from my feminist-era youth, to reassure me that, in our progressive, nerd-dominated culture, gender isn't so important. But now, almost four decades later, the songs sound like lies. There are no straight Williams out there who want dolls. Ladies do go first. You and me are not free to be you and me. You and me are going to be a mother and a father, and there are differences between those roles. And if I stay the kind of man I am right now, we are going to have a son who forgets to mention that dads were invited on the camping trip.

So I'm going to learn how to be a man. If I can just make it through some man stuff—go camping, play a sport, hunt an animal, fix stuff around the house—I'll gain some credibility with my son. If this goes really well, he'll never even know the wussy me. But if I can't, I'm afraid that instead of looking to me as his role model, he'll turn to his coach, his best friend's dad, or, worse yet, a professional athlete who eventually disappoints him, fueling a depression that leads my son to write a better book than mine.

I think I might even enjoy trying to become a man. After all, I've always suspected that by avoiding male activities, I've been missing out on something. Though I always assumed they were things I was glad to be missing out on. Now I'm not so sure. Maybe getting homoerotically hazed while barfing naked with frat buddies would have been great fun. Maybe getting concussed on a football field while my mom cried would have been a rush. Maybe a few street fights would have made me appreciate *West Side Story* even more.

I don't know why I avoided the experiences every other guy sought out. I'm not sure if that's because I got brainwashed by my feminist mom, had an overly contented dad, have wimpy genes, or simply grew up on a busy street without other kids my age. But I want to find out. That way I can blame someone. I'm hoping it's my parents. People seem to like books about that.

I am afraid of finding out the answers. I'm afraid of learning that I didn't do sports because I'm lazy, can't fix anything because I'm spoiled, didn't consider joining the army because I'm selfish.

I've had a soft life. I don't know what all this ease has let me hide. But because I'm untested, I also don't know what I'm capable of. Maybe after traveling the country and interviewing strangers as a reporter, I've toughened up. Even if not, maybe finally doing the things I've avoided will enrich my life by giving me more confidence, more interest in helping others, more assertiveness, more ambition, and less fear.

So, at almost forty, I've decided to make a list of tasks that I hope will turn me into a man. My list will not include anything I have ever read in *GQ* or *Esquire*: I will not learn to fold a pocket square, mix cocktails, build my triceps, look up the word *bespoke*, or get the right haircut for my face shape. That's being a dandy. This book could beat up that book.

When I tell my friend the comedian Jamie Denbo about my project, she gets very excited in a way that implies that her husband, John Ross Bowie, needs to buy this book right away. I know this because she says that the one thing I definitely need to do is rape a woman. I believe Jamie was touching my leg at the time.

Raping is something I'm going to exclude from my list. So is living in a prison, crossing the Mexican border with illegal immigrants, joining a gang, selling drugs, getting waterboarded, and riding motorcycles with the Hells Angels—though the last one is partly because the Hells Angels' website doesn't list a contact email address, and while I'm a dogged reporter, I have my limits.

I don't want to do extreme man stuff—ice road trucking, bounty hunting, steroid popping, oil drilling, heli-logging, Alaskan king crab fishing, mercenary fighting, stunt flying, Jamie raping. I just want to do what most men in our country already do, often for fun. I'm not looking to be the most manly man. I just want to catch up to everyone else.

Despite my wife's pleas, I'm not going to learn how to please a woman sexually. Most men in our country do not know how to do that. I'm also not going to follow her suggestion that I go on a silent retreat and discover the real man hidden somewhere within my chakras. These are things that men do only in women's magazines.

This isn't a reactionary list of antique man skills lost: I'm not going to farm, hang out at the Elks Club, or wield a two-handed sword. It's also not a modern list of stunted manhood: no mastering first-person-shooter video games, no fantasy football leagues, no poker tournaments. I do not need to loosen up and enjoy sloppy male excesses: There will be no going on my first spring break, being a roadie for a rock band, trying cocaine, partying with bikers at Sturgis, learning how to pick up women, or—as nine out of nine gay men who heard about this book suggested—hanging out at a gay leather bar. I'm not going to find out if, with all the lights on and people watching and the starting and stopping, I can successfully have sex on set with a porn star, because Cassandra explained that that's not being a real man; that's being a divorced man.

Cassandra, who still has several months to nail down this supportive, maternal thing, thinks my manquest is an incredibly stupid idea. "Nobody changes like that. It would be like me saying I'm going to drive across the country in three days and I'm going to learn about the country or my mortality or whatever the fuck it is. I'm just going to drive for three days." I understand what she is saying: She wants to drive across the country in three days. Pregnant women have weird cravings.

But I think she's wrong. I think immersing myself in the foreign land of masculinity is the only way to learn its language. Avoiding all these conflicts and challenges is how I got this way; confronting them must be the solution. I hope, at the end, to be able to show Baby Laszlo that fears are just a list of things to be done. I hope to say manly things like that out loud without giggling.

I have created a list of tasks that all future men will have to grapple with after this book: a test of strength, endurance, honor, dignity, bravery, and complicated travel arrangements. A list that will put fear into men and moisture into women. A list that, when I finish it, will allow me to stand back, examine it, and realize how dumb I am and how smart that *A Year in Provence* guy was.

CONTENTS

MAN MADE

1
SURVIVING OUTDOORS

Being a man seems a little intimidating, so I'm going to start off by being an eleven-year-old boy.

The only way to fix all the man damage I've done to myself is to time-travel all the way back to the moment where I made my first big mistake: not becoming a Boy Scout. If I had learned to tie a square knot, pitch a tent, and be constantly prepared, I'd have made lifelong friends who would have cajoled me into joining Little League, fraternities, and the boards of multinational conglomerates. Even if it's too late for all that, I hope to learn how to live without being dependent on modern comforts by spending a weekend as a Boy Scout.

For years people have told me that I have nice skin, and I didn't know what they meant. Eventually, I figured out that I have nice skin the way that vampires have nice skin: I've never been outside. Growing up, I'd spend months without seeing the sun, going from my room—where I never opened my black Levolor blinds—to the car in the garage to either school or the mall. Inside was for humans, outside for animals. Sleeping outdoors for fun seemed like mocking our ancestors.

But I'm probably missing an understanding of freedom and self-reliance. An access to some instinctual part of me that I'll probably need for all my other tasks. This is my chance to start fixing that. If I can't—at thirty-eight years old—earn my first Boy Scout badge this weekend, I'll have no chance on my other quests.

My camping weekend at Firestone Scout Reservation outside Los Angeles will be under the supervision of Rick Pierce, the Scout leader of Troop 773. I had no idea that being a Scout leader is one of those badass jobs, like professional wrestler, rapper, porn star, and Pope, where you get to pick out an action-hero name for yourself like Junkyard Dog, Ghostface Killah, Ben Dover, or Pope Hilarius. I am excited to be under the tutelage of someone who would make such an excellent choice for Scout leader nom de guerre. Then I find out that Rick Pierce's real name is Rick Pierce. My parents doomed me from birth. I wish I had known this before I agreed to name our son Laszlo.

When we talk about the upcoming trip, Rick Pierce tells me to bring a tent and a sleeping bag. Since I don't want to fail at my first task as a Boy Scout, I tell Rick Pierce I will totally bring a tent and sleeping bag. I, of course, don't own a tent or a sleeping bag. Worse yet, I am unsure whether it's socially acceptable to ask to borrow a friend's sleeping bag. I mean, you're really in that thing. Is it like borrowing someone's underwear or more like borrowing a blanket? And even if it is only like borrowing a blanket, is it okay to ask a friend to borrow his blanket?

Luckily, I do not have to deal with these delicate social issues, because, of course, not one of my friends owns a tent or a sleeping bag. So I call Rick Pierce and nervously ask Rick Pierce if Rick Pierce has an extra tent and sleeping bag. Of course Rick Pierce does, and of course Rick Pierce doesn't feel weird about sharing them. He sends me an email telling me that for our initial meeting at the campsite—for which he uses military time—I should "pack a sack dinner" to eat with the group. So, at 1700, I leave the house and pick up a braised short rib sandwich on my way. About forty minutes into the drive, and two hours before I normally eat dinner, I panic about being trapped in the wilderness without food and eat a few bites of one of the three PowerBars I bought, pacing myself through my reserves. This just makes me more anxious about being hungry, so I eat half the short rib sandwich. And even though I am already late, I stop at an In-N-Out Burger and eat a Double-Double cheeseburger and a vanilla shake. I consider buying a second burger and salting it so I can store it outdoors.

What I am really afraid of, more than death from starvation, are the Boy Scouts themselves. This may partly be my mom's fault. "I think the Boy Scouts are a fascist organization," my mom says when I ask her why I wasn't allowed to join. It's exactly what she said when I was a kid. "I don't like the regimentation. I don't like the rigidity. I don't like it any more than I like the army. I don't think it fosters creativity." That's right: My mom approves only of activities that foster creativity. I am lucky I can add.

My mom is a family therapist who went back to school when I was kid, at the height of the 1970s feminist movement. My mom is like a liberal suburban Zelig: She does not miss a trend. She spent the 1980s jogging, the 1990s in a book club, the 2000s in a monthly poker group, and now does a lot of yoga. So while I was not joining the Boy Scouts, she spent a year not shaving her legs or underarms and met at a monthly consciousness-raising group with other women in the neighborhood. She also founded a charitable organization called "Women Helping Women," which, in the initial brainstorming group, I'm sure they considered calling "Fuck You, Men."

My mom's resistance to the Boy Scouts was fine with me when I was a kid, since none of the Boy Scout activities involved reading or watching television. Instead, Boy Scouts are tiny little survivalists, the kind who carry knives and smash the eyeglasses of the asthmatic. To calm myself before the trip, I called my sister's husband,

Mike Browning, who had gone all the way through the program to graduate as an Eagle Scout at seventeen. Although Mike is a computer programmer, he's much tougher than I am: He drinks beer, hunts, watches the History Channel, keeps his hair short, loves super-violent horror movies, curses a lot, and stores a survival kit in his car specifically designed for the zombie apocalypse. When I asked my sister, Lisa, if she thought it was surprising that she married someone with the same interest in history and facts as our dad, whom she's always fought with, she said, without any intention of hurting my feelings, "I could never be attracted to someone who is soft and metrosexual like you." It feels very uncomfortable to be sad that my sister doesn't find me attractive.

Mike's main advice about my camping trip with the Boy Scouts is to bring earplugs. Not to keep out the sounds of animals, but to block out the farting and the laughing about the farting. He says the kids will try to trick me into hunting snipes, a fake bird that apparently is so hilarious to trick people into hunting that Mike believes it is probably still funny after twenty years. The highlight of the trip will be hanging out by the fire.

"You put everything you can in the fire to see what happens to it. They'll be burning stuff you know is toxic," he says.

I am going to spend the weekend with farting, knife-wielding pyromaniacs.

I drive past the gates of the Firestone Boy Scout Reservation with food all over my face. My cell phone signal is gone, my GPS shows nothing but unmarked green expanse, and it is getting dark. I drive blindly down dirt roads, more and more certain I will starve to death. My unborn son will be raised by Cassandra and a rotation of gay men.

Two miles later, Rick Pierce appears in front of my yellow convertible Mini Cooper in an SUV and introduces himself as Rick Pierce. Then Rick Pierce leans down from Rick Pierce's window and tells me to follow Rick Pierce. Rick Pierce leads me to the campsite, where, to my shock, Rick Pierce informs me that we are going to sleep right next to our cars. This seems less like camping and more like camping on a reality show. I am thrilled.

Rick Pierce brings me to a picnic bench to meet the boys, all of whom have good, solid, Rick-Pierce names such as Nick, Kirby, Chad, Tanner, and Wiggles. They are eating their sack dinners, so even though I am close to barfing from the two thousand calories I ate in the car, I pull out the second half of my short rib sandwich in order to fit in. I am three minutes into quietly eating when several kids ask if I want to hunt snipes. I look hard at them in the gathering dusk and tell them I know about snipes. They nod, impressed, like prisoners who've just noticed my tear tattoo.

Then they tell me about Beef. Beef is a man who lives in the shack down the hill and knows absolutely everything about outdoorsmanship. Beef owns a fire truck and is an expert with guns. Beef, obviously, is bullshit. A human snipe. When I ask Rick Pierce about why this fake person calls himself Beef, Rick Pierce plays along and says it is because Beef used to be a hundred pounds heavier, which sounds like it makes sense but does not. Rick Pierce says Beef isn't a park ranger exactly, but is sort of a volunteer ranger whom the other rangers let do ranger stuff and live in a ranger house every weekend. I tell the kids that I know Beef doesn't exist.

Then Beef comes by. It turns out Beef is not only a real person, but a real person who introduces himself by saying, "Hi. I'm Beef." Beef tells me that his family has been camping on this site since 1965 and that his dad was also a big deal in the Scout organization. "Some families are Kiwanis. Some are Masons. We are Scouts," he says.

The kids run around Beef and yell like he is Willy Wonka. He shows them an old soda machine he spent a lot of time retooling with car hoses and CO_2 tanks so it basically makes soda. But the kids call it "Homemade Coke" and pass around a cup tasting it and commenting thoughtfully like it was a 1945 Mouton Rothschild.

By the time the cup gets to me I think of it less like Homemade Coke and more like Cold-and-Flu Coke.

Beef starts throwing miniature boxes of Milk Duds and Reese's Peanut Butter Cups at the kids, who go wild with Beef excitement. He says his fire truck is under repair, but he has some special stuff in store for them over the weekend.

"My job is to build memories. And to make them all feel accepted," he explains to me about his role as the Santa Claus of Boy Scouts. I cannot justify this, but when you are around Beef, you are certain that he is not a child molester.

What I instantly love about Beef, and what my fellow Boy Scouts see in him, is the very manly trait of boyish delight. It comes built into most of us, and our job is not to let it get removed.

I walk outside and jot down that idea. When I look at it, I realize it's not good enough for The List. Ever since Cassandra got pregnant, I started writing a list of life advice for Laszlo. It's my philosophy: a combination of what I've learned by doing, seeing, reading, and listening. The List is the most embarrassing thing I've ever written. And I just wrote about owning an Easy-Bake Oven. But this idea about being born happy and having to exercise that happiness, while not being good enough for The List, does make me think about the day Laszlo was born, which, despite all the talk about it being the most memorable day of a person's life, doesn't pop in my head often. I didn't learn all that much that day, other than that women should definitely get the epidural right away, out of politeness to others. But I also learned that I had no idea how we start out.

I assumed women struggled and pushed and a baby popped out and everyone clapped and shook hands. What actually happened was that, over and over, Cassandra struggled and I saw the top of Laszlo's little fuzzy head poke out and go back into her vagina, like the worst Thai strip show ever.

Eventually, Cassandra pushed Laszlo out, and I couldn't believe how enormous he was. I went to go get him, when I realized that was only his head. The rest of him slithered out of her, red and angry and screaming. For three very long seconds I feared I wouldn't love this furious demon child, that I wouldn't be able to calm him, that he'd hate me. But then, because Cassandra had some excessive bleeding, the doctors immediately put him in my arms, and the red left him, and he calmed down. And as soon as he stopped crying, I started.

I'm not entirely sure why. Part of it was that I thought about all the people I loved who had died and would never get to meet him. Part of it was that, for the first time, all my decisions seemed to matter: meeting Cassandra, staying married, deciding to have a child. So much could have derailed this: other men, other women, a lack of forgiveness, one of a million tiny acts of cowardice of not saying how we felt calcifying into irreparable resentment. Part of it was because of how unmarked by experience Laszlo was. I fought an urge to run out of that hospital, leave Cassandra forever, and drive with him to a cabin in the woods and raise him alone. I didn't want anything to corrupt him, not even Cassandra. Everything was out to hurt him, to ruin him. This feeling lasted for several weeks. And, in retrospect, was something I probably should not have told Cassandra about. I got halfway through describing why I thought I might have these reactions and how it didn't reflect on her or my deep love for her or how great a mom I knew she'd be, and how animalistic and discombobulated your emotions get right after having a baby. She left the room, pondered the deep emotional experience I was having, and sent me this email:

"You do not have boobs! You do not have breast milk! I'm doing all the work. All! The! Work! You! Could! Not! I! Do! Everything! You are useless! You and your woods!"

I think the main reason I cried, though, is that I assumed being born was awful: You suddenly went from darkness, wet warmth, and a feeding tube that hooked into your stomach to bright, hungry coldness where you had to breathe yourself. I had a good childhood, but I remember it being really difficult and confusing and lonely and vulnerable and full of heartbreak in a way that adulthood isn't. But after those first three seconds of red-faced crying, which, in his defense, were probably due to the fact that his head had just been squeezed by Cassandra's super-tight vagina, Laszlo wasn't upset. He was curious, looking up at me with total trust despite the fact that I hadn't finished one parenting book and wanted to raise him in a cabin even though I'd never spent one night in a cabin. The Buddhists were wrong: Life isn't suffering. It's awesome. And that was making me cry.

Cassandra thinks this is the stupid ranting of a narcissistic parent, but I really could tell right away that Laszlo is a good person. Until he was born, my greatest concern was whether he would get into an Ivy League college. But right then I realized he was happy and kind, and that was more important. I could tell that he's a nicer person than I am. I don't know how I can prove that, but I will be very, very surprised if he perpetrates genocide.

All this crying over my newborn son would make me a pretty good person, if it weren't for the fact that I wasn't paying any attention to the fact that a bunch of medical professionals were working to stop my wife from bleeding to death.

I cry a lot now, and it's embarrassing. Before Laszlo was born I cried as often as I barfed, about once every seven years: when my grandfather died; when I was dumped by my college girlfriend; when I feared I was losing Cassandra. Now I cry over the part in children's books where the kid gives up his stuffed animal. My feelings are much closer to the surface, or maybe the skin around my tear ducts has thinned out. Either way, it's annoying.

I do not want to cry during my weekend as a Boy Scout. So I steady my nerves with a shot of Homemade Coke and join my fellow Boy Scouts outside Beef's shack. We sit on some picnic benches illuminated by electric lanterns, which is when I notice that these kids aren't as badass as I feared. In fact, they are wearing uniforms that include a neckerchief. They have flashlights strapped around their foreheads as if they're about to go spelunking in the nerd mine. Plus, they are eleven to thirteen years old. From El Segundo, a tony beach town in Los Angeles. Even Beef isn't all that tough: He teaches technology at Eagle Rock High School and coaches their athletic decathlon team under the name Glenn Laird. These were a breed I did not know existed: outdoors nerds.

Wiggles, a small, good-looking, obviously popular thirteen-year-old, asks me why a thirty-eight-year-old man is joining a Boy Scout camping trip in a way that informs me that his middle school is doing an exemplary job of warning him about child molestation. So I tell Wiggles about my lack of male skills and that I've just had a son and how I worry about passing my inadequacies on to him. I figure fatherhood insecurity is just the kind of thing to bore a thirteen-year-old out of asking a person any more questions about his creepy desire to camp with children. But it doesn't. Wiggles is the most empathetic kid I've ever met. He nods at everything I say to him and seems to process my middle-aged masculinity melt-down in a way that Cassandra did not. After waiting to make sure I've finished talking, Wiggles leans forward on his bench across the table from me and tells me something that makes me feel even less intimidated by the Boy Scouts than their neckerchiefs do: "We suck at sports," he says.

Looking around the table, I can see everything Wiggles is try-ing to tell me about the Boy Scouts. Sure, a group of them is having a manly conversation about sniper rifles, bazookas, and howitzers, but in that way dorky kids who like complicated games involv-ing painted figurines do. Boy Scouts are a lot more like me than I thought. They are playing Dungeons & Dragons, only they've replaced elves with American Indians.

A tall kid sits next to me and asks if I want to see something cool. Before I can decide, he shows me six knives he's hidden on various parts of his body. Then he tells me that his dad is in jail, which led him to join the Scouts. When I ask him what his dad got put away for, he tells me it was weapons sales. I mention that carrying around a Le Cordon Bleu number of knives isn't a great call for someone with his family history. He tells me that his dad was caught selling guns, not knives. There is clearly no Scout badge for non-linear thinking.

Since we are all hyped up on soda, candy, and Beef, Rick Pierce holds up three fingers, which is the Boy Scout sign for silence. Then Rick Pierce has everyone line up behind their senior patrol leader. I am not at all surprised that Wiggles is one of the leaders, or that his group looks the coolest—he is flanked by two boys with longish hair and a bit of an attitude, each significantly taller than Wiggles. The other patrols all have four kids instead of three, so I meekly volunteer to join Wiggles's, trying to half pretend it's a joke since I am at least twenty-five years older than them. But Wiggles sees through it and quickly waves me to the back of his line, like it's normal to have old, neckerchief-less men join them. He makes me feel like I belong, despite the fact that I'm a foot taller than my patrol mates, and two feet taller than my patrol leader. Then the groups state their patrol group names. One is the Red Hats. One is the Leprechauns. One is the Gummi Bears. Wiggles's group is the Master Exploders. I must have heard this wrong. Faster Decoders? Mister Explorers? No, we are the Master Exploders. Wiggles says he got it from the title of a Tenacious D song, the heavy-metal comedy band with hits such as "Fuck Her Gently." He shows me the Master Exploders patch on their uniforms; it is a drawing of a mushroom cloud.

Wiggles and the other kids set up their tents. It is dark and there are lots of poles and pounding of stakes with rocks. This is the stuff I was afraid of. On some level I know putting up a tent can't be too hard if an eleven-year-old can do it, but eleven-year-olds can also illegally download movies and shoot people in Halo. I have no mining-helmet flashlight. I have no flat rock. I am starting to sweat from embarrassment and ineffective pounding on stakes with round rocks.

Luckily, Rick Pierce comes over and sets up my tent with me, which isn't all that hard. I string a few poles through some holes, pound the stakes in the dirt with the bottom of my shoe, and suddenly there is a flimsy piece of plastic separating me from the earth, the sky, and, most importantly, the farts of eleven-year-olds. I go over to help Rick Pierce with his tent, when I discover that Rick Pierce has a cot. This is so incredibly wrong. Like finding out your favorite superhero sleeps on a cot.

When I ask Rick Pierce what the etiquette is on urination, Rick Pierce points me toward two Porta-Potties down the hill. I check the Porta-Potties out, only to discover that one of them has some Boy Scout feces on the seat. This confirms my plan to not defecate during this camping trip. I fear this might make my experience less authentic when Chad, a very chill, confident eleven-year-old with a shaved head and some kind of cool black neoprene Nike outfit, tells me that all the kids constrict their bowels until they get home. As far as pissing, Chad takes me aside, away from the adults.

"I always set up my tent near a tree. Just don't let the scoutmasters catch you," he says. "You can use a Porta-Potty in the city." We high-five in our minds, as people who pee on trees are wise to do.

The only thing I can't figure out is where the kids brush their teeth.

"In their minds," explains Mr. Wetmore, one of the kids' dads and one of four non-Beef adults on the trip.

"These boys won't brush their teeth or change their underwear until Sunday night," adds Rick Pierce. I can't figure out why, then, they had packed such enormous bags—bags that barely fit in their tents.

"Who do you think packed those bags?" Mr. Wetmore asks. Moms apparently either don't understand or refuse to accept just how disgusting boys are. Which I need to embrace. I need to lose some of what's made me so uptight, so afraid, so weak. I need to unbrush and unfloss. I do not need the bag I brought, either. The Boy Scouts are teaching me that being prepared is for chicks.

While the kids settle down to sleep at 2130, I chat with Rick Pierce and the other three adults. Rick Pierce, unsurprisingly, spent most of his career as an air force rocket scientist and is now employed in the private sector working on satellite weapons systems. His seventeen-year-old son just dropped out of the Boy Scouts but Rick Pierce has decided to keep going anyway. I think this is pretty weird. I can't imagine telling Cassandra that Laszlo isn't interested in baby music class anymore, but I'll be spending Sundays at a random couple's house singing hello to a group of babies teething on tambourines. But this is how Rick Pierce is giving back to the community, and Rick Pierce is even taking classes to become a more advanced Scout leader, son or not. One of the other dads, Wayne Torrey, also has a son who dropped out of scouting a few years ago, and he spent three of the last four weekends at this campsite. For his weekend off, Mr. Torrey watched a Civil War reenactment.

It's nice to learn that I'm not the only person with this fantasy of stealing his son and taking him to the woods: There's a giant international organization dedicated to it. Some guys like Rick Pierce, Beef, and Mr. Torrey have it so bad they're satisfied taking other people's sons into the woods.

I say good night to the four adults and get in my tent, where I put on two layers of socks and a hat and try to fall asleep in the cold. I am trying to get comfortable by twisting my body around the rocks under me when I hear a boy yelling, as loud as he can: "Go outside! GO OUTSIDE! GO OUT OF THE TENT!" I stay in my tent, remembering that you should stay still and quiet when a bear is around, no matter how many Boy Scouts it is eating. But I quickly figure out, by the rolls of paper towels Rick Pierce is requesting, that one of the boys barfed. This, apparently, is so common—because kids so often get sick and so unoften eat boxes of candy and Homemade Coke for dinner—that it's not even a big deal to the barfee, who went right back in the very same tent with the guy who just barfed on him.

"I barfed last time," explains the barfer's tentmate, Charlie. In fact, Charlie says, the barfer—who is actually my cool, piss-confidant buddy Chad—still owes him one barf after this. That's when I know I am in the right place. Dorks or not, these are the men I need to learn from. Men with a Mafioso-like sense of loyalty and repaying favors. Men who are comfortable sleeping in one another's vomit.

I do not sleep well. It turns out the outside makes a lot of noise. At about 0300, I gain an even deeper appreciation for houses, which are underrated in their ability to provide warmth, block noise, and keep dew off you. In the ranking of shelters, tent barely edges out no tent. I cannot get warm. I cannot get dry. I cannot sleep. My car is only feet away. I could easily sleep there, with the heater on and some classical music in the background. I could even drive to a hotel and be back before anyone knows. Is that any less manly than Rick Pierce's cot? Isn't it resourceful? Isn't there a badge for that?

But I can't fail this soon, even if no one else would know. Because I would. So I put on a third pair of socks in the dark and shiver on top of the tree root sticking into my back, putting together sets of twenty-minute naps.

Even though we agree to get up at 0630, the boys get up at 0530, which pisses the adults off by 0100 percent. I am not nearly as upset since I don't yet appreciate the subtle differences between sleeping in a tent and being awake outside of one.

Still, I feel like I've accomplished something. I've camped. I've beaten the elements. I feel connected to this grassy field. I know it in a way I haven't known a plot of earth since the backyard of the house I grew up in. Better yet, I've never woken up outdoors and had quite this quick a transition into my day. I feel like a man with important things to do. Like sleep.

Instead, I walk out of my tent in the clothes I showed up in and Mr. Wetmore offers me a cup of coffee. I admit that, in addition to never having camped before, I'm also not man enough to drink coffee. Mr. Wetmore informs me that most Boy Scout dads don't drink coffee, and suddenly my lifelong inability to handle bitterness becomes a Boy-Scouty, clean-body/clean-mind, too-tough-to-need-caffeine affectation. I head for my morning treeside ablutions when Wiggles asks me what I'm up to. I am not sure on all the Boy Scout rules yet, but I figure lying to your patrol leader is not okay.

"I'm going to brush my teeth," I admit.

"That's unheard of," Wiggles says.

In fact, only one kid has brushed since arriving, and he is a severely autistic seventeen-year-old. "I haven't brushed yet," Chad says to me. "And I puked."

Rick Pierce makes sure we look spiffy since, as part of Boy Scout diversity training, we are hosting a brand-new troop from South Central Los Angeles made up of poor, inner-city kids who are mostly black. Troop 1323 is going on their first sleepover, under our tutelage. When the nine nervous, quiet boys show up and introduce themselves and their patrol troops (Panthers and Sharks), we help them put up their tents. It is beautiful to learn that eleven-year-olds don't care at all about race and class when they are allowed to boss around other eleven-year-olds.

For breakfast, we are preparing several rugged outdoorsy entrées for our guests, one of which is muffins from Costco. Unfortunately, the kid with the six knives opens the muffin cellophane with one of them and Mr. Torrey confiscates it, since it is a sheath knife, which apparently is not permitted. The kid takes this pretty well, probably because he has five more knives hidden about him. He tells me that the hardest part of passing my test to be a Scout, which he believes I can do that very afternoon, is learning to tie a square knot. After a few tries, I get it, and he quickly shows me another knot.

"This is the hangman's knot. It's an illegal knot," he says, making me Richie to his Fonzie. "You're not supposed to use it. Especially around the new troop. It's offensive." Still, he makes it clear that in less racially fraught situations, illegal knots are way cooler than legal knots. I'm really worried about this kid's future.

Meanwhile, Andrew, a small Asian kid from our troop who knows the most about World War II weaponry, is standing near a slab of bacon holding a knife and spinning while screaming, "Blood circle! Blood circle! Blood circle!" like he is in a 1970s punk band. I think there is something very wrong with him until I learn that this is standard knife-operating Boy Scout procedure. Apparently, much of the fun of wielding a knife is that you get to yell "blood circle!" while holding it in your hand and swinging your outstretched arm to demonstrate, in the most dangerous manner possible, the risks involved in getting anywhere near you. It's as if every time you used a paper clip you unfurled it and threw it as hard as you could at someone's eye to warn them that there were paper clips around. I decide that I am totally doing this with my knives when I cook. It will make it seem so much more manly when I'm crying and chopping onions if I'm also screaming "blood circle!"

In addition to muffin-package opening, we are going to make eggs in a paper bag. We put raw bacon on the bottom of a brown paper bag, crack two eggs on top, and tie the bags to a rope above a fire. This will be of use if we are ever trapped in the wilderness with just a fire, some bacon, a carton of eggs, a lot of brown paper bags, and rope. We also fill ziplock bags with Egg Beaters, bacon bits, cheese, and tomatoes and drop those in boiling water. I do not know why there is such concern over the cholesterol of active, outdoorsy eleven-year-olds.

I assume we are loading up on a big man breakfast so we can do some serious scouting, finally putting a few feet between myself and my Mini Cooper. I am excited to check out the thirty-two hundred acres of wooded hills. I am ready to reconnoiter or bivouac or attack American Indians or befriend American Indians, depending on our mood. Instead, Beef comes by to teach us how to make paper rockets. The Master Exploders get two Troop 1323'ers added to our patrol, one of whom is a small, hyper boy named Robert. As we are cutting paper by the picnic benches, Robert keeps asking the same question: "When are we going to go over there and catch snipes?" Wiggles takes charge, calmly improvising that snipes don't come out until nightfall, are hard to find, and are extremely dangerous. Beef, clearly uncomfortable with the snipes lie but trapped in a classic moral dilemma between empathy and tradition, will only say, "They're very elusive." So are you, Beef. So are you.

Though I have not told Wiggles about The List, Wiggles gives me a lot of unrequested advice on fatherhood while we're carefully folding paper:

"Don't get involved in everything your son does."

"Be on him about grades."

"M-rated video games are okay. But don't get him games with sexual themes. No *Grand Theft Auto*."

"Don't always be there, standing with him and waiting for the bus. You'll embarrass him. Starting in sixth grade."

Wiggles is far better than any parenting book I've read, even if I'd read a parenting book.

I've always assumed people became leaders because they were power-mad. Which I am not. I even view my relationship with Laszlo as give-and-take, sometimes giving in to his desires and sometimes insisting he listen to my suggestions that he lie still and let me wipe his butt. But Wiggles is able to give advice and direction without seeming like a jerk. He doesn't ask what I want to do, but it feels like he's paying attention to my needs, whether that's advice on fatherhood or paper rockets. Wiggles is on my side, and because of that, I want to do whatever it takes to make the Master Exploders the best patrol on this trip.

Our next outdoorsy activity is putting Mentos in half liters of Diet Coke and watching them explode. Then we turn the bottles into yet more rockets. I'm starting to see that nature isn't something to explore as much as something to shoot rockets into. Luckily, Beef drives up in his ranger vehicle and offers me a tour of the campsite.

Beef, I learn, is a member of the Scouts' prestigious Order of the Arrow, where he has been given the Vigil Honor and the Indian name Lo Unsa Wesechumaid. There aren't many of his kind left. Scouting has been in decline for decades, ever since Vietnam, when people started associating the Boy Scouts with the military. People like my mom. In fact, the organization is still in such financial trouble that they had to sell the thirty-two hundred acres of Firestone to the City of Industry, which loans it back to the Scouts. The Scouts lost further membership in the 1990s when they decided against allowing gays or atheists. In other countries, scouting mixes both boys and girls, but in the United States they don't, and now the Boy Scouts are far more popular in Republican areas, while the Girl Scouts, who refuse to use guns at all, are bigger in Democratic regions. Ironically, one of the reasons that Boy Scouts are in decline, Beef tells me, is that boys think "it's gay." My sister's husband, Mike, was one of these "closeted Scouts."

"No one at high school knew I was a Boy Scout," Mike had said when I called him. "It would have been open season on my dorky ass. There was an unwritten rule that anyone in Boy Scouts never said anything about it at school."

Beef wants to take me on some real scouting. He leads me into the woods for the first time since I arrived and makes me taste some kind of dirty plant he picks from the ground and guess what it is. I take a tiny bite and say "watercress." Beef's face drops. Something is wrong. He has clearly realized that he gave me poison and the antidote is either far away or out of season. Instead he tells me that, yes, what I ate was baby watercress. I have found the one place where survivalists and pampered city folks overlap: identifying field lettuces used in expensive restaurant salads. I hope I get a Boy Scout badge with three Michelin stars.

Back at the camp, my fellow Scouts begin dinner preparation. Dinner, sadly, will not involve a roaring fire and sticks. Rick Pierce brought little electric burners that plug into outlets near the picnic benches. Even more disappointing, Rick Pierce organizes dinner as an *Iron Chef* competition among the patrol groups. I am baffled that gay kids aren't allowed to be Boy Scouts.

I am very excited, since cooking is something I can totally master explode at. Even though he knows a lot about food for a thirteen-year-old, Wiggles lets me take charge of my patrol. We make a two-course meal: chicken potpie and a dessert we call Grandma's House because it smells, for very good reason, like an entire canister of cinnamon. Wiggles makes cooking fun by acting like everyone's ideas are great, even as he decides not to pour everything in one big pot as the other kids suggest. He makes us believe our patrol's cooking superiority is so objective that the judging results are immaterial.

We win the *Iron Chef* cook-off and celebrate by eating a lot of cinnamon. Then we all dip bananas in sugar and caramelize them with a blowtorch, which is the most effete method of playing with fire possible.

After dinner, Rick Pierce brings me to a picnic table to take my official Scout test. If I pass, I will be an actual Boy Scout. If not, I'll need to take a step even farther backward in my man journey and learn how to burp and spit up masculinely. Wiggles tells me that I have nothing to worry about on the test. That I'm already a Boy Scout.

As Rick Pierce watches, I successfully tie a square knot, give the Boy Scout salute (three fingers), recite the motto ("Be prepared"), and demonstrate the secret handshake (can't tell you). Then Rick Pierce goes over Boy Scout law, asking how I demonstrate each of the Scout attributes. I am doing pretty well, especially when he asks, "Are you 'clean'?" If there's one place where "I am clean," it's with this group, where the autistic kid and I are the only ones who brushed our teeth.

Then Rick Pierce gets to "reverent." I explain that Rick Pierce is asking me to choose between scouting and my career. That's when Rick Pierce explains that reverent specifically means in relationship to God. I tell Rick Pierce that I don't believe in God. Rick Pierce puts down the manual. Mr. Wetmore, an editor for commercials who is used to dealing with guys like me in Los Angeles, says a belief in any higher power or energy will do. He gives both me and Rick Pierce a nod that implies we should go along with this. Which Rick Pierce grudgingly agrees to. But I am not going to build the foundation of my new manhood on a lie. Maybe it's the lack of sleep, but right now I'd rather give up this badge and abandon my entire journey than not be true to myself. So I tell Rick Pierce that, no, I can't go for the higher energy thing. Mr. Wetmore, who cannot believe he is parsing theological terms so a thirty-eight-year-old can get his first Boy Scout badge, suggests that just believing in myself is a kind of reverence. Rick Pierce gives him a weird look, but Rick Pierce has twenty-one kids and a live blowtorch to deal with, so he passes me on the test, for reverently believing in myself. I am now a Boy Scout. I get a square knot in my throat and shake Rick Pierce's hand in a way that I can't tell you about.

I told Cassandra I'd be home before she goes to sleep, so I get ready to leave when Wiggles grabs me. We're going on a snipe hunt with the new troop members to haze them.

Wiggles insists that I can't miss such a storied part of Boy Scouting. So I join him as we walk into the darkness down the hill, the kids from the inner-city troop nervous and quiet. One of the kids from our own group, Nick, who missed the memo about snipes being fake, gets scared and heads back. I go to stop him, but Wiggles signals to let him go.

Eventually, we walk three feet into the woods, the troop entering nature for the very first time on the trip. Chad, the unbrushed barfer, hides behind a tree. He tries to blink his two red forehead flashlights to replicate the eyes of a snipe, but he flashes it white the first few times and then finally red, which is way more robot than snipe. We all, I'm sure, see him fiddle with the thing. I figure the game is over. But then Wiggles yells that the visiting troop should attack the snipe, which not only works but seems, at least for Chad, like a cruel reversal of this elaborate practical joke. A particularly small boy named Christian yells, "I hate you! I hate you!," his fists wildly swinging in front of him as he rushes toward Chad. As they're beating the crap out of Chad, who goes fetal, they finally discover he is not a snipe. Chad, oddly, looks triumphant, as if he got the better of these kids who are punching him.

I should break up the fight, but I can't tell if this is just normal boy play or something more dangerous. Because I didn't participate in normal boy fighting. When I was five, my mom brought me over to play with her friend's two sons, who were older and Italianer than me. One of them started hitting me when my mom, apparently, went to save me from my first fight. "My friend said, 'No, no, no. You have to let them fight it out.' I thought, *Maybe she's right. You can't always run away. I can't keep protecting him*," my mom said. "And he punched you and pushed you down and you were crying. And I was so pissed at her." One clue to where I got my fear of fighting is that my mom is so afraid of her Italian friend that she won't let me print her name in this book.

Looking at this scrum of kids in the woods, I realize that by the end of my man journey, I'm going to have to fight someone. I don't know who, I don't know why, and I certainly don't know how, but I know I'm going to hate it more than anything else I have to do.

Confrontation is the most elemental part of manhood and the one I've worked hardest to avoid. Even seeing these eleven-year-olds fight, I want to run away.

By the time I react and decide to break up the fight, the pile of kids has already gotten off Chad. As we approach the tents on the long, quiet walk back to camp, Christian, the particularly small inner-city kid, looks at all of his supposed Scout mentors and says, "Whoever that snipe was, I hate you. That was not cool." I have a bad feeling we just confirmed a lot of what he already thought about white people.

I do not know how Wiggles is going to handle this debacle, to repair this fissure between our two groups that was the exact opposite of this weekend's purpose. Wiggles, though, doesn't see it that way. The mission was accomplished. The new kids, once they calm down, will feel included, like they're experts now in something, even if it's in fictionalized birds of wrath. Wiggles doesn't need to be liked. Wiggles follows his own code. Which is why he's respected.

Sitting on a picnic bench next to Wiggles, I say good-bye, thanking him for all that he somehow managed to teach me about outdoorsmaning without ever really going into the outdoors. Wiggles begs me to stay until morning, when they'll be cooking something called a Wagon Wheel that sounds to me like the same undercooked bacon and eggs I had this morning, only arranged on the plate in a different way. I explain that I have a baby and a wife and I can't stay away any longer.

"I get that," he says.

But he does convince me to stay for another hour so I can see the fire they're about to set. I find it hard to believe this will only take an hour since it is already 2100 and no one has gathered any wood. Beef explains that, because of the dangers of forest fires in Los Angeles, this will be a propane fire, just little jets of blue flame emerging from tongs of steel. It's tiny and lame and as evocative of the power of the elements as a paper fan. You can't make s'mores in this fire. It does not attract insects. It is like we're holding up Bic lighters waiting for an encore where real Boy Scouts come out and light a huge bonfire. I just got my Boy Scout badge hours ago, but I already feel like throwing it in the flame in protest. Especially since it has absolutely no chance of burning in there.

We gather around the not-fire and Mr. Torrey tells a very long Nordic myth about mistletoe that he segues out of by saying, "Now I have a story that you might enjoy." Then the boys put on skits that imply that they have attended a lot of vaudeville shows. Wiggles drags me out to the center of the group, next to the not-fire. He has me and another kid hold a stick for no reason and pretend we're at a candy store. The skit ends when all the other kids go back to their seats and Wiggles looks at us and says, "I've got two suckers on a stick!" Everyone laughs even though (a) I'm sure they've heard it before, (b) it's not funny, and (c) there's no way they know that lollipops were once called suckers. But I feel so glad to be included enough to be made fun of—to be sniped—that as the kids file off to go to sleep I consider getting back in that tent and abandoning Cassandra and Laszlo for one more night.

I thank Wiggles again, and he shakes my hand, and tells me that he'll mail me the cool mushroom cloud badge he says I also earned—the Master Exploder one. I know this is not the last I will see of Wiggles. That someday, somewhere, he's going to be my boss.

I could have stayed. I could have peed in the woods, worn that same outfit, and secretly brushed for another two days. I could become one of them. All I need to do is take my natural nerdiness and apply it to stuff I'm not interested in. The happiest thing I learned this weekend is that nerdiness is a big part of manliness: learning battle dates, perfecting martial arts moves, memorizing NFL passing percentages, knowing a lot of knots even though the only one you really need is the "shoelace knot."

I'll be back. With Laszlo. I like that time is slower out here. I like the freedom from feeling I should be doing something better or more interesting. It's my first appreciation of boredom, and if I like sharing that with Wiggles, I bet I'm going to really like doing it with a kid with a slightly less stupid name. And if Laszlo is anything at all at eleven years like he is at five months, then he won't mind barfing on himself and others.

When I get home from the campsite, I tell Cassandra that she was wrong, that already I've changed, that I've learned enough from earning my Boy Scout badge to take Laszlo and his friends camping whenever they want. I also tell her that I definitely don't need any dinner tonight, since the impacted short rib sandwich, cheeseburger, beef stew, cinnamon treat, undercooked eggs, and PowerBars are starting to hurt. Then in an act of magnanimity, I tell Cassandra that she can come to the woods with Laszlo and me.

"I'm not going camping. There could be spiders. I would go camping if I could be in a log cabin with running water."

"That's not camping."

"Oh. Then I won't go camping."

I told her that if she did come, I'd make sure any spiders, whether itsy or bitsy, stayed on the water spout, far away from her. These are precisely the conversations I wanted to have as a man. Ones in which my wife cowers in fear and I lean over, put my arms around her, and taunt her for her fears.

2

RESCUING THE HELPLESS

Though I think Cassandra is being uptight, I agree to take a shower before going to bed. I feel great, recounting my triumphs over raw eggs and tween barf, unsure why Cassandra is not setting them to verse. Instead, she tells me she cannot believe how empowered a person can feel after surviving one night of camping with eleven-year-olds. It is going to take more to impress her.

A big part of being a Boy Scout, perhaps second only to cooking, is community service. To become an Eagle Scout you have to complete a huge service project—my brother-in-law Mike restored trails at a state park. Beef's whole life seemed to be about helping children. That's because the Boy Scouts believe that after you learn to take care of yourself, you should help people who don't know how. I want to leap to the other side of that divide. And I want Laszlo to learn how to do that from me.

There are many different levels of sacrifice, none of which I know anything about. Risking your life for someone you don't know, someone you'll never meet, someone who very well may not even be worthy of this risk, is the most moronic level. And it's exactly what firefighters do. I need to find out why. And whether I could ever rush into a burning building to save someone. Or even be near people while they do it. Because by having a child, I suddenly went from protected to protector.

Bravery is not something I'm naturally gifted at. In fact, I cannot figure out why bravery wasn't the first trait eliminated via natural selection. Whenever people ask what items I'd save if my house were on fire, I look at them like the idiots they are. Why not ask which bill denominations I would request to keep from the guy mugging me at gunpoint? These are people who do not realize the importance of being able to identify an emergency situation and then run quickly away from it. These are people who think that before you get stranded on a desert island, you get to pack a bunch of records.

Firefighter is one of the few jobs kind enough to warn me away by containing two words I'm not interested in, unlike the deceptive *bookkeeper*. All the boys in my kindergarten class wanted to be firemen. When I used to ask them why, not one of them mentioned early retirement, days off, or excellent benefits. Instead they focused on the giant truck, ladder, pole, and hose. I realize now that this is because all the boys in my kindergarten class had tiny penises.

Firemen are different from guys with other man jobs: I respect them, but they don't intimidate me. That's because they get to be brave and badass without ever confronting other human beings. Their only disagreement is with one of the elements. That's why firefighter is the job closest to superhero. Actually, Mexican wrestler is the job closest to superhero, but since I don't speak Spanish and face masks immediately make my whole face smell like morning breath, I figure if I want to learn to conquer fear and help others, I'll try out firefighter instead.

Four months after the Boy Scout camping trip, a friend on the LA City Council puts me in touch with the guy who runs Fire Station 27 in Hollywood, one of the ten busiest houses in Los Angeles.

His name is Captain Buzz Smith. I cannot believe the names of real men are so real manly: Rick Pierce, Captain Buzz Smith. Did my parents doom me to wimpdom with my name? If I were Jack Hammer would I be the first man on the sun? Or, as a quick Internet search shows, would I just have been an imprisoned male porn star?

Just like Rick Pierce, Captain Buzz Smith uses military time, telling me in an email to show up at 0600. My life never calls for military time. If someone says, "Let's meet at six," I know exactly when they mean since I have only one six in my life. Also, just like Rick Pierce, Captain Buzz tells me to bring a sleeping bag. He suggests I wear boots with toe protection, too, which, of course, I do not own: I live a life in which my toes are never in any danger. He ends his instructional email by commenting on the idea for this book: "Not to dismiss your entire premise, but none of the activities or skills you plan on doing define becoming a man. A man is honest, kind, and courageous, protects women, is humble, bold, moral, seeks truth, loves children, and fights for what is right." He actually wrote that! Without one of those winking emoticon things!

I park my car in the morning dark and walk down the street to the firehouse in my vulnerable-toed shoes. Since I still don't have a sleeping bag, I carry my giant down comforter and a pillow, like a kid with an overprotective mom going on his first sleepover. I ring the doorbell of a huge, beautiful old brick building with a red, Mexican tiled roof, and a fireman leads me past an empty reception desk to an office in the back of the house where Captain Buzz Smith is sitting behind a desk. Captain Buzz Smith does not look like a Captain Buzz Smith, by which I mean he is not made of plastic. He has a gentle face, an easy smile, a mustache, and a general kindness to him; if he were cast as an astronaut he'd be the guy in charge of mixing Tang. Both his father and grandfather were firefighters in LA, and it is a safe assumption that at least one of his eight children will be. Shortly after getting married, he and his wife heard a sermon at church about how you should let God decide how many children you should have. I think this is a pretty good plan: let stuff just naturally happen and say that's how God wanted it. I am going to let God decide how much food I eat, how much wine I drink, and how much porn I watch.

Upon Captain Buzz's suggestion, I've brought boxes of donuts to win over the other guys. This does not seem like the healthiest way to start a day of putting out fires. I suggested some egg-white omelets, but Captain Buzz said the guys are pretty insistent about the donuts. I bring them to the kitchen, where, at 0700, men are eating fried pork skin and cucumber salad with ranch dressing left over from the dinner made by the previous crew. They are not doing this because they lost a bet. They are doing it because it is food that is there. My stomach can't even handle an oolong tea that's too dark at 0700. They are able to eat 0700 pork rinds without anyone commenting on how gross this is because there is not one woman among the house's three crews of sixteen firefighters.

The guys are really friendly considering God wants us to be asleep and they have no idea who I am. There's not one hostile "May I help you?" There aren't even any questions about what I'm doing here. I'm a guy who's not starting a fire, and that's good enough for them. Besides being friendly, almost every one of them is weirdly good-looking. I knew about the handsome firefighter stereotype, but I didn't think it could possibly be true about so many of them. I'm okay with bending employee discrimination rules for restaurant hostesses, but is it really a good idea to be choosing the people who save our lives based on facial symmetry? The good-looking firemen are especially a problem since, as we were going to sleep last night, Cassandra said, "Wouldn't it be cool if you made all these firemen friends?" This was disturbing, especially since a firehouse was used more than once as a setting in the classic 1990s series of films called the Gangbang Girl. Plus, everyone knows that, as far as occupations that get you laid, fireman is number three—behind drummer and male prostitute. I am definitely not going to be making "all these firemen friends."

I do, however, need to be liked by everyone at all times. So my plan is to indeed make all these firemen friends but never tell Cassandra. I will claim I'm going out for the night to play poker with my dork friends, but I'll really go out with my firefighter friends, and we'll spend the night drinking light-colored American beer and recounting stories of danger and gangbanging girls.

But these guys are way better looking than I feared. All of them are significantly better looking than the firefighters in the Gangbang Girl videos. Cassandra will never meet these guys no matter how much our house is on fire.

They are also excellent homemakers. The kitchen is immaculate. I had no idea men were capable of being neat without women around. Seeing a lot of fires, apparently, makes you pretty concerned about clutter.

It's not just the kitchen that's clean. The garage is spotless, too. It looks like a museum room displaying two ambulances, an SUV, and two fire trucks with exhaust pipes that hook into hoses that vent out the ceiling to keep the carbon monoxide out.

I am a little disturbed that the stereo is blasting Death Cab for Cutie instead of Pantera or Motörhead, but I figure that's an 0700 thing. After a long conversation with Captain Buzz about the difference between fire trucks and fire engines that I really should have written down, he explains that as soon as I hear an alarm, I have to put on my jacket and hat and get in the fire truck engine within sixty seconds or my team will leave without me. I think this is an excellent policy to institute with Cassandra for whenever we go out.

Captain Buzz introduces me to Herbie Johnston, the engineer who drives the—I'm guessing here—fire truck I'll be riding in. Herbie, fifty-five, has a slight limp to his step and looks just like Robert Duvall with a mustache. He was drafted at nineteen, and he has surprisingly positive memories of the Vietnam War, which focused his life and gave him confidence and discipline. It is 0700 and I am talking about Vietnam.

I instantly like Herbie. That's because everybody likes Herbie. He's one of the few people I've ever met who is calm and chipper—like Tom Hanks without the nervous need to please. Herbie seems happy about everything. He's happy to be here early in the morning. He's happy that it's his turn to cook dinner tonight. He's happy he was drafted into the Vietnam War. The only thing Herbie isn't completely happy about is talking about all the lives he's saved in his three-decade-long career. When I ask him about that, he instead talks about how much he needs to be a fireman. Herbie has put off his retirement several times, using excuses and technicalities to drag his career slightly past where the city normally allows: "It's not the fires," he says. "It's the guys." If I were being rescued from a fire, I'd be instantly calmed by Herbie's face.

Herbie shows me the rest of the house. Anytime I compliment something nice—the food, the TV, the computer, the lockers to store their equipment, the chairs in their TV room (which is now called the meeting room to impress inspectors), the extra side-view mirrors on the engine—Herbie tells me that they were bought by the firefighters out of the three-dollar-per-day house dues they choose to pay out of their own pockets. This is the first time in my life that I feel like my taxes are not high enough.

I'm just finishing the tour when the alarm goes off, which is less like an alarm than a soothing young female voice suggesting we get going. Apparently, the real alarm occasionally gave firefighters in LA heart attacks, so they moved to this pseudo-phone-sex system. I scurry into the middle of the backseat, Herbie takes the driver's seat, another guy jumps in shotgun, and two men sit on either side of me. Herbie blasts the siren.

None of the three non-Herbie firefighters ask who I am or why I'm smushed against them. Are they that unflappable? That focused on the fire we're headed to? Are random unshowered dudes in sweatpants always popping up in their fire trucks?

As we race out of the station, siren blaring, everyone looking forward, headphones over their ears, my heart pounds. Are we going to have to pull out burning bodies? Will I be called on to hold a hose or an ax or a trampoline? Will the donuts cause everyone to cramp up at some key moment? Half a block from the station, when my panic starts to crescendo, Herbie turns off the siren. He drives around the block and pulls into one of the firehouse's three giant garage doors. Confused, I get out of the truck and take off my firefighter jacket. Herbie tells me this was a false alarm, which is common.

When we walk back into the house, Captain Buzz introduces me to the guys I'll be with for the day, the ones who seemed not to have noticed I was in their fire truck. Captain Paul Silveri, a squat, balding, squinty guy with several destroyed fingernails who looks like he could be in a Steven Bochco show, is two years from retirement and second in command to Captain Buzz, which entitles him to ride shotgun. Sitting on either side of me were Trevor Cooper, a calm, patient guy around my age, and Brett "Sparky" Sparkman, a slightly older, six-foot-three guy with glasses who looks like Plastic Man. Sparky's dad and uncle were firemen, and his son wants to be. Trevor is a third-generation LA firefighter, and both his brothers are also in the LAFD. Firefighters, apparently, are selected using the same method as cobblers and blacksmiths.

Though no soothing lady voice has beckoned us, my crew heads toward the truck. Captain Silveri explains that we're going to read to children at the Vine Elementary School. This confuses me. Reading to children is something I do every day. It is not manly. It is often done in a high voice with fake excitement about anthropomorphized animals. Can't Vine Elementary find other people to read to children, like teachers? Or me? Captain Silveri says the firehouse likes to be a good member of the community, and assures me that they do this only once a year. Other fire stations in the city will show up for a kid's birthday party for free if you ask them, but this one won't because it's too busy. If kids want to see the fire truck, Captain Silveri explains, they are just going to have to stop by the house and that's all there is to it. Though they can do it anytime. Without calling ahead. I am dealing with a pretty hardened group.

My new firefighter friends give me a pair of headphones with a chin microphone so we can talk to one another without yelling in the truck, where the roar of the motor and siren drown out our voices. The headset makes everything sound astronaut-important. Captain Silveri reads a printout of the email from the school. Apparently, we were each supposed to bring a favorite book to read.

"I have a *Maxim*," Trevor says. Everything is much funnier when said through the headsets.

We park the fire truck in the school's parking lot, effectively ending its usefulness as a parking lot. In the school's tiny library we add our names to a list of other readers: two female cops, three managers from Vons supermarket, a manager from Shakey's Pizza, and four retirees. We are bringing way too much star power for reading day. We need an auditorium, some pyrotechnics, and Dokken to rock out as we spray the kids down with hoses, put out the fireworks, and yell, "Here's your book, kids! The book of saving your fucking lives!"

Instead we sit down on tiny chairs at tiny tables surrounded by tiny bookshelves and wait for tiny, old librarian ladies to decide which kids get to be read to by us and which get stuck with the supermarket manager. But the kids who go off with the supermarket guy don't yell and cry and slice their Achilles tendons in protest. No, they just happily go off with the supermarket guy. I am not sending Laszlo to this school.

While Herbie stays at the truck, showing it to rotating classrooms of kids, Trevor and I go to one classroom, while Sparky and Captain Silveri go to another one. Trevor, who is great with kids, picks out *Johnny Appleseed*, which, it turns out, is a story about me. Johnny Appleseed is a giant pussy, refusing to wrestle or hunt or do any pioneer stuff. He just wants to help the environment and grow local, organic fruit. Also, he's way, way, way too into apples. He does, however, want to live in the forest, which is something I would never want to do, though I guess if all the city folks were as into wrestling and hunting as they seemed to be back then, I might consider it. After the story, they don't ask Trevor a lot of questions about Johnny Appleseed. Or about axes and ladders and trampolines. They ask a lot about living in a fire station, which they think is weird.

"Are you married?" one kid asks.

"I have a wife," Trevor says.

"Why don't you sleep with her?"

Trevor explains that he sometimes sleeps at the firehouse because LA firefighters work a twenty-four-hour shift every other day; after three shifts they get four days off. Which seems to sort of satisfy the kids, but not me. Cops have to deal with emergencies twenty-four hours a day, too, but they solve that problem by assigning some cops to night shifts. Cops don't have sleepovers. Neither do emergency room doctors, 7-Eleven managers, power plant workers, or CNN anchors. Lots of businesses are open twenty-four hours without having bedrooms in their office buildings. It's as if firefighters received our country's one charter to start adult fraternity houses. When I ask Captain Buzz Smith more about this, he explains that big fires happen at all hours, requiring a fully staffed station, and can last longer than eight hours. Cops, meanwhile, do a lot more predictable daytime work, such as investigations and walking a beat. Also, firefighters love one another very, very much.

We finish with the class and go back to the library, where Sparky and Captain Silveri look a little down.

"We thought we were doing pretty good until the guy from

Shakey's showed up. And then it was 'Shakey's! Shakey's!' We got upstaged by a pizza guy," Captain Silveri says.

At 1030 we head to our next assignment: a breakfast meet and greet at Hollywood Presbyterian Medical to improve strained relations between the firefighters and the hospital. Again, not what I expected from a day as a firefighter. Los Angeles has no separate ambulance service; if you call 911 to go to the hospital, the firefighters take you. They all know CPR and some are specialized in emergency response. I assumed that putting out blazing buildings was enough of a job. Taking guys with heart attacks to the hospital, I thought, was the volunteer work of socially awkward dudes without girlfriends who you get stuck talking to at extended family functions.

But since LA firefighters do have to bring people to hospitals, they want to get along with the people who work at those hospitals. Especially because they have to wait in the emergency room with their heart attack sufferers until the hospital admits them. Not simply until the hospital signs them in to the waiting room, but until the patient goes into the examining room. Which takes hours. Which doesn't make the firefighters happy, since they didn't sit in their kindergarten classes dreaming of one day driving in a fire engine to make small talk with people who need rides to emergency rooms. The hospitals aren't happy with the firefighters, since they wish the firefighters would talk these patients out of coming here, since they not only don't have insurance, but almost never have an actual emergency. But to avoid lawsuits, the city's policy is that the firefighters have to take anyone to the hospital who calls 911 and asks. So the hospital and the firefighters don't get along that well. I can see now how the American health care system leads to inefficiencies like firefighters eating breakfast at a hospital.

Herbie tells me that more than 80 percent of their calls are for ambulance services, not fires. And that 85 percent of those calls are for injuries so trivial, I would never think to even see a doctor for them. Sparky has been to a call where someone had a cockroach on him. Two of the guys promise me that they have separately been called to apartments where the person wanted to have their television remote control handed to them. More shockingly, they did it.

"When it comes to dialing 911, there are no urban myths. Think about it: How easy is it to call three digits?" firefighter Justin Draeger tells me later. Justin said that a hazmat unit was sent in for a poisonous leak that turned out to be a skunk. Most of the people who call 911 for stupid reasons, he says, are either really poor or really rich. "It's people who don't know how to take care of themselves. The unfortunate and the pampered. Celebrities will call us for the same things as poor people."

The lame-ass calls are only increasing. "Cell phones have doubled our load," Trevor says. "You or I would stop someone on the street and see if they're okay. They'll walk by and call. Or they'll call and say, 'Hey, I see smoke in the sky.'" I like Trevor's assumption that I wouldn't call 911 after seeing something awry because I would deal with the situation myself. I wouldn't call because I don't care.

Heading to the hospital, Trevor points out that a guy in the car next to us is smoking crack.

"There's no law against that," Herbie jokes into our headphones. It's pretty cool to work for the city and not have to enforce any of its stupid rules about smoking crack while driving.

We arrive at the hospital late, due to our full morning of reading *Johnny Appleseed*. There is no one from the hospital to greet us, but someone leads us to a little area outside with a few covered metal trays of not-so-great food, which is not surprising since it's from a hospital. If the hospital really wanted to improve relations, they would have offered free drugs. We eat alone, not doing a lot to mend the relationship with Hollywood Presbyterian. Especially because about ten minutes into our breakfast, the firefighters' radios go off and we have to run to the fire truck like we're in a movie, tossing plates into the garbage as we run. There's a possible DB, which is a dead body, but said in code so it won't freak out people who try to overhear things on firefighters' radio signals, who are probably a pretty easily freaked-out group. Also, apparently, not master code crackers. Sparky and Trevor put on latex gloves, which apparently they carry around all the time. I'm definitely not telling Cassandra about that.

I'm not sure why we have to turn on the siren and race to a body that's already dead, though I guess if there was a dead body in my house, I'd want it out of there pretty quickly. Herbie drives fast and smooth, slowing down for reds but never stopping. He shows no annoyance at the shocking number of people who don't pull over, pull over to the left instead of the right, or just continue driving along rocking out to the radio, unaware of the enormous red truck blaring its siren right behind them.

When we get to the building with the possible DB, we are waved off by a small ambulance from another fire station that beat us there. I am completely unsure about whether I'm supposed to feel good or bad that we lost the race to a dead body. It turns out: totally psyched. These guys aren't so different from me after all; we both prefer not to pick up dead bodies. Captain Silveri decides that we shouldn't return to the hospital, since that situation seemed awkward and donutless.

Instead, we stop at a store to buy some glass for Trevor's project. You put real men in a house together, and each of them is going to create a little shop project to work on. Trevor is making a glass box to put the house's American flag in at night. Really. For fun. With his own money. I ask Herbie if he has a project, and Herbie explains that he's done some construction work. I tell him about my lack of skills; if I were a firefighter my project would be making a spreadsheet of all the other firefighters' projects.

"It's all exposure," Herbie says. "If someone said, 'You're not going to eat until you put up these two-by-fours,' you might get a few black-and-blue fingers, but you'd figure it out. You've just never been exposed." I am deathly afraid that Herbie is about to tell me that I'm not going to eat until I put up these two-by-fours, but he is more the Yoda flavor of mentor than Mr. Miyagi.

Right after returning to the station, we head back out for lunch at In-N-Out Burger, which I've avoided since my preemptive binge eating with the Boy Scouts. But this burger will be far manlier, eaten out of confidence instead of fear. Sitting at a picnic table in a park next to the Hollywood Heritage Museum at 1158, I eat my first-ever morning cheeseburger.

"We burned it down," says Herbie of the building we are sitting next to.

I am not sure why our firehouse would have done that, but I am guessing that someone at the Hollywood Heritage Museum messed with us bad, totally ignoring our heritage. Instead, it turns out that *We burned it down* is a phrase firefighters use when they fail to put out a fire, kind of like when doctors say "We lost him." I like that they take such responsibility. At my job, I tend to say things like, "That sentence wrote itself stupid."

Other than Captain Silveri, my firefighter friends are Republicans. They care about the homeless, whom they deal with constantly, and think health care needs to be reformed, and that more money should be spent on government services such as firefighting, but they're big on self-reliance, family values, and Jesus Christ. Being a liberal just isn't very manly. In fact, the firefighters generally think that society has become so liberal, manliness is disappearing. The LAFD has banned hazing new firefighters, including dropping buckets of water on them from the roof. "We can't do that anymore because people have feelings now," Sparky says.

While I pretend to agree that a society where buckets of water are dumped on people's heads for no reason is a far better one, I begin to wonder if manliness isn't that necessary anymore. Maybe as technology makes life easier, manliness is doomed to fade away.

For most of history, human life didn't change much, and men were indeed men and women were indeed beaten. But in the last five hundred years, society has been evolving exponentially faster, and most of us have shed our need to hunt, build, fight, and farm. So we've gotten softer. Each generation before us was more badass. In hunter-gatherer societies more than 15 percent of people died due to violence; in the twentieth century, despite the invention of submachine guns, despite the Holocaust and Stalin, the chances of a European or American dying due to violence were less than 1 percent. Our grandfathers, silent and distant as they may have seemed to us, would have been far too sensitive and emotive for their dads, who came home spent and angry from physical labor at the mine/field/barn raising. And their ancestors, if the Bible is any guide, would have been even more surly and silent, having spent their day being invaded and enslaved by the tribe one town over. Though masculinity drives progress, progress is the enemy of masculinity.

These firefighters seem retro in their love of guy stuff and guy time, like they want to form a lodge and memorize oaths and wear fezzes. Living together several days a month isn't enough; they take guy trips together on their mutual days off: motorcycle races, ski trips, waterskiing.

"We have the same days off. If we stay at home, we get lonely," says Herbie. "I've got two families. One here and one at home. Only this one is dysfunctional."

We leave our picnic and are parking the fire truck in the street in front of Ralphs supermarket to shop for dinner when we get a call to go to a fire. Not a sick guy or someone who saw a mouse. A real fire. We go screaming up a hill near the HOLLYWOOD sign to a house where a guy is standing outside, waving his arms and shaking his head. "It was just a toaster," he explains. It turns out that this is not the first time my new friends have been to this stringed instrument repair shop. None of the firefighters seem suspicious about why people working at a stringed instrument repair shop make toast so often and so poorly.

Back at the supermarket, Herbie can spend only seven dollars per person on dinner, which seems hard, but he's got a plan: his famous chicken chimichangas and Mississippi mud pie. I assume every firefighter recipe is preceded by the word *famous*, but everyone assures me I'm lucky to have come this night. Which seems unbelievable due to the quality of ingredients Herbie is buying: canned refried beans, jarred salsa, fake cheese, instant chocolate pudding mix, Cool Whip, vanilla wafers. I had better ingredients when I cooked with Wiggles.

I would have thought there would be more room in the fire truck for groceries, but the firefighters have wasted all the storage space on stuff to save people's lives, so we have to put the bags on our laps or on the floor near our feet. That's when we get a call that there's a DB a few streets away from us. We head to Santa Monica Boulevard near Highland Avenue and get out, but I don't see anything on the sidewalk. Trevor, however, walks right over to a large cement flowerpot, pushes it aside, and there it is. The first dead body I've ever seen. He's wearing a huge purple sweatshirt, black sweatpants, and Air Jordan sneakers, facedown on a garbage bag holding everything he owns. Trevor puts on his latex gloves and flips the body over gently. There are bruises all over the dead man's wide stomach, which is peeking out over his sweatpants. When Trevor turns the man's head and pulls aside his long hair, I see black and blue all over the man's face. He looks like he's sleeping, but he's not. He's still got a hospital bracelet on. Trevor says the man probably died during the night. He goes through the man's bag looking for identification. Sparky throws a white sheet over the body. Everyone is quiet.

I expect to vomit or cry, but I feel nothing. Maybe it's the culmination of living in cities where I've seen too many homeless people and walked by them unguiltily, which is far worse than not feeling anything now. Or maybe there's just not much to feel about a person you've never met who died nonviolently, whether his body has been dead for ten hours or ten years. Or maybe I've soaked up a little of the firefighters' toughness. But weirder than not feeling anything is that I don't feel anything about not feeling anything. I'm fine with it.

The only thing I do feel, standing there in the sunshine, is that there are probably dead bodies behind cement flowerpots all over the city, that I've been seeing some fake clean bright surface of the world without bothering to look closely. That there's this small group of men who spend their days cleaning these streets so I can maintain my false assumptions about everything being okay. It makes me feel distant from the real world I suddenly realize I'm oblivious to, as I stand in sunglasses with my arms crossed, awaiting pickup on a dead body.

Unfortunately, it's nearly 1500, and all these city buses keep dropping off scores of kids at a bench that serves as some kind of transfer point on their way home from school. At first they don't notice the body under the sheet, and all these giggling teenage girls squeal about the cute firefighters and, even though I don't feel anything about the dead man himself, I do feel like this scene is awful, just highlighting the fact that this death is invisible. Then the girls see the body with the sheet over it and it's even worse, since they stop and grab their chests and yell "ohmigod" like teenage girls do about everything and ask if it's a dead body. Trevor, who has put on his sunglasses, slowly nods yes as if trying to impart the seriousness this deserves, but there's more yelling and nervous giggling and it's just horrible, both for the dead man and for the girls.

When they get on their bus, Trevor turns to Sparky.

"You know that guy Marshall?"

"Tom Marshall?"

"I think it's him. It's hard to tell."

Tom Marshall was the guitarist of Pacific Gas & Electric, a

bluesy band in the 1970s whose hit "Are You Ready?" has this cho-
rus: "Are you ready to sit by His throne? / Are you ready not to be
alone? / Someone's coming to take you home / And if you're ready,
then He'll carry you home." There's a documentary in which Marshall's old bandmates try to get him off this very corner, where he's
lived on the street for decades, but they fail.

A group of boys comes off a bus, throwing a basketball at one
another. Tony Prouzinin, thirteen, short, with braces, sees the
white sheet first.

"Is that a dead body?" he asks.

"Yes," Trevor answers.

"That's crazy. I would think something more would happen
when someone dies."

"Like what?"

"Like hundreds of cops. That's crazy. Is there blood?"

"No."

"That's crazy. I want to see what happens. No one even cares.
All these people are sitting right next to him. That's so weird."

Trevor asks the boys if they knew Mr. Marshall and they say they
did, since they get dropped off here, on his corner, every weekday.
There's not much more to say, but the boys want to see what happens
next, so they stand off to the side, waiting. We're just standing there,
too, waiting for the cops to arrive. We're not talking, which makes all
non-real men like me uncomfortable, so I ask Trevor if he remembers
seeing his first dead body. He thinks about it for a long time. "No,"
he says. But after a little bit of silence, he tells me that the first corpse
he does remember was a thirteen-year-old who hanged himself on a
backyard swing set after getting in a fight with his mom about home-
work and she went to the market. I wish he had left it at "no."

Finally, two cops arrive. Trevor has been patiently answering
various kids' questions for nearly half an hour. But five seconds
after the cops arrive, they yell at the kids: "Hey, guys, get out of
here! Go! Go!" Which the boys do. Firefighters seem like entirely

different people from cops, who spend all day getting in conflicts; firefighters only encounter people asking for their help.

The cops put up yellow caution tape and wait for the coroner. We, meanwhile, have milk sitting in the fire truck. So we go back to the house, where I help Herbie cook. Since I've never cooked right after seeing a dead body, I fail to follow basic etiquette by keeping the dead body out of the conversation. Herbie can't remember seeing his first corpse, either. Then, after a pause, he adds: "I remember the first child call I went on. The first and probably only time I almost threw up on this job." It was a nine-year-old girl. Her mom had gone out and her stepfather had molested her and shot her in the head. The lesson is to never ask a firefighter if he remembers his first dead body.

While we scald milk for the mud pie, Herbie tells me about all the great pranks he's pulled over his long career, probably to distract me from my concerns about getting sick from milk left on the fire truck too long. Herbie once convinced his wife that the trailer he owns was full of rat droppings. But they were actually chocolate chips he had put there. So he ate one off the floor in front of her. Herbie enjoyed that one. Another time, after another firefighter fixed an outlet in the wall, Herbie pumped smoke in it. So the guy had to pull out all the wiring and try to figure out what went wrong for the rest of the day. Herbie senses my confusion over why that was cool, probably because I don't laugh and instead say, "I'm confused over why that was cool." Herbie explains that guys bond over pranks. It's exactly what Wiggles was trying to explain to me when we tortured those inner-city kids: that the snipes were just as important to the Boy Scouts as square knots or blood circles. It was affection masked as hostility. Just like Yoda, Herbie is teaching me how to use forces I can barely understand. Like being a dick.

I tell Herbie about snipes and he tells me that, even though his kids have long since grown out of Boy Scouts, he is a scoutmaster, too. In fact, a lot of the firefighters here are either scoutmasters or were Eagle Scouts. I fear that even though I planned to meet a bunch of different types of men for advice—firefighters, hunters, marines—I'm actually just going to wind up traveling among the same fifty last real men.

It's almost dinnertime when the soothing lady voice goes off again and we all pile in the fire truck. Herbie stays behind to finish cooking, so some other guy drives, and I don't feel quite as comfortable. Especially because this time everybody is quiet and super-focused. That's because this isn't a medical call: There's a house fire. We're going fast down Sunset Boulevard at rush hour, driving in dead-still traffic on the wrong side of the street, finding gaps I don't even see, slowing down at the reds just enough to make sure no one does anything stupid. Then we head up into the hills—twisting, skinny roads where cars don't see us behind them and glance in shock over the tiny spaces we find to get through. It's like we're driving the Indy 500 in the biggest car in the world, and there are obstacles on almost every inch of the track. It's a beautiful thing to witness.

We're a block away from the house that's on fire when we turn around. Another station's fire truck got there a minute or two before us. Everyone in our fire truck is truly bummed. This confuses me. I figured a good day for a firefighter is when you don't have to walk into a burning building. That firefighters would scold people about using candles and failing to keep fire extinguishers around. No. These guys are rooting for fires. They've trained their whole careers for fires, and they rarely get to put one out. They're careful not to complain about a lack of fires, but when they talk about the effectiveness of the LA law requiring buildings of more than two stories to have sprinklers on every floor, they don't say it with a lot of enthusiasm. They didn't become firefighters to take people to the hospital or deal with dead bodies. That's why every fire station in any area remotely close to this house sent their fire trucks racing here, trying to be first to the fire so they could go in, rather than standing back and pointing hoses or going on the roof to chop escape holes for the smoke.

"We're like dogs. We train and train and train for this one thing, so when it comes you want to do it," says Captain Silveri. The only thing manlier than firefighting is being upset about a lack of fires to fight.

When we get back to the house, one of the firefighters from another fire truck tells us that the house we just rushed to is owned by some actor.

"It's Justin Bateman's house," he says.

"Who?" someone else asks.

"The actor."

"Not Justin. Justine? No, that's his sister."

"Jason?" I ask. "Jason Bateman?"

"Yeah. The actor."

I've interviewed hundreds of celebrities, and Bateman is the only one who stayed in touch with me, inviting me to a few Dodger games. And his house was on fire. And I failed to save him. I send him an email asking if he's okay. This is what he wrote back:

"Ha! Wow, what a coincidence!

They were unnecessarily dispatched. We called them to ask their advice. We had a raging fire going in our fireplace then realized that the chimney was shut—and STUCK!—so the house was filling with smoke.

The lady on the phone advised us to put it out with water instead of our fire extinguisher. We did. Then, as I was getting ready to get in there and manhandle the thing, the trucks showed up.

Overall, a very emasculating event.

This is tremendous. Most conversations Bateman and I have are contests to see who is a bigger pussy. Yes, Bateman has season tickets to the Dodgers and brings a glove and has a fantasy baseball team, but that's one step away from being a forty-year-old whose birthday cake is shaped like a Dodger cap. Sure, Bateman watches the UFC and has a dog and races cars, but I have been with him when he's bought scented candles, expensive soap, and those soft, expensive designer T-shirts. Still, I've always won our biggest-pussy contests. So I email him right back to make fun of him. He responds immediately:

> And the capper is that I probably could've figured the g-damned thing myself, without the phone assist, if I wasn't on week three of a triple gay, very Hollywood, mother fucking CLEANSE! I'm so hungry that my body is now eating my own brain, clearly having finished off my balls earlier in the day.
> I hate my wife . . .

He is totally winning the pussy contest. Being a firefighter even for just one day is making me manlier.

I sit down for dinner, which the firefighters call Family Time, next to Captain Buzz, who is easy to talk to but never starts a conversation. He's oddly quiet, calm, and non-threatening. The main thing I've seen him do is paperwork. He stands back and lets other people make a lot of decisions. He is not the guy I would have thought would be chosen to inspire men to risk their lives. But he's got what Wiggles has: the ability to listen, and a greater interest in living by his own rules than in being loved. You don't want your leader to be the toughest, the coolest, the funniest, the most charismatic. You want him to represent something bigger than himself.

Herbie's chimichangas really are illogically delicious and the mud pie is even better, like some white-trash meal I'm going to crave all the time. I eat two helpings of everything. I would be a fire-fighter for the day again just for the food. I happily pay my three-dollar house dues and seven dollars for dinner. I wish I could have tipped, but manly jobs never involve getting tips.

The firefighters invented a series of games to determine who cleans the dishes. These games all take far longer than it would take to clean the dishes. Women could live together in a house for years and they would never come up with this system, or even understand it. But I love it. I love that boys turn something lame into something fun. It's like an anti-complaining gene.

Unfortunately, the game involves a basketball and a hoop, instead of what I had hoped for, which was graph paper, medieval figurines, and a twenty-sided die. I am bad at all sports, but I am worse at basketball than any other sport including hockey and I don't know how to ice-skate. The worst part is that we had a basketball net on our driveway and my dad, who played for his high school team, taught me how to shoot. He told me that the only way to get good was to stand there and take shots for hours. I can't do anything for hours except sleep. It's why I don't know how to play an instrument, speak a foreign language, or give decent oral sex.

Everyone is pretty excited to play, until the Chief shows up. The Chief of the district, who has his own car and driver, works out of this office. He is squat and bald and, needless to say, mustachioed and very tough looking. Everyone seems a little nervous, like they're not sure whether the Chief is allowed to do dishes. Worse yet, the Chief absolutely sucks at basketball. He's one of the few people I've ever seen play basketball where I thought, *I could be in a league with that guy.* He is so bad at basketball that he stops looking tough when he's playing. Picture John Wayne getting on a horse and waving his hands as if they were made of jazz and yelling "yipes" and you'll get an idea of what the Chief looks like playing basketball. He is sent to the dishwashing line after one shot.

For reasons that I assume have to do with adrenaline left over from my triumph over Bateman, I play so well that I am one of the last people sent off to the dishes crew. I believe these five minutes can make an inspiring sports movie. However, the game is not nearly over. The dishwashers are actually just a pool of potential dishwashers. So when I somehow make a three-pointer in the second stage of the game, I am not only freed from the line of dishwashers but also allowed to banish one of the winners to the loser team. I have learned from other uncomfortable guy situations that I have to pick the most powerful person here. That way the other guys will think I'm tough for taking on the alpha dog, but, really, the alpha dog longs to fit in by being picked on. Unfortunately, the Chief is already on the loser team. So I pick the next guy down the alpha dog chain: Captain Buzz. Everyone makes an impressed noise at my gutsy selection and Captain Buzz smiles. He beats me, and I am sent back to the losers.

But—and this is something cops would never do—we all do the dishes. We played a game more complicated than cricket for half an hour, and everyone does the dishes anyway. And fast. Without a dishwasher. There's a military efficiency to everything these guys do.

After dinner, fireman and paramedic Brian Quick tells us the dead body we found was not Tom Marshall, the guy from the band Pacific Gas & Electric. It was another homeless man. I walk outside with Brian and sit by an unlit fire pit filled with wooden palettes ready to be set ablaze. These guys really like fire. Brian talks to me, first about Boy Scouts, but then about the Bible and how the end of the world is coming soon. This is a part of being a man that I am not so interested in.

It's 2100, so we should really go to sleep, since we were at work at 0600 and are likely to be woken up during the night. But there are no moms or wives to tell us to go to bed. We can work out at 2100 if we want to. And we do.

In a little gym off the garage, there's a TV hanging in the corner of the room. *Showgirls* is on Cinemax. Someone declares a moment of silence for the lesbian makeout scene. Then Dave Grijalva farts. "Did you eat a dead baby?" asks Tom Macintyre.

Even among firefighters, Tom is really good-looking; of all the firefighters Cassandra will not meet, she will particularly never meet him. Tom went to Cal State Fullerton, where he eventually decided he didn't want to be a writer.

"I was reading Sartre and Kierkegaard and all these people who had done stuff before they started writing," he says. "I started to think, *I want to stop thinking about stuff and start doing stuff.* I thought about being a cop, but I didn't want to be a douchebag for my whole life. I decided to do stuff that was awesome." I add "stop thinking about stuff and start doing stuff" to The List of advice for Laszlo.

His first week on the job, Tom pulled a guy from underneath a subway car he'd been pushed in front of. When he got him out, Tom discovered he was just pulling the guy's torso, since his legs had been sliced off. "I'm only twenty-five, but I've seen a whole life," Tom says.

Captain Buzz had told me that they don't use the pole anymore, since it caused some injuries and it doesn't save much time over the stairs. Many stations throughout the country, in fact, don't have poles anymore. Dave, the dead-baby farter, tells me that this thing about not using the pole is bullshit. Oh, they use the pole. Not because the pole is so much faster than stairs but because the pole is so much awesomer than stairs.

Dave tells me to jump onto the pole, grab it with both hands, wrap my legs around it, and just slide down by letting up on my leg pressure. This sounds impossible. Dave insists it isn't. So I jump into the void. I'm slowly sliding down the pole, feeling manly, like whatever the exact opposite of a stripper is. I go right back up and do it again. Dave tells me that I've had enough.

The soothing lady voice goes off yet again. It's a medical run, so the guys tell me to stay behind at the house, since this is a nothing deal. But I go anyway. They don't even bother turning on the siren.

We walk into an elderly Filipino woman's apartment. It's decorated with a lot of Asian knickknacks, many of them representations of the Buddha. But she also has figurines of Jesus, one of those mounted Big Mouth Billy Bass things that sings Al Green's "Take Me to the River," and two collectible *Star Wars* cups filled with Samuel L. Jackson Jedi puppets on either side of a lamp. It's like she hired a decorator whose aesthetic was American Immigrant Experience Mockery.

The woman, who is eighty, tells Dave that she is dizzy and wants to go to a hospital.

"I want to go to the Philippines to die," she says.

"You want to go to the Philippines to die?" Brian asks.

She sits up straight and looks at him like he's an idiot. "Of course."

We get to the hospital, where the woman tells us about her husband, who died a few years ago and fought in the Korean War. This woman is neither sick nor happy with us, but Brian says he doesn't mind helping her, compared with his usual calls. Her husband served the country, he explains, and she deserves whatever she needs at this point in her life. Still, we're glad to be rid of her.

I'm not back in the station for long when I get back in the ambulance for another medical run. We park outside a halfway house, where a ragged, old guy stands in the street, saying his nose got hurt in a fight. His nose looks fine. In fact, his nose is so okay that he's threatening another old guy who lives there. I am hardly an expert in street fighting, but I don't think you can intimidate someone while standing in front of an ambulance you called for yourself.

Even this pathetic form of fighting makes me tense. The darkness, the summer smell of the asphalt, it makes me picture my last fight. It was the summer I turned seventeen, and it was technically half of a fight, since only one guy was fighting while the other guy stood still and got punched. I was walking down the street with my friend Mike Gorker in Long Beach Island, New Jersey, where my family rented a house every summer, when a guy literally called me "four-eyes" from the pizza parlor across the way. I ignored him, but he and his friends crossed the street to where we were, and he pushed me. I don't know if he thought I was dating this girl Stephanie whom I later heard he liked, or if he really just hated the bespectacled. I wrestled him to the ground and got up, thinking it was over, since that was as far as I'd ever seen people fight. Then the guy who hated eyeglasses and all they represented stood up and punched me in the face. I fell. I got up wanting to discuss whatever misunderstanding we were having. He punched me again. I fell again. We did this pas de deux three times. Gorker stood there with the guy's friends and watched. I had surrounded myself with even bigger pussies than I was.

I touch my eye, remembering the black eye I had from that fight, and how I refused to let my father teach me how to box that night, as desperately as he wanted to. I should have let him but I just wanted to forget what had happened and figure out how to never let it happen again. I'm going to have to fix that. I don't know if I need to just let my dad finally teach me, or take a martial arts class, or find a bully and stand up to him, but I've got to get over this fear. It's going to be the culmination of this quest.

It does not seem appropriate, however, to make my first opponent this elderly schizophrenic man with nose hypochondria. While it would probably be a fair fight, I think my firefighter friends wouldn't appreciate all the emotional baggage I'd suddenly be dropping on this old guy as I punched him in the eye and yelled, "I got LASIK, bitch!"

Instead, we take the hurt-nose guy to the emergency room at

Hollywood Presbyterian, where we wait for a nurse to admit him. The guys who drove me here are more impatient than I've seen any firefighter today.

"The worst thing is when you're here and you missed an actual fire," Justin Draeger says.

Missing a fire, I'm starting to understand, is like missing free blowjob day and then having to live in a house where all your friends talk about how awesome free blowjob day was.

We're eventually ushered out of the waiting room into the hospital, but we still can't leave until a doctor shows up to take hurt-nose guy. The waiting takes so long that the hurt-nose guy starts to feel bad for us.

"How about you get out of here and leave me here?" hurt-nose guy asks.

"I wish it were that easy," says firefighter Robert Cole.

To which the hurt-nose guys responds, "Tell me this: Is Mel Gibson an actor or am I crazy?"

Without pausing, Cole says, "How about a little bit of both?"

As soon as a doctor shows up, we drive away from the hospital, going much faster than we drove there. We pull the ambulance into the firehouse around 2200, get out, and immediately see two guys welding. Yes, welding. I join them, putting on a welding helmet, burning some metal into some other metal, and feeling great about it, when the soothing lady voice goes off again at 2230. I join two firefighters as we drive an ambulance to a corner where a super-gay, super-skinny guy with no shirt is standing bloody-mouthed while his pimp looks on. I know he's a pimp because he is dressed exactly like a pimp. He is dressed more like a pimp than my buddies are dressed like firemen. If he did something else for a living and showed up in his outfit, everyone would say, "Hey, you must have mistakenly thought this job involves pimping." Eventually, Brian walks over to the shirtless, super-gay-looking, bloody guy.

"Who did this?" Brian asks.

"Some faggots," shirtless, super-gay-looking, bloody guy says.

Brian offers some bandages and performs a brief examination, and the shirtless, super-gay-looking, bloody guy says he doesn't need to go the hospital. Driving back, the firefighters point out a whole world I've never seen right in my neighborhood. The Donut Time in a strip mall on Highland Avenue and Santa Monica Boulevard is known as Tranny Donuts; everyone besides me, it seems—even weight-conscious transsexuals—eats donuts. There's a bar for gay ranchero cowboys. There's a gay bathhouse and a huge apartment full of elderly, first-generation Russians. There are female hookers right out on Santa Monica and Highland as if Craigslist doesn't exist.

What else am I oblivious to? Are there guys rolling dice in sewers, betting one thousand dollars against their souls? Are there choreographed knife fights between Italians and Puerto Ricans? Are there drunk orphanage matrons abusing children? Is my knowledge of society's underbelly really limited to Broadway musicals?

The house is pretty quiet when we get back at 2330, so I, too, head up to bed. Herbie is already asleep in a bed about ten feet from me. I turn on my little light, put a glass of water on the ledge next to my bed, look at the alarm, and wrap my giant comforter around me. I am really happy.

I know we didn't put out any fires, and I know I'm not a real firefighter, but it feels like I accomplished much more today than I usually do. Even when we weren't doing much besides the dishes, we were doing it as a team. I know I'm not brave enough, athletic enough, or calm enough under pressure to be a firefighter—that my natural skills don't jibe nearly as well with firefighting as they do with writing dumb jokes about firefighting—but I honestly think I'd enjoy this. I don't want to stay away from Cassandra and Laszlo for nights at a time. I don't want to risk my life. But I think that if I did, I'd be happier. I am right now.

An hour later the soothing woman alarm goes off and I am

out of bed, my mouth somehow already as gross as if I'd slept the whole night. I get in the fire truck and everyone is fully awake, with a hopeful energy. We are driving faster than we have all day. Every few blocks another fire truck gets in front of us, or behind us, until we are stretched out down Sunset Boulevard like a funeral procession. I feel the same dry-mouth nerves I felt the first time Herbie drove this morning, not sure how I'll be able to handle a real fire, if I'll get confused by the chaos and get in the way, or if I'll just get scared and run back from the burning building.

We arrive at a strip mall on Sunset and North Crescent Heights Boulevard, and for a moment we don't know where exactly the fire is and where to park, so we lose just a minute to the other fire trucks, but that's enough. By the time we park next to Kura Sushi, guys from another station have pushed a hose straight into the building. Another station has gotten the second-best gig: axing through the glass door of the second-floor dental office to get to the restaurant's ceiling. It's just a kitchen fire, and we've got enough equipment in this parking lot to put out a forest. Everyone is frantic, pushing to get to the fire, and a few of our guys somehow get in, but most of us are stuck out here, looking for stuff to do. Herbie holds me back from heading toward the building and brings me to find a hydrant that no one has spotted. We hook up our hose and point it at the restaurant. The fire is out before we even get to turn the hose on. Standing there in the light rain, Herbie looks a little down.

I am, too. I'd always assumed when firefighters rushed into burning buildings, they willed selflessness to overpower dread. But that's what happens when they sign up to be firefighters. At an actual fire, they are driven by selfish excitement. And I feel it. It trumps fear, this thrill. I wanted to be in that building. I have no idea what purpose I could possibly serve there, and I doubt I would have felt this way if it were a towering inferno instead of a kitchen flare-up at a sushi joint, but at least I felt the cave shadow of bravery.

After some minor arguing over jurisdiction and some pulling out of maps, all the firefighters from the other stations go home, since the restaurant is technically in the area we cover. As soon as I see an opening, I push through the smoky sushi restaurant, which is surprisingly intact. The sushi case has been broken, but the fish looks fine. The floors aren't that dirty. Not very much water has been sprayed in here at all. It doesn't look like a fire. And it certainly doesn't smell like the smoky wood barbecue smell I expected. It smells like burned plastic.

I wonder why a sushi place has a kitchen. And why would it burn down at 0030? I am not the only one with such questions. The Chief with poor basketball skills has floodlights and flashlights pointed everywhere. Guys from the gas company show up to check things out. I wonder if they have a little house they sleep in, too. Eventually, the Chief calls for the arson unit.

I did not know that after putting out a fire, the firefighters stay to clean up. They are separating destroyed items from salvageable ones, sweeping ash in garbage bags. This seems insane. People don't even clean up after coming to your party. It's like they were apologizing for coming into the place and putting out their fire. You know what would have made the place easier to clean up for us? If we let it completely burn down.

Half of the guys are staying behind to finish cleaning, which will take hours. And despite my arguments, they refuse to even take any of the sushi, which is going to go bad anyway. Cleaning seems pretty unmanly, so I get back in the fire truck with Herbie and head back to the station with half the group. Everyone is too excited to go to sleep, so we go to the kitchen, and at 0130, Dave Grijalva, the very nice firefighter who had not long ago farted in a way that caused others to ask if he'd eaten a dead baby, pulls

Herbie's famous chimichangas and Mississippi mud pie out of the refrigerator. I grab a spoonful and sit next to Herbie, excited to talk to him about the fire, but Herbie is a little sad about it. I get the feeling he fears he's lost a step. And that every fire might be his last. He's glad to have gone on a run with his crew, to have one more story to bond over, but I sense he wishes that fire had been just a little bigger and he had gotten just a little more of it.

Herbie and I head upstairs to sleep. Except that every thirty minutes, the front doorbell rings. At 0600 I get up to see what's going on. Brian Quick is at the front door, talking to the old man who has been ringing the bell all night. He yells at Brian: "Your mother's a jughead!" An exhausted Brian stays polite as his mother is impugned over and over. Doorbell Ringer spits out a string of curses that I can't print here because it is 0600 and I didn't remember to bring my pad to write them down. The guy is coughing all over Brian, and Brian just says, "Sir, cover your mouth," followed, after more mother-baiting, with "Sir, watch your mouth." Eventually, Brian agrees to take him to the hospital, because it will get rid of him.

I go upstairs and pack up my stuff. I haven't made my own bed since junior high, but I do my best to make sure the sheet is on perfectly straight. I expect there's some final meeting, some discussion of the fine job we did, maybe a group hug. But there isn't. Everyone just heads to their cars. Which are trucks. I carry my down comforter and pillow to my Mini Cooper. Everything is too bright and shiny, right back to the surface world I saw before. I thought what I'd like about firefighting was feeling like a superhero. But they are more like social workers and chauffeurs for the poor. They have house projects, elaborate dinners, and dishwashing games because there aren't nearly enough fires to bond over. And the bonding is the best part. I've always hated all-male environments. Whenever one demographic hangs out exclusively, they start acting dumb, since no one is around to tell them they're dumb. It's why sorority girls sing in public, members of all-white golf clubs eat tasteless food, and so much creepy stuff takes place in Japan. But I love the cheery, orderly, polite, boy-like world these guys have built. I think that's because their guiding purpose, even though it's been stifled by lawyers and sprinkler systems, is sacrifice. And I sensed, at that sushi fire, that while I have buried that instinct, it's somewhere in me, possibly ready to come out if I ask it to. These guys have made me glad we had a boy. I just hope Laszlo turns out like these guys. And not the guys who call 911 all day.

A few months later, I bring the guys dinner to thank them for letting me spend the day with them. Plus, Captain Buzz offered to let Laszlo climb around a fire truck, and he's been getting oddly excited about fire trucks—all kinds of trucks really. It's his first sign of manliness and I want to encourage it. The problem is, I cannot convince Cassandra not to come. I also cannot convince her that a freak cold front has hit LA and she has to wear many layers of clothing.

Laszlo is very excited to see the garage full of fire trucks, but when Captain Buzz opens the door of one and puts Laszlo behind the wheel, he instantly cries. I did not see this coming. Captain Buzz says this happens all the time with boys his age. "It's just his personality. He's a cautious dude," Cassandra explains. "He likes fire trucks in miniature form or from a distance. He knows that real men drive these big trucks." Non-real-men hold their sons tightly and feel more and more sure that bringing their wife was a big mistake after hearing her refer to the firefighters as "real men."

When I walk into the kitchen and see the guys, it's awkward—quiet and stilted and formal. No joking, no making fun of one another, no farting. Herbie seems like a friendly, old, shy guy, stripped of all the wisdom and bravery, like Yoda without puppeteers. At first I think they're all acting like this because I'm a foreigner again, no longer part of the day's routine. Then I realize: It's Cassandra. I don't think she notices, so impressed is she with the manly handsome men who save lives and clean dishes. I am wrong.

"I don't need to do that again," Cassandra says as soon as we get in our car.

"What?" I ask, confused. "They weren't good-looking? They weren't nice?"

"They were," she says. "But when you're talking about a bunch of LA firefighters, I think of cosmopolitan dudes who have this added bonus of manliness. But really they were just small-town, Middle American dudes who just happen to be in LA." Cassandra realizes she's searching for a unicorn: masculinity and urbanity in a straight dude. I'm not that far from what she wants. Coming here to make Laszlo cry was totally worth it.

"When a woman walks into a situation like that, and there's no sexual possibility, dudes like that treat you with awkwardness," she says. "I felt like these dudes don't socialize with women much, as opposed to the parties we go to where it's not a big deal. If anything we flirt with one another's spouses."

I did not know that we flirt with our friends' spouses. But it might explain why Cassandra says that every decent-looking couple we meet—including one we talked to on our mutual honeymoons, for all of ten minutes, *about wedding guest lists*—wants to swing.

I have to keep manning up for Laszlo's sake. Not just so he can handle himself in the world without crying at fire truck interiors. Not just so he can see the bravery that I might have seen in me for a moment at that fire, and know that it's in him, too. But so I can be man enough to satisfy Cassandra so his parents don't get into a creepy alternative lifestyle.

3

ENGAGING IN COMPETITION

Every time we drive by a fire truck, Laszlo and I both get excited, but for different reasons. I'm hoping Herbie and the rest of the guys are in there so I can stop and talk to them. I have no idea what Laszlo is so excited about. I suspect he's just overcompensating for crying at the firehouse.

I miss the firehouse, not because of the excitement, but for the reason Herbie did: hanging out with guys. Which I've avoided since childhood. It isn't just that boys were into stuff I didn't like, such as sleeping outside and wrestling and having to touch one another during the wrestling. It was their energy. It was feral, unpredictable, intense. So instead of playing games with boys, I read the entire Judy Blume collection, including *Tiger Eyes*. Most of my friends are guys now—largely because making a lot of new female friends is frowned upon by Cassandra—but I still don't feel comfortable around groups of men the way I do around groups of women.

But I don't want to be left out anymore. I suspect that I could have learned more at the firehouse if I didn't feel so self-consciously different. I just needed to find some small way to connect. Even one night of being a Boy Scout opened up conversations with the firefighters. I need more of those entry points. Because I don't think I can become a man without becoming relaxed enough around other men to learn from them.

The problem is that real men are uncomfortable to be around. Even for other real men. It's not that they're purposely alpha-dogging you. It's that they're uncomfortable in social situations. Which is why, when they are forced into a group, they will do exactly what newly socialized children do: play a game. And when, for some reason, they can't play a game, they talk about games other men play professionally. Men like Shawn Green.

Shawn, a two-time Major League Baseball All-Star, has agreed to show me how to throw, catch, hit, and coach baseball, all of which there's a good chance I'll have to do with Laszlo. After hitting forty home runs in three different years, tying the record for most homers in a game, and knocking in more home runs in a season than any Dodger in history, Shawn retired in 2008 to spend more time with his wife and daughters. I know that's what everyone says when they get fired, but Shawn actually quit being a Major League Baseball player so he could stop traveling. That's because Shawn is more well rounded than most baseball players. Or most people. Shawn went to Stanford at the same time I did, and he didn't get in for baseball. He got straight As in high school, graduating third in his class at an enormous middle-class Southern California public high school. He is into meditation and Buddhism and wrote the least manly titled book about baseball ever: *The Way of Baseball: Finding Stillness at 95 mph*. He is also so polite that all of his emails to me start with "Joel," as if he were penning a Victorian-era letter to a viscount. Shawn found some way to live in a very masculine world while still being a guy a lot like me. I'm hoping that, in addition to showing me how to hit a baseball, he could teach me how to do that, too.

I've avoided organized sports because comparing myself physically with other men seemed like another opportunity for humiliation. Also because most sports take place outside and often require running. Plus, sports, like so much of scouting and firefighting, are completely earnest. There's a code requiring players to talk about opponents with generosity and their own accomplishments with humility. I would do even worse at sportsman-like conduct than the actual sports.

When Cassandra was eight years old, she loved the song "Memories," which contains the lines "I can smile at the old days / I was beautiful then," which I pretended not to know when she told me the story. Those lyrics made her realize that while society valued her for being smart and artistic, the most important quality for girls is being hot. The pretty girls were popular, treated better, required to do less. When she posited that there is no equivalent for boys, I argued that there is: sports. Unlike the squishy science of hotness, boys have a quantifiable measurement for human value. If you're good at sports, you're confident, aggressive, competitive, coordinated, and unfat. And just as women look at celebrity magazines to envy and mock the beautiful, men watch sports to idolize players for successes and chastise them for failures.

Sports are the male lingua franca. Ask a guy if he saw the game. You don't need to know if there was a game. There was. His answer will tell you what kind of guy he is: angry, optimistic, cocky, judgmental, loyal, anti-authoritarian, paranoid. When I meet men and have to admit I don't know anything about football, I'm rarely able to recover conversationally. It's as if I'm telling them that I'm not interested in having male friends.

I arrive exactly on time at the strip mall in Santa Ana, California, outside Proball, an indoor baseball training facility that's owned by Shawn's high school buddy and is used by lots of major leaguers. Just as I park, Shawn pulls into the space next to me in his black Lexus. We shake hands and he smiles. Unlike with the Boy Scouts or firefighters, I'm instantly comfortable. He's also the first person I've interviewed for this book who has great hair—a gelled cloud of brown sloping straight off his forehead. Before we even leave the parking lot, I ask him about his hair product. Like me he is using Pomade by Crew, but he prefers something called Unite Creamy Paste when he can get his hands on it. "It smells so good," he says. "Like cookies or cake." If he had been wearing it, I like to think I would not have smelled his hair.

After all that camping and firefighting, I am happy to relax in the comfort of a fellow Jew. There are badass Jews, who are not comforting at all, but Shawn is not one of them. Woody Allen has made neurotic, frail, high-strung Jews seem like all we've got, but I can't blame my lack of manliness on my religion. Not only are there tanned, Uzi-toting, unsmiling, Maccabee-tough Israelis, but there are the haggling, arguing, lawyering Jews that Larry David has brought back. My dad is one of those Jews. Just like Larry David, my dad sparks to life during a confrontation. When he gets angry, which is rare, my dad Hulks, becoming louder, standing closer, his confidence complete, his speaking voice slower, lower, and more like that of a deaf weight lifter.

My father has scars on his knuckles, one of which is permanently bent. This is not something you would think is easy to work into conversation. Yet I have been told many, many times how he got them: As a teenager in the Bronx, he took on the duty of protecting smaller Jews from large, anti-Semitic Italians. I figured, despite the physical evidence, that the number and severity of these fights—some of which involved knives—was an exaggeration. It's not that my dad lies; it's that he never tells stories in which he doesn't come out looking really good. I am deeply suspicious of this, since I do not have any stories in which I come out looking even moderately good.

But he wasn't exaggerating. A few weeks before my baseball training camp with Shawn, my dad and I went to visit my eighty-nine-year-old grandmother, Mama Ann, in her condo in Fort Lauderdale. I asked her what my dad was like as a kid. "As soon as he learned to walk, he only walked one way," she said. When I asked Mama Ann what that meant, she explained that my dad was not conflict-avoidant: "Your father would walk up to kids and hit them. He'd get in trouble. Then he learned. He'd say, 'They hit me first.'" My father's aggression was so severe, that—and this is back in the 1940s—his pediatrician recommended putting him on drugs to calm him. Which my grandmother had to talk my calm, patient grandfather out of doing. While Mama Ann told this story, my seventy-year-old father kept interrupting her with: "You mess with me, I'm going to mess with you." I now believe there are a lot of knuckle-scarred seventy-year-old Italians from the Bronx talking about the violent, racist Jew.

The day after seeing Mama Ann, I took my dad and sister to the South Beach Wine & Food Festival in Miami. We were waiting in a long, slow line for crepes when a guy and two women cut to the front. My dad told the guy, in his early thirties, to get to the back of the line. Line vigilantism is something I deal with a lot, and not just with my dad. Cassandra is often telling people to get to the back of the line who, she then discovers, have been in line a lot longer than us and she just didn't notice them. I do not understand the obsession with line justice. People are born in war-torn countries where they starve to death while others get free passes to food and wine festivals, and line order is where people demand fairness? When I was thirteen, my dad made me use my skills on my Apple IIe and Epson dot-matrix printer to create a fake receipt for a non-existent fur coat that he claimed to have donated, and yet the rules and regulations of the crepe line cannot be compromised. I'm more than willing to put in thirty extra line seconds in exchange for not having to serve as a line border patrol agent. But once people form a single file they are suddenly fully committed to the ideal of equal treatment for all sisters and brothers. I honestly believe that the civil rights movement would have happened years earlier if instead of sending black people to the back of the bus, they made them wait at the end of the line.

When my dad told the guy at the food and wine festival to go to the back of the line, the guy and his two female friends boldly refused, standing there with their plates out, crepe-expectant. My sister and I had already decided that thirty minutes for a crepe wasn't worth it, but my dad wouldn't leave. When we returned with lobster rolls and conch chowder, my dad, to our surprise, was not only still in this endless line, but also still in a feud with the line-cutter. In fact, he was in the line-cutter's face, calling him "buddy." When Buddy ignored him, my dad asked Buddy to "take this out-side" and fight. Let me remind you that my dad was seventy. And at a food and wine festival. And waiting for a crepe. Not a savory crepe, but a chocolate crepe with whipped cream.

Buddy, in response to the challenge to fight a seventy-year-old man with glasses dangling from a rope around his neck, said he was a lawyer and would sue if my dad hit him. My dad got a few inches from Buddy's face and told him that he was a partner at one of the biggest law firms in Manhattan, which is not at all true. My dad then repeated his offer to "take this outside." Buddy did not move, but my dad blocked him from any hopes of a getting a crepe, thus becoming the hero of the crepe line. My father handed crepes to several peo-ple behind us before taking our crepes and departing to everyone's approval. It was one of the finest moments of civil rights the crepe line at the South Beach Wine & Food festival would ever witness.

My dad will work pretty hard to get his justice. He has spent the last ten years exacting revenge on his local Waldbaum's super-market because they scanned a half gallon of Breyers ice cream at three dollars instead of the posted sale price of two dollars. He takes dairy items that have passed their expiration dates and returns them so they're put back on the supermarket shelves. These rancid products, he hopes, will be purchased by customers who will complain. This is his method of recruiting for his army. Sure, it's a sickly army doubled over with food poisoning, but it is an army nonetheless.

If someone gets a fact wrong in front of my dad, he cannot help but argue indefinitely with him, as if his dignity depends upon it. When someone gets a fact wrong in front of me, I spend five minutes wondering if I'll hurt his feelings by telling him.

I can tell that Shawn isn't a fighting Jew. He's more like me. But unlike me, Shawn has never been in a fight. Not even one where he just stands there and gets punched. Which is insane because fights do break out in baseball. In an off-season league in South America, Shawn got hit twice by a pitch from the same pitcher, and knew if it happened again he'd have to rush the mound to fight him if he hoped to keep any respect from his team. So he told a teammate to grab him before he got to the pitcher's mound to make it look like he was holding Shawn back. Luckily, the pitcher didn't hit him again. The few times he's been part of a bench-clearing brawl, Shawn walked to the outskirts of the fight. "You just talk to a buddy on the other team. It's exciting. It's a nice change from the norm," he says.

Shawn can't fix anything in his house and would never go hunting. While he did buy a fishing boat after signing a contract with the Dodgers for eighty-four million dollars over six years, he says it was simply because he didn't know what to do with the money and his teammates had boats. He took it out a few times, barfed a few times, and sold it. He is such a pussy that after he barfed, he probably brushed his teeth.

Shawn claims to have gone camping, but the story falls apart under questioning: "I've slept in a tent as a kid. In my family room. I guess I can't say I camped then, huh?"

Shawn doesn't watch sports. Not even baseball. And definitely not football. "I try to watch football every year and I can't get into it," Shawn says. "I couldn't name all the positions. If I ask a kid what position he plays and he says, 'Left tackle,' I wouldn't know what that is." The only man thing he does is play poker, which I know does not count because I play poker, too. I like Shawn.

While he did join a fraternity at Stanford, he did it only because he left school every spring to play minor-league baseball and didn't want to leave a dorm roommate stuck with a random dude replacing him. And he regrets it. "I hate that whole mentality. The whole macho attitude," he says. He's the only adult I've ever met who is still angry about being hazed.

"I'm pretty unmanly. I have three girls in my house and I wouldn't know what to do with a boy. I have a vagina now," he says. He doesn't seem sad about not having a son. Or about having a vagina.

But Shawn wasn't an outcast who sat alone in locker rooms doing the *New York Times* crossword puzzle, like All-Star pitcher and Stanford alumnus Mike Mussina. He's a guy with my personality who figured out a way to interact with men who don't have my personality.

Shawn opens the door to the giant, pristine warehouse filled with batting cages. We walk over to a strip of Astroturf, and Shawn grabs a bucket of balls. I brought a glove, which I bought in the early 1990s, when I worked for *Martha Stewart Living* magazine and played on our coed softball team. Even on the Martha Stewart coed softball team, I played catcher and batted late in the order. If it were any other coed softball team, I would have played catcher, batted late in the order, and had to prepare refreshments.

I was even worse at sports as a kid. My parents did insist that I play a sport, so until I was old enough to lawyer them into believing that bowling counted, I played soccer, the sport for the least tough kids. I always played defense, which is the position in soccer where they put the least tough of the least tough kids. But I was wimpy even for a soccer defender. I would get to the ball quickly but run away if any kid was getting close. When the ball wasn't around, I picked dandelions. Really, literally. I had no interest in flowers. I just wanted my parents to see how bored I was.

So throwing a ball with a Major League All-Star is intimidating. Especially since I've always loved baseball, even though I was too afraid to play Little League. It's a great sport for nerds to follow, with all the statistics, the slow pace that allows you to talk about statistics, and the lack of any violence, which is hard to put into statistics. But actually playing is nowhere near as appealing as watching, since when you play there are moments of intense pressure—hitting, catching, tagging—which people judge more harshly than your long division in figuring out Value Over Replacement Player.

I face Shawn from across the Astroturf, try to picture a Major League All-Star throwing a baseball to another Major League All-Star, and throw it like he would. Shawn catches it and walks right over to me. He is smiling. I am expecting compliments on my innate ability. Perhaps he will want me to sign the ball for him.

As he gets closer, with his arm outstretched, I realize that Shawn is going to show me how to throw a baseball. I am wrong. Shawn is going to show me how to *hold* a baseball. This is something I thought I would have learned from having watched thousands of hours of baseball in my life, or from being an American, or from having fingers. But I am never sure if you use three or five fingers to throw a baseball when you're not pitching, and I absolutely don't know that you put your index and middle finger on the stitches, perpendicular to them. It allows me to make a nice loud popping noise when the ball hits Shawn's glove. I've thrown balls before, shot basketballs at the hoop in my driveway like my dad suggested, but it felt like drudgery, and I never improved. There's a satisfaction I'm now feeling, though, in focusing on a physical task over and over when I'm doing it right. I would have thought concentration on repetitive action would be exhausting, but it's invigorating, making the chatter of my brain momentarily disappear. It's what Beef was trying to show me in the woods during our walk searching for edible plants, only throwing this ball is far less boring. I am finding stillness at about twenty-two miles per hour.

After a particularly good throw, I ask Shawn at what grade level I was throwing before he taught me the stitches trick.

"Probably third or fourth grade," he says.

"Third- or fourth-grade girl or boy?" I ask.

"Boy. First throw—girl. But you're a quick learner."

This is the kind of man banter I assume takes place on Major League Baseball fields everywhere.

When he played baseball, Shawn did twenty minutes of daily meditation, practiced yoga, and traveled to away games with Hermann Hesse's *Siddhartha*, which is much easier to pack in a suitcase than Herman Hesse's *Hey Other Baseball Players, Come Beat Me Up*.

I took two Buddhism classes at Stanford, and I learned there's something incredibly manly about it. Not just that Zen monks can sit still for hours without food or drink. Or that some head monks will hit them with sticks when they sense their concentration faltering. It's that their philosophy is acceptance. Which our society has been calling repression. We've been taught that controlling our emotions is just sublimation, and those emotions will lie in wait and collect interest and then come out in horrible, uncontrolled fits of anger, sadness, depression, and disease. But expressing emotion exaggerates your feeling of it: Smiling actually makes you happy, and yelling makes you angry. Controlling your emotions separates children from adults, and all of us from the British. It's what the firefighters did all day as they politely drove angry people to the hospital who didn't need to be there.

Repression isn't simply civilized; it's the mechanism to express dignity, honor, respect, and self-discipline. It's not that you shouldn't let people know how you feel; it's that you should decide how and when you express it. I want to be the kind of man who drinks tea with a stiff upper lip as the bombs fall around London, mostly because it's the only manly way I can think of to enjoy loose-leaf first-flush Super Fine Tippy Golden Flowery Orange

Pekoe Darjeeling, which I like very much. Both Captain Buzz and Wiggles had this calmness, and Shawn has it, too. I thought it was just good leadership, making others feel important. But it's more than that: It's humility. It's not needing to express everything you feel immediately, because you're not the most important person. By not reacting to my awful throws, Shawn is making me feel like with a little practice, I could throw a baseball just as well as he does— that I'm just as smart, good-looking, and successful as him, that our hair is equally lustrous. He makes everyone feel this way. It's a true confidence that comes from both not caring what other people think about him and caring about them. It's superiority stripped of dickishness.

I want to be more like this. Our culture celebrates the other half of masculinity, the fiery destructive half, where you brag, threaten, and fight. I want to stay on the other side, even if being controlled, thoughtful, competent, and good at math doesn't attract women.

After throwing the baseball pretty well for a while, I go to the bathroom, where I am pleased to find pomegranate-scented hand soap. When I return, Shawn gives me a batting glove, which seems a shame to put on since my hands smell great. Then he puts a baseball on a tee. I don't have a problem with being sports infantilized, but a batting tee is going too far. You stop hitting off tees right about the age when you can walk. Then someone throws the ball to you. But Shawn says he brought a tee with him to every ballpark for batting practice. The stationary ball let him freeze time and eliminate the variables so he could focus on his breath and be in the moment, instead of asking a coach to throw practice pitches to him.

He fixes my swing by having me harness power from my legs and chop down on the ball. When he teaches me to catch, I learn that outfielders put two fingers in the pinkie spot in the glove and none in the index finger hole because it makes it snap closed much more easily. This seems insane. With all the expensive, specialized equipment in sports, professional outfielders use gloves where they put two fingers in one hole? I own a kitchen gadget that just slices mangoes.

Shawn knew all of these baseball tricks as a little kid because our dads, while both Jewish salesmen who played basketball, raised us differently. "My dad pushed a little bit. Most guys who make it, their dads pushed a little bit," Shawn says as we pick up all the balls that I hit hard into the net. "He'd say, 'do twenty push-ups before bed' and I'd do it. He'd tell me to swing for fifteen minutes every day and I'd do it—to the second. I was obsessive." Even though he made his dad's vicarious dreams come true by playing big-league ball, he still didn't become precisely the player his father wanted him to be. "He always wanted me to have more of a temper and be more aggressive."

If Shawn had a son, he wouldn't make him practice every day. "When you're playing sports for a career, you see the difficulty of traveling and the pressure. A lot of baseball players think it would be nice to have a normal life," he says. Shawn is glad his dad pushed him because of the career it gave him, but he didn't enjoy practicing all the time as a kid. And he feels a little bit like his parents, who clearly love him, are as excited about the professional baseball part of him as the son part of him. He feels like their son, but he also feels a distance, like they're also his fans.

Shawn and I go to a sports bar called Spoons, where we sit near a TV showing the Phillies-Reds play-off game. Neither of us orders a beer, because it is still early. Also we don't like beer. We really only drink wine. Recently, Shawn enjoyed a particularly refreshing rosé. "It was called Pink Girl. I dug it. It was really good. The bottle was all bedazzled," he says. We also don't drink coffee. "I don't like it. It's too acidic," Shawn says. "I drink tea. Mostly green."

Shawn orders a cheeseburger, and I am about to do the same until I see my big chance to outman him. I ask for the Macho Burger: one beef patty topped with a hot dog, chili, American cheese, and BBQ sauce. Only I get it without the hot dog. I never liked hot dogs. Still, it's more macho than his plain cheeseburger.

In the third inning, while I'm wondering if chili on a burger is really necessary, Shawn looks up at the TV and calmly says that Roy Halladay is about to pitch a no-hitter, much like Rain Man states how many toothpicks have fallen from the box. Only one person has ever pitched a no-hitter during the play-offs, and that was in 1956. But Shawn says he can tell by the way Halladay is throwing that no one is going to hit him.

We return to our unmanly contest. We are tied on never smoking a cigarette, but I trump him in drug taking because I had a really intense pot-brownie experience. I cannot believe, however, that after a career in baseball, he's never tried chewing tobacco. My disbelief is so loud that a bearded, slightly older, pudgy guy eating alone in a booth pulls out a can of Kodiak and offers it to us, like we're in an Afterschool Special about chewing tobacco and peer pressure. This is clearly my moment to chew tobacco for my first time—in a sports bar with a Major League Baseball player and a bearded, slightly older, pudgy guy. Maybe I will become instantly addicted. I'll walk into *Time* magazine meetings with some kind of spittoon and kick dirt on my editor when he rejects my article idea. I'll have to carry around chewing tobacco, the spittoon, and dirt. I am going to need some kind of satchel.

Shawn, though, refuses to try any. He promised, back in high school, that if he ever chews tobacco it will be with his friend Ben who owns the batting cages we were just at. But he does get a Styrofoam cup with napkins origamied inside so they'll absorb my spit. This is an official Major League Baseball Styrofoam spit cup.

I take what I assume is a little bit of Kodiak and thank the bearded, slightly older, pudgy guy for the chew. He, however, says it isn't chew. It is dip. I do not see the importance of this distinction, so the bearded, slightly older, pudgy guy explains that I shouldn't chew it. I should put it in between my cheek and gum and let it sit there. I put a pinch in the back right top of my mouth because that's where I thought I've seen tobacco bulges. But the bearded, slightly older, pudgy guy says I should have put it between my lip and bottom front teeth, but it's too late to move it. He also tells me that I've taken about one-ninetieth of a serving.

Dip, I am thrilled to learn, comes in flavors, and not just "tobacco" and "very tobacco." This tin of Kodiak is wintergreen—minty and delicious, like earthy gum. I am barely enjoying this first rush of flavor when Shawn leans over and peppers me with questions. "Are you getting an adrenaline rush?" "Are you addicted?" People who don't dip tobacco just don't get it.

I am feeling much better about being a man, and I don't think it's due to dip-induced endorphins. I like the way Shawn is unapologetic in his smiling, Zen manliness. We talk about having non-Jewish wives and how we had to negotiate our family's discomfort with that, and our spouses not wanting our families to show up at our houses all the time. Diplomacy is not unmanly at all. Neither is talking, in a drama-free way, about how you feel. I tell Shawn that he doesn't need to ever try dip. Which he already knew.

Shawn and I exchange email addresses and he gives me a signed baseball for Laszlo. We say good-bye and I get into my Mini Cooper with my now-brownish Styrofoam cup, spitting away happily. When I get home, I turn on the end of the Phillies game and see Roy Halladay finish pitching the second no-hitter in post-season history. And looking at him, I feel, for just a second, that maybe I'm not as different from a star athlete as I always assumed.

In fact, Shawn made me think I don't need to change to become the man I want to be. I can still be a total wimp inside. I just need to expose myself to a broader world, like Shawn did, and like I'm trying to do with these adventures. I need to expand, not change.

I'd like to expand enough to like football. Which is going to be difficult. Not liking football is a key part of my identity. Football is tribal, warlike, and anti-intellectual. No one shows up to a book club meeting with his face painted.

My dad watched New York Giants games on TV when I was little, but I was both bored and confused by the staccato blurs of violence. I'd go to high school football games to find out where the party was afterward, but I spent the whole time ignoring the game and talking to kids in the marching band who all hated football too, which was odd, considering attending football games was a key part of their job description. My freshman dorm would go to every home game at Stanford, but I'd leave at halftime, feeling disconnected from the chanting and cheering. At Super Bowl parties, I occasionally ask what's on other channels.

I've gotten some ex-pro-football players to let me spend a Sunday watching games with them, so they can show me what I should be enjoying. The day before, to prepare, I'm getting a lesson at the NFL Network headquarters in Los Angeles from Steve Mariucci, a TV analyst who is a former head coach of the San Francisco 49ers and Detroit Lions. He's a super-confident, fast-talking, energetic, blue-eyed man with lots of combed-back dark hair who goes by the nickname "Mooch." He touches my arm a lot and, I'm pretty sure, is about to sell me an expensive car. He brings me to a conference room where the table is scattered with soda cans and tiny empty bags of chips. Nutrition, I am learning, is not an important factor in watching football.

The first tip he gives me for watching the game with him the next day is to shut the hell up. "When I'm watching a football game at home, like *Monday Night Football*, my message to my family is: 'Shut up! I'm watching the game!' "

I want more details. Like what formations are, the names of the positions, and what I should be looking for. Mooch stares at me in silence. "Oh man. This is going to be Beginners 101."

Mooch walks over to the giant whiteboard and wipes it clean with his fist.

I ask him what a nickel defense is, since I have seen the term on football video games. He draws a bunch of X's and O's on the board—X's are for defense and O's are for offense. Why, I wonder, don't they use D's and O's? By the brevity of his answer, I discover that Mooch is less interested in etymology and semiotics than I am.

A regular defense has four backs, Mooch explains. "In a nickel, instead of four you have five. It's a nickel, Stanford!" A dime, he says, has six backs. When I complain that this doesn't make any sense, Mooch gets exasperated. "Because there is no coin that is six cents!"

I press Mooch for more formations, and he draws diagrams of the 26 Power Thrash, the 96 Stretch, the 2 Jet Flanker, and the Zebra. As I am furiously copying these sketches down, Mooch explains that NFL fans don't know any of this. If a fan saw his favorite team's playbook, Mooch says, it would be incomprehensible. "I'm watching for who's winning and how. I'm not rewinding to see who blocked the power play," he says. Mooch is not happy when I then make him draw out the power play.

What Mooch is able to show me by describing the details of an ordinary play is that there's an intimacy to football that I didn't appreciate. Sports take away words and force men to communicate in a more basic way—physically showing respect, concern, and anger. Laszlo hasn't said a sentence to me, but I know him better than I've ever known anyone—through wrestling, kissing, throwing, carrying, laughing, and crying. I don't think I'll ever be this intimate with anyone: I wipe his ass, I wash him, I feed him, his tears wet my cheeks. He's the only one I don't feel self-conscious around naked, although that's largely because my penis is so much bigger than his. And I've got to enjoy that while I can, if that obstetrician knew what she was talking about.

I wake up early on Sunday morning, totally unsure what to wear. I don't own any jerseys with other men's names on them and wearing a jersey with my own name on it seems weird, especially because it says MARTHA STEWART on the front, so I put on jeans and a white button-down, but a wrinkled one. A little before 8 AM, I walk into the giant, two-story studio where the analysts tape their pre- and post-game shows. Everyone is moving equipment and talking about games, and I'm not sure what to do. I stand by the wall, slightly squinting, my right elbow resting on the back of my left hand, my right index finger above my lips, my middle finger under them, my thumb on my jaw. It's a weird, uncomfortable position, and I'm not sure why I'm standing this way. Then I realize: This is how my dad stands. When I don't know how to act like a man, I act like my dad.

Eventually, Mooch calls me over to sit next to his big comfortable reclining chair facing a wall of televisions, which I am supposed to somehow watch all at once. Analysts Marshall Faulk, Michael Irvin, Warren Sapp, Deion Sanders, and Rich Eisen sit alongside us. They all played pro football except for Eisen, a Jewish sports anchor, who somehow is Shawn-Green-level comfortable around these guys.

I introduce myself to Sapp, who won a Super Bowl, played in seven Pro Bowl games, and came in second on *Dancing with the Stars.* Sapp is six foot two, way over three hundred pounds, and by far the largest man in a room full of former professional football players. I assume that most of Sapp's day is spent responding to emails from friends who want help moving. Sapp, who has lots of energy, takes me aside and puts an arm around my shoulder. I am very, very glad we are at the NFL Network studios and not in prison.

Sapp tells me that watching the ball is an amateur move. Instead, he tells me, I should focus on the lines of guys facing each other. Coincidentally, Sapp spent his career as one of those guys facing each other. "Linemen don't lie. When I go to reach block you, I'm going to reach block you." Sapp repeats this thing about linemen not lying several times and laughs each time. I look up at him and nod, unable to decide whether to laugh or not. It turns out that Sapp laughs after most things he says, less a nervous tic than a courteous signal that he isn't going to beat you up.

For the first time, I am able to follow an entire play. I see some movement on the line and see a guy break toward the quarterback and tackle him. "You just watched a sack! I set it up and you saw it!" Sapp yells. He removes his hand from my shoulder and uses it to slap my ass. I do not see this coming. No one has ever slapped my ass before. It is suddenly clear to me that, while slapping another guy's ass is manly, being the slappee is not at all manly. I have no idea if I'm supposed to slap his ass back, like a high five. For several reasons, I decide not to.

Sapp says the whole point of football is sacrifice for a shared goal. "The biggest misconception is that football is a family. In a family if a baby lags behind, you wait for him. Football is a brotherhood of men. We have a job to do. We will move on without you," he says. "We'll be in the middle of practice and someone will get hurt and he'll be laying there and we'll move the drill five feet over." Sapp would make a horrible college football recruiter.

I sit back down in my comfortable chair to prevent any more ass slapping. A few minutes later Mooch slaps my arm because some guy made an impressive play, and he tells me the guy is a "Cal Bear." I'm confused, until I realize that Mooch coached at the University of California–Berkeley for a long time, and I went to Stanford, Cal's rival. In fact, whenever a player does something impressive, everyone yells out any personal connection whatsoever they have to him: the area he grew up in, the college he went to, where he lives now. When those players screw up, no one says anything. It's kind of like how you're a lot prouder to be someone's friend during his wedding. Which is all sports is, really: the tribal joy of identifying with an arbitrary group. These athletes from my college, my town, my country, my religion are representing me, unless they mess up, in which case I'm sure I can figure out some other group they also belong to that I hate.

The biggest fan-and-player connection in the room is between Mooch and Minnesota Vikings quarterback Brett Favre, whom he coached and is good friends with. Things are not going well for Favre. Deion Sanders puts down his phone for the first time all day in order to focus on antagonizing Mooch about this. But with just two minutes left, Favre somehow passes for two touchdowns and ties the game. After the second one, Mooch and Michael Irvin run to the TV with their arms up in the touchdown call, laughing like little boys. During overtime, Mooch is so stressed, he walks up a stairway to this little bridge that overlooks the TVs so he can pace. Which is like putting a duck in one of those little areas where he can get shot more easily.

Deion: "Don't jump!"

Rich: "You have a lot to live for!"

Deion: "Your son has a dime!"

I am not sure if a dime meant six or ten in this context, but either way I am glad to learn that a man is supposed to take pride in the hotness of his son's girlfriend.

"I can't handle it!" Mooch yells before descending the stairwell. He sits next to me and slaps my arm with the back of his hand. "We got two overtime games, Stanford!" And I am excited. Because it's fun to be with a group of guys experiencing something together. Even if I don't care about that something.

Favre wins in overtime, and I'm happy about it. Happy for Mooch, but also happy that I got to be there for this.

Later, I go back to Sapp's office, which is decorated with a swimsuit calendar on which his girlfriend is the cover model, and an airbrushed painting of her on her knees in a cat-like pose against a black background, done by an artist named Ghost. Besides canvas, Ghost paints on cars, guns, and naked women. I do not know what he paints on naked women, but I'm going to guess it's more naked women.

Sapp is so manly that he taunted opposing football players

during pre-game warm-ups by skipping in between them and singing the theme song to *The Smurfs*. This is not something I could
pull off. Partly because the only non-perfect grade I got on my
second-grade report card was in gym, for not being able to skip.
"Run and hop" still doesn't make sense to me. Sapp also intimidated opponents by dancing like a stripper and shaking his ass in
their faces. "I did the Beyoncé dance with the booty poppin' and
they're like, 'You dance on us? Like a ho?'" I do not understand
male taunting at all. Would the ultimate touchdown dance involve
putting on full makeup, singing Sondheim songs, and curtsying?

Sapp is so clearly uninterested in humility that I suggest he
commission a Sapp family crest. He looks at me like I am insane.
Because he already has one. There's an Old English S on the gate
to his house, the mats inside his house, and the theater chairs in his
screening room.

Clearly, I don't have the personality for football. But Sapp says
that the reason I'm not interested in the sport is that I had so many
other choices that came with growing up with money in the sub-
urbs with intellectually engaged parents. "Brad Culpepper said to
me, 'You think it's hard coming to the NFL out of the ghetto or the
country? Try being a silver-spoon baby. I don't need this shit. I've
got a law degree.'" Besides, Sapp says, I had different goals than
winning football games. "You covet what you see every day. You
see your dad put on a suit and tie every day, you want to have a
nine-to-five job."

My dad never threw a football to me. Which is why, during my
first week of college, my two roommates would not let me come
inside until I finally caught a pass across the lawn in front of our
dorm, even as it got dark and the dining hall started to close. "Dad
was athletic—he was strong and built well—but he just didn't do
much of that later," my mom said. "He's got this very intellectual
part of him. Whatever free time he had, he would read and then
bore me with what he read." My dad had the same explanation of

his fathering strategy, minus the purposely-boring-your-wife part. "You can't do everything and be everything," he said. I wasn't interested in throwing a ball, so he didn't force me. He did force me to work hard in school, because that would help me avoid a difficult life. But other than that, he let me pursue what interested me. He read my articles in the school paper and showed up to watch me embarrass myself in a school play, but he never got overly involved. He let me build my wimpy self. It's incredibly similar to the parenting advice Wiggles gave me: "Don't get involved in everything your son does. Be on him about grades. M-rated video games are okay. Don't always be there, standing with him and waiting for the bus." Shawn's father didn't follow those guidelines, making him practice hitting a ball every day, and it worked out pretty well for Shawn. But I doubt it would have worked if Shawn didn't like baseball a lot. And it didn't work out so well that Shawn would push like that with his own kids.

I ask Sapp if his dad pushed him into football. He says he didn't have a dad. When he got his first NFL paycheck, Sapp retired his mother, who worked two full-time jobs simultaneously during his entire childhood. He used seventy-two hundred dollars of that check to buy her the house in Plymouth, Florida that she lived in—the one he grew up in. His father left him and his five older siblings when Sapp was eleven. Because his paternal uncles and cousins didn't talk much about his dad, the only information he had about his father came from NFL player Edgerrin James, who grew up in Immokalee, Florida, where Sapp's dad had moved. James said his father would brag about Sapp's career, saying that James wasn't nearly as good. Which sounded sweet to me. That's how little I understand about how it feels to have been abandoned by your father.

When Sapp was thirty, his mom said his dad had called asking to see him. "I said, 'You know I don't use that word around here.'" But Sapp told him to come over. "I said, 'You can stand in the driveway and talk to me like a man. You can't walk in that house because I bought that house. You'll never see that house or your grandkids. You had the balls to brag about your son but not to see your son.'" When his father made excuses, Sapp interrupted: "I want you to get in the car and leave like you did that day."

Sapp believes not having a father didn't hurt him. "You worry about things you can control. I can't control that he was standing on the corner getting high instead of being with his kids," he says. "Do you want an excuse for your life? One of the most wasted things in America is potential. You know what potential is? Potential is 'You ain't done nothing yet.'"

My anti-masculinity is so strong that every time I meet a real man, I wind up talking about his emotions. I'm like the Man Cooler. In addition to father issues, we talk about dancing. Sapp tells me I should watch Chris Brown on *Dancing with the Stars* that week, since he's the best dancer since Michael Jackson. I tell Sapp I can't enjoy Chris Brown because he hit his girlfriend Rihanna. This is something I might not have said if I had known that, a year earlier, Sapp was put in jail for domestic battery when his girlfriend accused him of choking her, though she later dropped the charges.

"Oh, so you're one of those people who think Michael Vick shouldn't be playing football?" he asks, leaning toward me.

I explain that Vick's dogfighting ring hurt only animals, which I eat every day. Brown hit a woman. Again, I cannot be sure I would have taken such a principled stance had I known I was talking to a three-hundred-plus-pound man who had been arrested for domestic battery. But somehow I get a high five out of it.

I compliment the airbrushed painting and Sapp tells me the kneeling woman is not his wife. He and his wife couldn't make their marriage work, largely because during away games, Sapp would have a woman fly into whatever hotel he was staying at, order up their favorite drinks and food, and have really freaky sex, which, on one occasion, caused her to become pregnant. This is the kind of thing that's hard to explain to your wife when you then do the exact same thing with another woman and impregnate her, too.

I ask if he'd learned anything since then about loyalty, honesty, and staying out of situations he isn't strong enough to resist. Absolutely not. "We're not rational. We're not made that way," he says about our gender. "A lot of people know what to do. Very few people do what they know." If he gets remarried, Sapp says he won't cheat on his wife. But not because he's wiser. Just because he's older. "I'm on the porch. I want someone that sits on the porch with me," he says. At nearly forty, a man shouldn't be attracted to twenty-year-olds he can't relate to. "You want someone who loves you. That's what you learn in the long haul," he says. "The grass on the other side is artificial turf. Do not lay down in it because it's going to hurt like hell."

I do not believe he would have told me any of that if we hadn't talked about football first.

I feel pretty sure that this is the exact right moment to slap Sapp's ass, but I hold back and shake his hand instead.

After that conversation, I feel ready for my challenges. Just being around these guys is making manliness less foreign. None of it will be that hard to do with Laszlo. I just need to keep taking more courses.

So I'm a little bummed out that I have to take a break from all this man stuff. A jarring break. For my mom's sixty-fifth birthday, I got her a trip to the beautiful Lake Austin Spa Resort. With me. I am the only man roaming the giant grounds. The place is populated solely by sixty-plus-year-old women floating by in white robes and flip-flops, each of whom, at some point, I walk up to thinking she's my mom.

While my mom is getting wrapped in roses or mud or coffee grounds, I go to the gym. I climb on an elliptical machine, place an herbal iced tea in the cup holder, and start switching channels on the little TV. I stop on a mixed martial arts fight. It's some kind of minor-league version of the Ultimate Fighting Championship, and two shirtless guys are attacking each other in a chain-link-fenced cage in front of a tiny outdoor crowd. There is blood dripping down both of their faces and bodies. One guy is holding the other guy's head and repeatedly kneeing him in the face, which, I deduce, is the cause of much of the blood. I had no idea there was a sport where face kneeing was allowed. Watching them, I get sad in the way that women get sad when watching porn. I feel bad that these guys have to do this for attention, undoubtedly due to bad fathering. It makes my citrus hibiscus iced tea taste bitter.

I haven't watched this much of a professional, or, in this case, somewhat professional, fight in a long time. When I was little, I used to lean against the foot of my parents' bed with my dad as he stared up at the TV in their bedroom, watching big fights. And I saw a few pay-per-view Mike Tyson fights with big groups of high school friends. But I never liked it. From 1995 to 1997 I was the sports editor of *Time Out New York*, which would seem like a manly job except that the sports section was nothing but listings of when the New York Road Runners gathered to jog. But I could use my title to get free tickets. My friend Marc Einsele loves boxing, as does Mike Gorker, which was not at all surprising since, back in high school, Mike had so enjoyed standing at a comfortable distance and watching while that guy beat me up for no reason on Long Beach Island.

So Marc, Mike, and I went to a bunch of fights. Up close, boxing is quite violent. Worse were the fans, who were mostly white men who booed when the black or Hispanic guys weren't hitting each other often enough. The last fight I took them to was between Riddick Bowe and Andrew Golota in 1996 at Madison Square Garden. Though I'm sure they had many differences in boxing style, the most obvious one was that Bowe was black and Golota was white. Golota, whose nickname was "the Foul Pole," was Polish, and so were a lot of the people sitting around us. Gorker, Einsele, and I joined them in these cool Polish chants that consisted of just the word *Poland* in Polish over and over and did nothing to discourage Polish stereotypes. It was really fun until Golota got disqualified for punching Bowe in the balls for the second time. This, by the way, is how he got the nickname "the Foul Pole." The Bowe and Golota camps then entered the ring to discuss the ball-punching disqualification. The disagreement got heated after a member of Bowe's entourage cracked a two-way radio over Golota's head and he started spurting blood. That's when fans entered the ring and a race riot broke out in the seats. Four black guys sitting in front of us turned around and said, "I think Golota shouldn't have been disqualified," which was code for "We would rather not engage in a race riot with you." We said something nice about the way Bowe took a ball punching, and the seven of us hurried out of the arena while the riot police came in. We were the kind of people Martin Luther King Jr. would not have to bother explaining his theories of non-violence to.

Thinking about how much I hated that night, I switch the TV channel away from the fight to *The Ellen DeGeneres Show*, which has an excellent segment about stopping bullying. But then I turn back. I see kicking, elbowing, arm twisting, and more face kneeing. A guy sits on another guy's chest and punches him in the face over and over. A man chokes another one—with his legs. It's the most repulsive, frightening thing I've ever seen. I am about to turn back to *Ellen* when I have a thought I never thought I'd have.

I need to do this.

Maybe I've overexerted myself by setting the resistance too high on this elliptical machine. Maybe hibiscus tea isn't hydrating enough and I'm hallucinating. Or maybe I'm having a weird reaction to breathing in my fellow hotel guests' estrogen—or, more accurately, the fumes of their past estrogen. But at least at this moment, what I have to do feels clear. If I can fight in a mixed martial arts match, even just for one round, maybe I'll get over my fear of fighting. If I can do what these guys are doing, just once, maybe I'll be able to stand up for myself anywhere. Maybe I'll be more confident. Maybe I'll understand rage and retaliation. Maybe if Laszlo starts fights like my dad does, I'll understand him a little better. I'm absolutely positive I'll lose some weight.

As I get more and more sure that I indeed have to do this, I realize I have no idea how to set up a martial arts fight. Do I go on Craigslist under "Men seeking men" and ask if there are any guys looking to get together and beat the shit out of each other? Do I walk into a bar and start dancing with an Asian guy's girlfriend? Is this something that my local Boys & Girls Club handles?

When I get back home from the spa, I am less enthused about my idea to drum up someone to knee me in the face. So I call the Ultimate Fighting Championship and ask if one of their professional fighters will get in the ring with me for one round. There is no way they will say yes. They must have a lawyer who will warn them of the obvious risks of being sued by the family members I'm survived by.

The UFC, however, thinks this is a great idea. All I need to do is sign a release and they'll throw me right in the ring with one of their trained killers. In fact, they say I can fight Randy Couture.

Couture has been both the heavyweight and light-heavyweight champion of the UFC, a league that was banned in thirty-six states in the early 1990s and called "human cockfighting" by Senator John McCain, who tried to outlaw it. Its tagline was "There are no rules!" though, in actuality, fighters were not allowed to bite or eye gouge. Also, differential calculus was probably frowned upon.

The UFC has more rules now, but it's still more violent than any sport in which both participants are not trained by Michael Vick. Two men enter an octagon cage made out of chain-link metal fence and use their hands, feet, elbows, and knees to knock each other to the ground, at which point they really start to beat each other up.

In addition to being one of the best UFC fighters of all time—he's already in the Hall of Fame even though, at forty-seven, he's still competing—Couture was a three-time alternate Olympic wrestler. He's an action hero, acting in *The Scorpion King 2: Rise of a Warrior* and *The Expendables*, movies that are so manly I did not even consider seeing them. A few years ago Couture won a fight despite suffering a broken arm early on.

This seems like a very bad idea. But I need to know what it feels like to fight. Male creatures have been fighting one another since the first amoeba grew a penis. Understanding evolution is not at all crucial to being a man.

Before I agree, I show Cassandra a photo of Couture, his head shaved, his center browline deeply sunken, his jawline sticking out, his red three-day beard not at all patchy like mine gets. She looks at his picture for a while and says, "Oh yeah, you're totally going to beat the shit out of that guy."

She does not believe I'm actually going to do this. But I am. Because if I'm going to learn how to fight, then I want to learn from a UFC champion. Just like if you want to learn how to be a total woman, you've got to get sex tips from a porn star. I am really hoping Cassandra reads this book.

4

BONDING WITH MEN

Knowing I'm going to fight one of the most dangerous fighters in the world makes me want a drink. Actually, it just makes me want to want a drink. I'm not much of a drinker. I don't like the loss of control. And not losing control has cost me. Not doing beer bongs meant I never went on spring break. Not drinking meant I left frat parties an hour after arriving, avoided bars, and didn't dance. Basically, it meant I didn't hook up with girls. I like having Shawn's and Wiggles's calm self-control, but I should at least find whatever rage, wildness, lust, and violence are beneath my sobriety. I should know how much of that I have in me, and be able to access it at will.

It's not just that I don't like drinking; I'm bad at it. As you can tell by the quality of our wines, Jews are not into drinking. But even for a Jew, I'm a bad drinker. In twenty-four years of trying, I don't have one positive story about alcohol. Not one "Remember that time we got wasted and built that school in Haiti?" All of my very few drinking stories, starting sophomore year in high school, end with me barfing like Chad on a Homemade Coke bender. Only, unlike Chad, who barfed only in his own tent, I always found somewhere inappropriate: in between exchanges with Chris Levy's mom on her front steps after she came home early and broke up a high school party; on the top bunk of a college dorm bed, after my first kiss with my freshman-year girlfriend, who turned out to be a lesbian, perhaps due to that very experience; on the corner of Twenty-Third Street and Tenth Avenue, after hopping off a bus on the way home from a fiftieth-birthday lunch for my boss, while a huge group of teenagers pointed and laughed at the nerd messing up his suit.

Worse yet, some of that barfing was from my drink of choice in high school: the wine cooler. Which I learned to make myself. The only thing wimpier than drinking a wine cooler is coming up with a recipe for a wine cooler, and then bragging about it to high school girls. I was stuck in the pathetic guy's mentality that doing what girls were doing would cause me to be around girls and eventually hook up with them. This also happens to be the strategy gay men use to not hook up with girls.

Until I met Cassandra, I barely drank. I didn't have a sip of alcohol from the middle of my freshman year of college until a year after I graduated. This was an even worse strategy for hooking up with girls than trying to gossip with them about hot boys while mixing homemade wine coolers.

Cassandra didn't understand how I met friends at bars and just stood there, hands unoccupied. She also didn't understand how I sat in my apartment without a drink in my hand. So we compromised: I went from drinking zero nights a week to drinking seven nights a week and she went from getting drunk to getting drunk. I am not a good negotiator.

Now I drink only wine, which is a pretty big step up from wine cooler. But I almost always stop before I get a buzz. Plus, there's nothing manly about knowing a lot about wine. I need to drink whiskey. That's what cowboys, dandies, and every other kind of man drinks. Which is why I fear it. That, and anything over 15 percent alcohol, tastes like napalm to me.

The Macallan, one of the great Scotch distillers, offers to send Eden Algie, the Global Brand Ambassador for The Macallan, to my house to teach the art of drinking to me and my wimpy sitcom-writer friends who can't handle alcohol. I picture Eden as an old, ruddy-cheeked Scotsman so pickled from alcohol, not only would I not be able to understand him, but other Scottish people wouldn't be able to understand him. So when Eden pulls up to my house in a Porsche Cayenne and comes inside—hair gelled perfectly, giant watch, paisley on the inside of his cuffs, smelling like something you put on to smell great—I know The Macallan is not the kind of beverage that lets the punks like me make the mockery of it for having the article in front of the name. Eden, the Global Brand Ambassador for The Macallan, brought twelve-, fifteen-, and eighteen-year-old bottles of The Macallan, and also whiskey glasses, Lindt 90 percent cocoa chocolate bars, and a bunch of Payne-Mason cigars, which were made for us by Cuban master rollers the afternoon before. I give Eden a glass of water.

I ask Eden what the deal is with the chocolate. He says it brings out some of the chocolate notes of The Macallan and pairs well with the cigars. When I subtly throw around hints like *"Sex and the City,"* "menstruation," and "suffrage movement," Eden says, "Chocolate is not girlie at all. It's educated. If the definition of a man is a Neanderthal, you probably want to drink cheap whiskey." I do not want to drink cheap whiskey. I am pretty sure I do not want to drink any whiskey.

I take Eden to the back of my house, where I can vomit freely. He guarantees not only that I will be able to drink The Macallan, but that I'll enjoy it. I won't, however, get to make that manly face where I scrunch up my mouth and violently shake my head one time. "People make that face when they're drinking a whiskey because they're drinking a shit whiskey," he says. "Drinking Scotch is not about looking like a bulldog chewing a wasp. It's about enjoying the flavors." When I ask if those flavors are pain and burning, he says they are chocolate, citrus, and cinnamon. Eden made a beverage that is 43 percent alcohol sound like Christmas cake.

He does admit that I'll feel a little burn: "When you first started drinking beer you thought that was a man's drink. You went through the pain to drink the beer and discover the taste of it," he says. I don't have the heart to tell him, as we drink beers outside my house in the late-afternoon summer heat, that I'm still trying to get through that pain and figure out what beer tastes like.

Scotch, Eden explains, is the manliest of drinks, because it's from a rural country where people like to fight, and when they fight their first move is the head butt, and when they're not head butting each other they merrily call each other "cunt." It's also the manliest of drinks because it's 43 percent alcohol.

I should be a great drinker. At restaurants, when I was barely old enough to see over the bar, my dad taught me how to lean on the foot rail and spit out the names of classic cocktails. He worked for a liquor distributor, and our basement was stacked with bottles I didn't have the guts to steal because I was so afraid of what they tasted like. So when I asked my dad when he learned to drink, I was surprised it was on the job. "I never drank. Your grandfather never drank," he said. When he first tasted Pinch Scotch, which his company distributed, he didn't like it.

"It tasted like medicine," he said.

"But you learned to like it?" I asked.

"No. I learned not to say anything."

All those three-martini lunches he told me about when he was an ad exec at Ogilvy & Mather in the 1970s happened, but not the way I thought. "I'd drink half the first one and someone else would finish it for me. Then I'd drink a quarter of the second one and an eighth of the third one." I finally found a man deficiency I could blame on my dad: my inability to enjoy alcohol. But this was also an opportunity. I could order Scotch around my dad, slam it back, and outman him. If I could figure out how not to cough, cry, and barf.

My wimpy comedy-writer friends start arriving, and each seems to make the same confessions to Eden about not being able to deal with hard liquor. Matt Selman, a writer for *The Simpsons* who works out every day and eats a lot of salad, doesn't drink because of the empty calories he'd rather spend on multicourse meals at expensive restaurants. Matt's main reference for whiskey is Tintin, the series of charming Belgian comic books. Dan Sterling, who was the head writer on *The Sarah Silverman Program*, brags about having upped his alcohol intake. "I've been drinking beer lately," he says. Then he gets a little quieter. "Sorghum beer. It's wheat-free beer. Beer makes me feel gassy and full."

We sit around a giant, Viking-like wooden slab of a table, right next to my grill, beside an outdoor fire pit, near my wine cellar, and close to this adorable fountain birds like a lot. Eden pours us some Sherry Oak Twelve Year Old, which is the second-youngest Scotch Macallan sells after the ten-year-old, other than a seven-year-old that's marketed only in Italy.

"We refused to give them anything older than that because they were pounding it with Coke. They were nightclubbing it," he says. It feels manly to be making fun of Italians. My dad would be proud.

I hold my Scotch up and look at it and swirl it and smell it, not so much to appreciate it as to buy time. I'm not afraid of the pain so much as my reaction to the pain. I see myself taking a sip, jumping up from my chair, running in circles, and waving my hand in front of my outstretched tongue, trying to put out the fire in my mouth with my own tears.

I close my eyes and take a sip. There is a slight burn at the very front and the very end, but mostly it tastes good. The second sip doesn't hurt much at all. Then Eden tells me to add an ice cube, but I tell him that I can handle it straight.

"It bugs me when people at a bar are like, 'You can't drink that with an ice cube or water because it's girlie.' Ice opens the palate and reduces the alcohol level as well," he says. One ice cube really does make it taste better, removing the burn while intensifying the other flavors.

I should have been less afraid of the taste and more afraid of the effect. Unlike wine, Scotch gets you buzzed right away. This is due to a combination of the facts that it's often consumed without food, is sipped quickly, and is 43 percent alcohol. I am not used to this sudden feeling, and I don't like it. So to be safe, I take a break and walk away to put the rib eyes and potatoes on the grill.

One of the few manly things I can do is grill meat. That's because I can cook lots of things, most of which involves slow braising, deglazing pans, and delicate plating. Grilling meat is much easier. Which is why every man loves to do it. Warren Sapp, who owns an apron that reads GIVE THE COOK HEAD, said men make two things: grilled meat and breakfast, for when a woman sleeps over or to impress children. There is no room for modesty in male cooking. So just as Herbie the firefighter made "My Famous Chimichangas," Sapp makes "My Famous French Toast and Eggs and Cheese and Bacon." It seems that a man cooking a meal for others is so impressive that the entire world finds out about it. Sapp's Famous French Toast and Eggs and Cheese and Bacon, as I'm sure you know, involves pouring both maple syrup and hot sauce over everything. But besides grilling and breakfast, men aren't supposed to get involved in any other food preparation. "You going to tell me you bake? It's a delicate thing. You have to have the proper ingredients," Sapp said.

I've barely put the steaks on the grill when Eden yells for me to come back so he can pour the fifteen-year-old The Macallan.

"You've got to finish that off," Eden says, pointing to my glass of the twelve-year-old The Macallan.

"Yeah, Mrs. Stein," says my screenwriter friend Alex Grossman, pushing my glass at me.

I finish, and Eden then pours the Fine Oak Fifteen Year Old, which is more robust and has more of a burn to me because it is aged in former bourbon casks, instead of sherry ones, which bring out a citrus flavor. I add a splash of water when Cassandra—who has been banned from my mancave—walks downstairs, picks up some cans from under the house, and goes to stain some furniture. She hands me Laszlo.

"No wonder you're not a man," Alex says. "She did that just to make you look like a pussy. To emasculate you. And she gave you the baby. She just butched the shit out of you."

Most of my manficiencies predate Cassandra, but her willingness to fill the role—painting the walls, hanging curtains, ordering drinks, killing mice, cursing—isn't helping. Neither is Laszlo. He's whining because I won't let him drink my glass of The Macallan. When I let him smell it to dissuade him, he pulls his head back, looks up at me, smiles, and nods in approval. "That's incredible," Eden says. "I'm going to sponsor his college education."

This is not the first time that Laszlo has purposely emasculated me. He's starting the Oedipal thing way ahead of schedule. I don't even think he's interested in Cassandra. I think he's just into destroying me.

A couple of months ago, when Laszlo turned eighteen months old, Cassandra showed him a picture of me on the refrigerator when I was away on a trip.

"Mama," he said.

"No, Daddy."

"Mama."

"No. Dada."

"Mama."

"Dada."

"Mama."

Now whenever he sees me, he calls me "Mama." Cassandra tried to convince me that this was because the *m* phoneme is easier to say than the *d*, but Laszlo already says "du" to refer to his rubber duck. He calls me "Mama" because I don't go to an office, because I run to comfort him as soon as he cries, and because he sees me cooking all the time. Also I tend to stand with my weight on one leg, so my hip juts out.

He's also emasculated me by doing better with women than I have, in front of me. When he was nine months old, I brought him to our supermarket where this attractive woman told me how cute Laszlo was. She came by three times, and it was not a small supermarket. Eventually she told me that she was a Jewish aunt who had been a nurse and loved kids, and thought Laszlo was pretty special. It turned out she read my columns and knew about Laszlo's circumcised penis, which I had written about. It was when this nice Jewish lady said "penis" that I realized she was Nina Hartley, the porn star. Laszlo was nine months old and porn stars were circling stores to talk to him about his penis.

Sitting on my lap now, Laszlo eats more steak than you'd think he could, and eventually Cassandra, pants splattered with either wood stain or the remnants of my testes, takes him back upstairs. Eden opens the Sherry Oak Eighteen Years Old and I like it. A lot. So much that I stop taking many notes. My notebook says "Joel" in someone else's handwriting and under it there's a drawing of a heart and then a drawing of an erect penis. I find it pathetic that men fall back on lazy homophobia to bond, which I assume I said out loud but just didn't bother writing in my notebook.

I do write down that there is a long discussion of the pleasures of making love to overweight women, which is passionately spearheaded by my friend Ross Novie, whom I've known since we were sixteen and has only, to my knowledge, dated thin women. Apparently The Macallan knows better.

Ross: "Is that a tit? Is that a stomach? Is that an ass? It's like climbing Everest!"

Duncan Birmingham: "I've certainly woken up to find out she's a little larger than I would have liked."

Ross: "No. I'm talking two hundred pounds."

This is the David Mamet play I wanted The Macallan to write.

Right now, I want to mount a lady of much avoirdupois. It sounds great, like a theme-park ride and a carnival guessing game all in one. I have not lived a full life. Because I have not drunk enough.

I'm not sure if this conversation ends before Cassandra finagles her way into the group and Eden gifts her with a bottle of Fine Oak Twenty-One Years Old. The bottle costs $250 and comes in a silver satin-lined case, which would look manly only if Barbara Eden lived in it. It is delicious, and I drink quite a bit of it, though I like the eighteen-year-old even more. At some point my friend Michael Thomas shows up in a kilt. He also has a bag of French *macarons*, these airy, colorful, meringue sandwiches with frosting in the middle. They are leftovers from an event for the shoe designer Jimmy Choo, and Michael put them in a canvas reusable shopping bag festooned with the logo of *The Kids Are All Right*, a charming independent movie about lesbian moms. I eat seven *macarons*.

Before he leaves, Eden shows me how to cut a small hole in the back of a cigar and slowly puff it to life. I am doing him justice, one in each hand, sucking on them back and forth and making happy noises, much like the women in the Gangbang Girl movies. Which I hope I didn't mention to my friends, Cassandra, or Laszlo. There are no notes of anything that happens from that point on and I can't remember anything with clarity. But I recall the cigar smoke making me nauseated. I recall feeling dizzy. And I recall telling myself that I cannot let myself barf.

At 10:30 PM I go upstairs, brush my teeth, take off my shoes and belt, get in my bed, and fall asleep. Shortly thereafter, Cassandra comes upstairs.

"Is the room spinning?" she asks.

"No."

"Do you have to go to the bathroom?"

"No."

"So this is it? You're not coming back downstairs?"

"No. How do we handle this—socially?"

By all accounts, Cassandra handled my sudden disappearance with aplomb, drinking with my friends and laughing until all hours of the night before joining me in bed. I handled it even better: by not barfing. Despite that triumph, it is a little embarrassing to be so unable to handle Scotch that I had to leave my own party without saying good-bye. But none of my friends thought my departure was rude. In fact, Ross said I left at exactly the perfect time, while I still was fun and not a sickly burden. "The only thing you could have done to be more manly was take a swing at me before going up to bed," he says.

Hanging out with guys is actually pretty easy, especially when drunk. They don't get hung up on tiny social graces, like going to bed in the middle of your own party. These are the faux pas that fuel entire episodes of reality shows about housewives. They're deconstructed by women in long, painful conversations about their friends and ex-friends and frenemies and ex-frenemies. We don't have those. We have people who are fun to hang out with, until they drink themselves sick and then, if we're lucky, fall asleep somewhere instead of getting us into fights. I had actually been a great host.

But I wasn't a wild man. I didn't have any desire to fight or argue or do anything besides nap. If a really beautiful, scantily dressed, enormously overweight woman came on to me, and Cassandra gave me the go-ahead, I don't think I would have even kissed her. It wasn't sobriety that kept me from all those adventures. I don't have any wildness in me. I'm just layer after layer of cautious decision making. There's nothing to tap into if I need it on these man adventures.

A few days later, though, my sense of my manliness is improved. It could just be Laszlo's natural cerebral development, a sudden mastering of the voiced alveolar plosive phoneme, but a few weeks after I learned how to drink Scotch, Laszlo points at my chest and says "Dada." It could also be that I've been working out a lot and have finally worked off my man boobs. Either way, I love it. I tickle him, hold him upside down, put his socks on his ears—whatever I have to do to hear him laugh and say, "No, Dada." It doesn't make me feel like a man in the way I've been working toward. It makes me feel better.

5
MAKING MONEY

I want to feel the rush of making lots of money and then snorting cocaine off a hooker who is snorting cocaine off another hooker.

Sports are a terrific way to dominate other men and a Scotch-fueled argument has its place in determining male hierarchy, but money is a lot more practical. Even if the apocalypse comes and we are reduced to hunting, fishing, fighting, and tying square knots to survive, about two hours after the nuclear bomb goes off some guy is going to have the most rat meat and the most cat pelts and he's going to trade them for witty observations about whatever pop culture emerged in those two hours. At least that's how I hope it goes.

I have no idea how women keep score of who is doing best, but I get the feeling it's complicated and involves shoes and delivering compliments that are actually insults. When men graduate from school, we switch from being judged on athletic ability to being judged on how much money we make. Taking care of yourself and providing for your family are so tied to being a man that unemployed guys have problems getting it up with their wives. This was true even before they could spend all day watching Internet porn.

Of all the man jobs, finance seems like something I might have actually done. Business guys don't have to be athletic, outdoorsy, or mechanical. They were in my AP classes in high school, my dorms at Stanford, my apartment building in New York. Yet I considered being a stock trader as much as I considered being a lion tamer. That's because there are nerds like me—writers, lawyers, professors—and nerds like them—bankers, consultants, venture capitalists. They're the lion tamers of nerddom. They use virtual whips and chairs to walk out of the cage with a pile of cash. My friend Matt Tupper—who retired at forty-one—graduated college a year before me, and when I visited him at the San Francisco office of Bain & Company in 1992, he walked out of an elevator, slapped another guy on his back, and told him to "have a good one." That, I was pretty sure, was code for "have a good night watching your Asian sex slaves entertain you while petting a black cat on your lap."

I need some back-slappiness, some jolt in taking money from someone else, in risking it all on a drive-through pasta chain—which Matt Tupper once considered. I want to learn from people who make a lot of money because they have certainty and self-confidence, and, more importantly, because they know how to make a lot of money. The people who make fortunes took unnecessary risks. The only risks I took were in Hebrew school, where I often got sent to the principal's office. Before I took those risks, I asked my parents, four times, if Hebrew school counted toward college. I was ten.

Unlike me, Laszlo is going to want to play football, jump dirt bikes over ramps, skip school, try drugs, and go on spring break, and I'm going to have to try to understand why he does those things, so I can at least talk to him about them. To help me do that, I'm going to see if I can take the bravery I sensed in myself at the firehouse and the confidence I got from Shawn Green, and use it to take other kinds of risks. Financial risks. Big ones.

I think it's prudent, though, to take those risks with someone else's money. So I post a message on Dealbreaker, a Wall Street gossip website, saying I'm looking for a man who not only will teach me how to trade stocks but will then give me one hundred thousand dollars for the day to see how I do at it. Will I panic from the pressure and make mistakes, blowing it all? Will I not be able to make decisions quickly enough and lose my opportunity to cash out on top? Does Hallmark make cards that say, "Sorry I lost your hundred thousand dollars"?

I do not worry about this too much because obviously no one is going to give me one hundred thousand dollars. But within a day, I get an email from Matt Nadel. Only twenty-five, Matt is the man of immense balls I've been hoping to find. He has already made a small fortune as a day trader, risking not only his own money but also money loaned to him by his firm. If that doesn't prove his voraciousness for risk, he has agreed to give me one hundred thousand dollars to trade for a day.

When I meet him at his office in Chicago, I instantly know Matt is not the guy I was hoping he'd be. Matt is the kind of guy that parents hope their sons grow up to be. He's optimistic and polite and has been dating the same woman since his senior year of high school. He has never drunk alcohol. He eats the exact same protein shake from the exact same restaurant for breakfast every day, and usually goes there for his afternoon chicken wrap. He works out a lot. He has never been to a strip club. His hair is not slicked back, he has no watch, he is not wearing cologne, his clothes are from J.Crew; he is, in every way, the opposite of The Macallan global brand manager Eden Algie. On Tuesday nights Matt is a Big Brother to a disadvantaged kid and, when he talks about it, he doesn't even say that he gets more out of it than the kid does. Matt is not going to take me out hooker snorting.

Matt is also a genius. His Vulcan mind calmly solves complicated logic problems in milliseconds that most people couldn't do in an hour with a spreadsheet. Matt got a full scholarship to USC *in debate.* You know how good you have to be at debate to get a full scholarship? You have to be pretty good at football to get a scholarship, and college football is on television. The only way college debate would be on television is if it got so heated one guy stabbed another guy and the debate was held in the stands during a college football game.

In addition to having a brain that computes crazy fast, Matt is devoid of laziness. He is all willpower, all curiosity, all eagerness, all the time. During college, Matt got bored of debate and really into online poker. So into it that when he graduated—in just three years—he had seventy thousand dollars in poker profits. Then he got bored of poker. So he moved back home to Chicago and applied to be a day trader at Great Point Capital. Matt can tell that not too long from now, he'll get bored of day trading. "I like the challenge of getting good at things more than the actual thing itself," he says. This is why men hunt moose, build model cars, and don't call women back after first dates. I'm much more of an actual-thing-itself guy. When a woman slept with me, I became instantly monogamous, thrilled to spend time with a person willing to have sex with me, instead of talking to women who almost definitely were not. I am more gatherer than hunter.

The markets have always interested Matt. For his assignment to write a book in first grade, Matt didn't write about his dog or baseball: He wrote a guide to the stock market.

"Some of my most memorable conversations with my father when we were younger was him just telling me about stocks and bonds and finance," he says. My dad did the same thing. Although they were low on memorability, other than the unforgettable fact that I was really bored. Unless that was his lesson, that investing is best done in the most boring way possible, by not touching your index funds and letting compound interest do its work. My dad might be a genius.

At least I thought I was always bored by the markets. But when

I look at the charts on Matt's computer, I remember I spent a lot of time when I was thirteen on my Apple IIe playing a video game called *Millionaire: The Stock Market Simulation* in which I read fake news about Sears and Tandy and put in orders for buys, sells, calls, and puts. Maybe I could have been Matt. Then again, liking a video game isn't a great career predictor. It's not as if I almost grew up to wear lipstick and a hair ribbon and eat dots and get chased by ghosts.

Great Point Capital, the city's biggest day-trading firm, is on the fourteenth floor of a building just across the street from the Federal Reserve Bank of Chicago and next to the Chicago Board of Trade. It's located in a large empty office space filled with long desks where men sit next to one another and work on computers that are each hooked up to many monitors. There's not a woman here other than the receptionist at the front desk, way far away from the office. Matt has never heard about a woman day trader, anywhere. His co-workers are young guys because of the stress and the fact that it's hard to raise a family when you don't know if you'll make or lose money that month. And they're badly dressed guys. I'm the only one in a suit, and I'm immediately mocked for it. Guys greet me by calling me "suit." Matt is wearing a green sweater and jeans and he's got a good shot at second-best dressed.

This is, I think, a nice office. But I'm not sure since it's really dark in here. All the time. No one ever turns on the lights in the office, because it would cause a glare on their screens. Which adds to the empty feeling of this giant space, where most of the desks are empty—abandoned since the market's downturn a few years ago. I am no human resources expert, but I believe Great Point Capital might have a much easier time recruiting female employees if it didn't feel so much like Rape Point Capital.

Matt, cheery and smiling, brought me a power-shake and a protein bar. He's going to spend the day teaching me how to day trade before handing over the hundred thousand dollars tomorrow. He's cautious that way.

He starts with the basics. Like what day traders do. Before this morning, I assumed it had to do with analyzing sales figures and doing math and talking to China. That is not what they do at all. They gamble. When Matt decides to buy stock in a company, he has no interest in the price-to-earnings ratio, who the CEO is, or what the sales figures are. He's only going to own these shares for a few seconds before selling them, hopefully, for five or twenty cents more than he paid. All he cares about is how the stock price is moving. At one point Matt points to one of his lists of companies' fluctuating stock prices: "I'm watching SINA, Sina Corporation, which is, I don't even know."

An enormous part of our financial system is just dudes making straight-up bets against one another. "This is gambling. It's educated guessing with an edge," Matt says. "It's just more prestigious than being a poker player." Day-trading firms are called "proprietary trading firms" by the people who work there. Everyone else in finance calls them "arcades."

Studies have proven that you can't beat the stock market over time, and the more you trade, the less you'll make, due to fees. One of the few truly practical aphorisms on The List of advice for Laszlo is "Don't try to make more than average on your investments." The best policy, as my dad taught me, is to buy boring index funds that mimic the entire market, and hold them. It's why women are better investors than men: They don't have the same cockiness and competitiveness that makes them believe they can beat everyone else. But making 10 percent per year, the historical average, is for women and children. Matt makes more than 1,321 percent on his money. He is doing something that's supposed to be impossible.

And he's going to teach me how, or lose a hundred grand trying. I pull up a chair next to his computer before the markets open, and Matt teaches me that the simplest and most important day-trading move is trend following: If a stock is shooting up, buy some and ride it up until it falls. "Fading a move" is where you think a stock has ridden far enough up, so you bet against it by shorting it, hopefully predicting its downward movement. You can look for another person's large upcoming order at a specific price that hasn't been reached yet and use it as a buffer, so that if you're wrong and the stock hits that guy's price you'll have time to get out while his big order is filled at that price. I cannot believe that no one has invented a more efficient system than capitalism.

They have, however, built a more efficient system than day traders. Guys now program computers to do the exact same thing Matt does, coming up with algorithms to find what day traders spot through intuition and experience. In 2010, 70 percent of all purchases and sales of all stocks and bonds in the world were made by high-frequency trading programs, called algo-bots. And it's increased since then. Algo-bots place way more orders than they do purchases, canceling 90 percent of them nearly instantly, which makes predicting their actions difficult. Computer programs have also created ways to hide large purchases—called dark pools of liquidity—giving them another advantage.

Most importantly, the algo-bots can buy a stock in 150 milliseconds—fewer if their Internet connection is near the New York Stock Exchange. Doyle Olson, the president of Great Point Capital, tells me that the amount of time in which the human brain can see something and tell a finger to hit a button is 250 milliseconds. "Some guys here are below two hundred milliseconds," says Doyle. But it's not nearly fast enough. Two years ago a hundred guys sat in this office. Now there are forty. It's not only that the Great Recession caused America to stop investing in the stock market, severely limiting the action to gamble on. It's that these forty guys are getting replaced by technology.

That's why the day traders here talk about the Flash Crash like it was the Battle of the Bulge. On the afternoon of May 6, 2010, the Dow Jones Industrial Average suddenly dropped more than one thousand points since its height that day—losing more than

9 percent of the entire market's value in its biggest intraday plunge ever. Then it gained nearly all of it back twenty minutes later. Several large companies had their stocks drop all the way to one cent for no reason. The high-frequency programs got triggered to either sell or stop trading, but the day traders soaked up the money the computers spit up. It was the day when the computers got their asses kicked.

During the market's free fall that day, Matt kept buying as he saw some blue-chip stocks lose nearly half their value. At one point, in those minutes when the market was falling irrationally and Matt was buying, he was ninety thousand dollars down. "I get a little sick still, just thinking about it," he says. He ran to the desk of Adrian Nico, the firm's risk manager, and begged for more leverage, which Adrian gave him, allowing Matt to put twenty million of the company's money into the market. "It seemed like it was the end of the world. No one was buying," Matt says. "I feel really proud of what I did that day. I stepped in when no one was willing to." He made $220,000 that day. Another guy at the firm made more than two million. Another guy was at the dentist.

Most of his colleagues have even worse stories. Of the eighty people who were hired by Great Point Capital between 2005 and 2007, only Matt and two other guys are left. When you first start working here, the firm lets you invest with their money. They give you a salary of two grand a month and let you keep a percentage of your winnings. If you keep losing, Adrian—a chubby, smiley guy who actually wears a button-down shirt—comes to your desk, cuts you off, and sends you home. He's been threatened more than once.

If you do well after about three years, you get the deal Matt has: He invests his own money, keeps all his winnings, sucks up all his losses, and pays the firm about four dollars for every thousand shares he trades. In return, he gets to play with a lot more money than he puts in—the firm gives him leverage of twenty-five times his investment. They also give him a great proprietary computer program to trade with (when you punch in your password, instead of seeing "******" you see "$$$$$$"), a bunch of other guys sitting near him to give him advice, and that four-buck trading fee, which is lower than what he could negotiate alone. He also gets TVs set to CNBC and a speaker system in the ceiling that plays Trade the News, a "squawk" service where a guy reads stock-relevant breaking news all day, which the guy unsuccessfully tries to make sound interesting by raising and lowering his voice a lot. Every time I try to picture the guy who reads that, I see a man holding a sheet of paper, tied to a chair with guns pointing at his head.

At 8:30 AM in Chicago the opening bell goes off in the New York markets and everyone in this quiet, dark room instantly gets Tourette's.

"What the fuck? Oh my God. What the fuck is that? Unbelievable! Unbelievable! So fucking ridiculous!"

"Pay me, motherfucker! Pay me!"

"Take a motherfucking offer, you cuntbags!"

They also might get more women traders if they cut back on that "cuntbags" thing.

The stock prices on Matt's screen are scrolling down so quickly I cannot read them. All I know is when he's ahead one number is in green, and when he's behind it's in red. Matt is punching buttons hard and fast. I cannot figure out why his keys look so new.

It's because, after an hour, it stops. All the real action is in the first hour of trading, and the last half hour. In between, guys go to the gym, get lunch, surf the web, throw around a Nerf football, or just go home and skip the last half hour of trading. But that first hour is intense. Tony Chlada is a sweet, quiet husband and father who cannot believe what he said at the opening bell when I read it back to him, and refuses to let me print it. "I don't swear at home. At home, I'm very well adjusted. This place makes you an animal," he says. "I've been here eleven years and I still get the heartbeat and the sweaty hands. When Google had big imbalances I would walk out of the office for the day, and three minutes later my hand was still shaking. I'd have to hold my hand." I want to hug him. Everything seems poignant when it is said in near-total darkness.

Somehow in the first thirty-one minutes, Matt loses $2,926. He is completely calm. Matt has the same centered temperament as Shawn Green. He also doesn't care much about money. He rents an apartment that he shares with his girlfriend, he doesn't own a car, and his diet consists mostly of protein shakes and chicken wraps. He could live the same exact way on the salary of the loser reading the stock news through the speakers. Though he's gambling his own money, it's only about 20 percent of what he's amassed; the rest is either in cash or in an indexed mutual fund. He's upset about the $2,926 he lost not because it's $2,926, but because it shows that he played badly.

"I like this job because of the number aspect, the competition," he says. It's why he liked debate and poker, and why he's into first-person-shooter video games and has a fantasy football team.

Matt has six screens in front of him, the second most in the office. The number of screens you have at a day-trading firm is a good approximation of how much money you make. A better approximation is this database Matt has of exactly how much money he makes. Over the last two hundred days, Matt has somehow profited about $3,000 a day; after fees, he's taken home an average of $2,114 a day—which is $528,500 a year. There were a lot of days where he lost thirty or forty thousand, but his big days made up for it. Right now, though, he's having his worst month since he started day trading, down an average of $465.03 a day. It's only his third losing month since he started in December 2007. It sucks to come into work early every morning, do a really stressful job, and go home with a weekly paycheck of negative $2,325.15. It is even worse, Matt says, to try to explain that to your live-in girlfriend.

The last half hour of trading doesn't go much better for Matt, but after the market closes, Apple announces its quarterly earnings, and they're big. Matt pounds on his keyboard for thirty minutes of after-hours trading and erases all his losses, making more than a thousand dollars on the day. We talk for a while and leave the office at five thirty, the latest he has ever been there. Matt has no boss, no paperwork. Matt has never gotten a work email, been on a business trip, or worked a weekend.

I take Matt to dinner at Next, one of the best restaurants in the country, to celebrate his last-minute win on the day. He indulges in copious amounts of deliciously prepared mixtures of tea and fruit juice.

Matt is one of the finest dinner companions I've ever had. He appreciates everything. He finds everything I say fascinating, everything the waiter says fascinating—even his non-alcoholic drinks are fascinating. He's not faking it. He's got a way of slowing time down by being completely present. He's not at all what I expected from a day trader. He makes me calm, just like Wiggles, like Captain Buzz, like Shawn, like three glasses of The Macallan. I thought Matt would be constantly consuming, bragging, teasing. But he's not interested in any of that. Matt has even trained himself not to get excited about gains and losses so he can keep his decision making clear. He day trades simply because he likes to fire the pistons in his mind. Money is just a way of tracking his improvement. It's absolutely wasted on him. Which makes me feel a tiny bit better about what I'm about to do to his money.

Still, you should never go out to dinner with a man whose fortune you're about to waste for no good reason. I lie in my hotel room bed thinking about all the things Matt was going to do with the hundred thousand dollars I'm going to lose. Probably give it to that Big Brother charity he works with. I could never feel okay after losing a hundred thousand dollars of his money. I am here to take risks, but I am going to take only the risks that Matt tells me aren't too risky. The ones I think I can handle. I hope I don't screw it up.

At seven forty-five the next morning, I sit in front of the computer next to Matt, who has the eager chipperness of a man who ate a twelve-course meal accompanied by juice, not the dread of a man who is about to lose one hundred thousand dollars.

I am about to find out if I can use just my instincts and my guts to take money from other men sitting in front of some other computer with nothing but their instincts and guts. Matt flows the cash into an account on my computer and I instantly feel the pressure. I want to ask for less money, maybe just a couple of thousand, but I know that won't prove anything about my ability to handle this pressure. And there's no time to change it now anyway.

The opening bell goes off on the TV screen showing CNBC above us, and Matt tells me to hold tight and avoid investing for the first few fastest minutes until I can figure out what I'm looking at. Of course I will. But then I notice on one of the lists Matt set up on my screen that Teva Pharmaceuticals is hitting record highs. I want to just dip in and quickly ride the trend while it's going up. Only I press Shift-S to sell instead of Shift-B to buy and accidentally short a hundred shares of Teva Pharmaceuticals. But my guess was wrong, and it's going down, so I actually make some money before I find the buy button to get rid of my Teva Pharmaceuticals. But in my panic I press Shift-B twice instead of once, so I actually do buy a hundred shares of Teva Pharmaceuticals, and it's suddenly going up now, so I make some money that way, too. I'm good at this. And I don't even know the right buttons. Or how they can make pharmaceuticals out of hippie shoes.

Matt is too busy to notice what I'm doing and in just a few minutes I have swapped back and forth more than $150,000 of Teva and made $40.70. It's a rush and I yell "fuck" a few times, mostly to fit in. I can't follow nearly as many stocks at the same time as Matt does, but I keep track of two of the ones on the lists Matt has set up for me: Abbott Laboratories and BorgWarner, which I assume is Time Warner's division that makes cyborgs. Unfortunately, I can't even handle watching two stocks at once. I think my cursor is in the Abbott box but it's really over at BorgWarner when I press buy. And suddenly I own a hundred shares of BorgWarner. I try to sell but accidentally press buy again, so I've got more than $15,000 invested in cyborg manufacturing. I make $1.50 on the cyborgs overall.

I love this. It's a rush, like sex, gambling, or tricking underprivileged eleven-year-olds into hunting snipes. I trade BAX, CPX, FO, ILMN, ISS, PCP, TSLA, and WLT—without knowing what any of them are. It is exactly the thrill I was hoping it would be. And then it stops. The first-hour morning action is over, and I've made Matt close to one hundred dollars, enough for three to four nights on the town drinking non-alcoholic beverages. Now I just have to wait until the closing half hour. Yesterday Matt taught me the day-trading mantra: The best trade made in the middle of the day is the one not made at all.

I'm doing a good job not trading. Then I start thinking about Herbie, standing there in the rain outside the sushi restaurant, sad that he didn't get to turn the hose on one of the last fires he might see in his career. I think of all that unmanly cautiousness in me that not even The Macallan could wring out. I think of lots of things that will convince me to gamble some more.

Everyone in the office starts talking about a Chinese cloud-computing initial public offering. Matt tells me to stay away. It's going to be fast and hard to follow, and I could lose a lot of money. His money. But come on. China? Cloud computing? IPO? I am going to be rich! I buy four hundred shares at $20.50 each and the numbers move so fast, I can't see if I'm up or down. I'm down. A hundred dollars down in five seconds. Matt tells me to sell, get out as soon as I can. It's the first day-trading rule I was taught: Get out when you're losing. But China! Cloud computing! IPO! I hear my heart beat. My investment is three hundred dollars down, and it comes back a little and I press Shift-S, so I wind up a little more than two hundred down. China. Cloud computing. IPO.

Now I'm down for the day. I hate computers and China and clouds. What was I thinking? I mean, China? Cloud computing? IPO?! What was Matt thinking in letting me do this?

Matt suggests we take a midday break to get sandwiches to keep me away from the keyboard. On the way back, I buy the other guys in the office cookies from the Amish family that sells baked goods on a foldout table in the lobby all the time. The Amish daughter tries to convince me I want all five plates of cookies, and she almost does it. I have no idea if the Amish are allowed to day trade, but I'm guessing as long as she doesn't trade in anything with caffeine or alcohol, it would be fine.

Upstairs, there's a lot of midday Facebooking and YouTubing and wild, excited Googling after I tell the guys that Amish girls get to do whatever they want for the year of their *rumspringa*. But I have no time for *rumspringa* fantasies. I need to make up for my Chinese cloud-computing errors. I hear some guys in the row ahead of me talking about Quepasa, a Latino social networking company, and I know from experience that Latinos are a particularly social people. I buy in as it shoots up. Then I hear the newsreader guy say something into the speakers above me about Microsoft, so I buy sixteen thousand dollars' worth of shares, riding it for a tiny spike. But I'm still in the hole when the closing bell rings.

I did fine. Matt still has nearly all his hundred thousand dollars. I didn't freeze up when things moved fast. I didn't avoid the big chances. If anything, I took too much risk. Better yet, I liked it.

As I'm starting to pack up my stuff, Matt tells me he's not done for the day. A few companies are going to be announcing their earnings after the markets close. And for some reason we can still trade those stocks in after-hours trading. I do not understand the concept of after-hours trading. What's the point of closing markets if you're going to let people trade afterward? Is that loud clanging bell just a suggestion bell? If so, instead of a bell, shouldn't a middle-aged woman come to the floor of the exchange and say that it's starting to get dark out?

SanDisk, the leading manufacturer of flash memory cards, is about to announce its earnings. Matt says I can definitely not trade it. It's too unpredictable, too fast, too dangerous. It's going to make that cloud-computing IPO look like an abacus IPO. Matt looks at me and realizes I am going to trade it. So he tells me I can only buy and sell in increments of ten shares instead of a hundred.

I'm in the zone. I cannot go wrong with SanDisk, which is insanely volatile, fluctuating more than three dollars a share for nearly twenty minutes. I'm buying when it's going up, selling while it's going down, riding wave after wave. I manage to trade 1,040 shares of it—nearly fifty thousand dollars' worth—possibly by not following Matt's ten-share rule. Thanks to SanDisk, I'm up $76.36 on the day, though after my trading fees that's just $20.60. Still, that's better than Bank of America made this quarter. Matt, however, has lost several thousand dollars today. Though it's several thousand minus $20.60.

At three thirty I walk outside. After a day in the dark, the sun is blinding. I'm in the middle of Chicago, but everything feels slow. I want to trade more, gamble on the ponies, put so much of my savings into SanDisk and BorgWarner that they could buy spaces in their names.

Maybe I do have more desire for danger than I thought. Maybe I can learn to be better about embracing the unknown. I'm not so good with the unknown. I'm more of a known guy. I'm usually ready for change about two years after it happens. I don't see the need to mess with anything that isn't completely broken. It took me years to decide to propose to Cassandra, and more to have a kid. Cassandra and I lived in a 475-square-foot studio in Manhattan for six years even though we could afford a bigger place, because I think moving is so awful. I'm not an overthinker; I just don't see the need for all this constant change the universe seems to be so into.

To defend my fear of sudden change, I chose to believe that life was incremental, that the tiny decisions you make every day determine your fate, that your job is to captain an enormous ship subtly into ever-clearer waters. But that's not how it works at all. Life occurs in moments. You get into college. You propose. You get the job. You get cancer. You get fired. She leaves you. You get her pregnant. That last one, because of the time of night and the fact that it had been a while, took only half a moment.

Because I was born in a stable country at a stable time, I falsely extrapolated that change is incremental. But if you zoom out just a little bit, you see that life is soccer, not basketball. It's revolution, invention, war. It's big bangs, exploding stars, asteroids killing the dinosaurs. Which means that all the action is in the risk taking, whether I want it to be or not. When I ask Cassandra if I'm a risk taker, she pauses. "I mean, you like to try new food," she says. "But you're not going to go skydiving or anything."

I used to think of taking on risk as inviting danger. But after meeting Matt I see that you can control risk so it expands your opportunities without sacrificing anything too precious. Not taking risks is a risk, too, just like not proposing to Cassandra would have been as much of a decision as proposing, since the tension that comes with being uncommitted could have broken us up. Not deciding whether to have a kid for so long was an enormous decision, since it might mean we'll have only one, and I might never know my grandchildren.

On The List, I had written down this advice for Laszlo: "Nothing is going back to how it was, so embrace how it is." But now I see that's not quite right. No, you can't stop all this change, but you can manage it. And from now on, I'm going to manage risk more actively, less warily. I'm going to let Laszlo know that it's okay to sometimes buy a few shares of SanDisk in after-hours trading. But not after drinking The Macallan. After seeing him smell that stuff, I think he might have a problem.

6
USING MACHINES

Laszlo is the kind of boy I was afraid he'd be when I first saw that sonogram. He is already seeking answers I don't have, expressing enthusiasm about things I know nothing about. He is nothing like me. He is obsessed with cars.

At nine months old Laszlo crawled into the kitchen, opened the cupboard, pulled out a shrink-wrapped package of two mustard jars, and started pushing it across the floor while making noises with his lips. That's when Cassandra and I realized we had to buy him some toy cars. And that *Free to Be You and Me* totally lied to us about gender being a social construct.

Car was his third word, after *no* and *this*. He'll pass by a photograph of people in Hawaiian shirts and sombreros sacrificing a goat and yell, "Cah!" and, if I look long enough, I'll find a car deep in the background. He sleeps with a Matchbox car in his hand like it's a stuffed animal. He shakes his head violently in opposition whenever he sees a picture of a tow truck, since accepting assistance is beneath the dignity of a car. Laszlo saw a commercial with a monster truck and his whole face lit up, until the truck crushed a car and he screamed as if he were watching a live execution. He cried

on and off for thirty minutes, essentially asking why we would
bring him into a world where such a thing can happen to a car. If
puberty suddenly hit Laszlo now, at a year and a half, he would
definitely fuck a car.

I need to learn about cars, and fast, so I can bond with him.
And so I can give him guidance to prevent him from embarrassing
himself by liking the wrong shapes of cars or the wrong colors of
cars. I don't even know what I don't know about cars.

Learning about cars shouldn't be hard. I've always loved
driving—the freedom, the speed, the control, the opportunity
to sing show tunes as loud as I want without anyone knowing.
My dad got me to cut the lawn every week by buying me a trac-
tor mower before I could drive. I volunteered to be the designated
driver in high school because I liked driving more than drinking
and because I stupidly thought that showing responsibility would
turn on drunk teenage girls. But I don't know anything about how
cars work, or what makes some better than others. To me, they're
all great. The Oldsmobile station wagon I had in high school hit 110
miles per hour in South Dakota when I drove it across country, so
I don't see the advantage of a Ferrari. Except that, unlike my station wagon, a Ferrari probably doesn't smell like puke every time it
rains. I'm assuming here that, back in high school, Neil Friedman
would have had the good sense not to barf in the back of a Ferrari
after drunkenly eating three slices of pepperoni pizza.

I'd like to blame my lack of automotive knowledge on the fact
that I spent eleven years after college in Manhattan without a car,
but it started before that. I never had Matchbox cars. In high school
I covered our furnished basement walls with stuff I liked—photos
of the Who; Garfield comic strips; porn posters from the video
rental store my friend worked at; a completed thousand-piece puzzle of a dragon—and stuff I thought I was supposed to like—two
posters of Iron Maiden, whose songs I've still never heard; beer

coasters; ads for cars. I was so clueless about cars that I tacked a photo of a Renault to the wall.

The problem is that cars are machines. Guys love to talk about how powerful machines are. I have no appreciation for power, whether it's tools, rangers, or bottoms. Sure I love gadgets, but gadgets aren't machines. Gadgets didn't dig the Suez Canal. They didn't build my house or pave my street. Gadgets, like so many things I know about, aren't essential. They don't connect you to the physical world. Which I've spent too long not connecting to.

When I moved to LA six years ago, I bought a yellow convertible Mini Cooper because it was cheap, opened up to the warm California sky, stayed low to the ground, took sharp turns, parked in small spaces, and was in the lot, unlike less embarrassing colors that I'd have to wait months to get. Within two months of owning my car, a group of teenagers in a Mustang passed me on the highway and yelled, "Faggot." My car got gay-bashed. Unless they were able to somehow hear the show tunes.

But Laszlo wants to know how everything works, so now, for the first time, I do, too. So I get to studying. Hard. Upon my twenty-eighth reading of Richard Scarry's dense and authoritative children's picture book *Cars and Trucks and Things That Go* to Laszlo, I learn that roads are made by flattening dirt, pouring gravel on them, and topping it with asphalt, which is oil mixed with sand. In *Cars and How They Go*, Laszlo and I stare in wonder at pictures showing that a car is powered by a bunch of tiny explosions that force the pistons up and down, which turns the crankshaft, which turns the wheels. I fear the amazement in my voice when reading this out loud may not convince Laszlo that I'll be the guy to go to with car questions.

So I'm pretty excited when I meet a woman who does public relations for Lamborghini, and, unexpectedly, she offers to let me drive one of their cars. I explain that I'm not nearly experienced enough as a driver to handle one; for instance, I don't know how to drive stick. That being the case, she suggests I keep a Lamborghini Gallardo Superleggera for three days, so I have time to learn and enjoy its simple paddle shift system. The more I tell her how unqualified I am to handle a Lamborghini, the more she insists I take it. I wonder if lots of women would have slept with me if I had just gone around talking about how I have no idea what the hell a clitoris is.

My goal isn't to tame this car. I don't need to drive 250 miles per hour, or take a sharp turn around a cliff face. I just need to learn how to love this car as much as Laszlo does.

I bring Laszlo inside the Beverly Hills dealership where I'm meeting my new PR friend. Laszlo walks into the showroom and goes straight to a Lamborghini. He walks in a circle around it and then gets on his stomach to check out the tires. It is the first time I feel he understands something much better than I do besides nipples.

Unlike my yellow convertible Mini Cooper with racing stripes on the hood, the Superleggera is not a friendly car. It is an evil car that looks like the Batmobile, if the Batmobile were pissed off. It has ten cylinders to my Mini's four; 570 horsepower to my 115; gets to sixty miles per hour in 3.4 seconds to my car's 8.9; and weighs just six hundred pounds more. Also, it costs $210,000 more. It is inches from the ground and has a glass panel on the top of the back so you can see the engine. The buttons inside are all marked in Italian, but I'm pretty sure they translate to "drop tacks," "shoot lasers," and "eject naked blonde."

Amateur race-car driver Richard Antinucci takes me for a drive to teach me how the Superleggera works. He turns the key and it starts with a rumble that, Antinucci tells me, the engineers put in just to sound cool. We inch out of the driveway onto the street and as soon as he hits the accelerator, I laugh. It's that same thrilling, giddy nervous shock I get when going down a roller coaster and that women get when having sex with me. My head is pinned to the headrest and it sounds like someone put an airplane engine behind me. It is the only car I've ever been in that comes standard with a fire extinguisher behind the seats.

Before I picked up the car, I went to see car expert Adam Carolla for advice on how to handle it. I know Adam from the manliest week of my life: When I used a week of vacation to work as a writer for *The Man Show*, which he hosted and where I sat at a desk getting made fun of. Now Adam hosts *The Car Show* on the Speed network. He's got four vintage Lamborghinis as well as a 1966 Ferrari. He told me the most important thing about a car is how fast it goes from zero to sixty miles per hour, and that less than six seconds is great. My Mini Cooper takes 8.9 seconds; still, I couldn't see how, even over years of driving, those 2.9 seconds were going to add up to a lot of saved time. But now I get it. The 2.9 seconds are the difference between driving and taking off.

I can't wait to take the car away from traffic, but first I have to drive through crowded Beverly Hills, during which, at stoplights, two women take my photo and a guy in a PT Cruiser jokes that he wants to race in a way that emasculates himself and not me. A boy asks if he can take a photo of my car. I feel like I'm hanging out with a celebrity.

This car changes my personality immediately. I am now magnanimous. I wave people across the street, let cars into my lane. It's not that I want to change some image of selfish Lamborghini drivers. I simply want to express my immense power by bestowing kindness on the little weak 115-horsepower people—just as Nietzsche predicted the superman would exert his power. I want them to feel not my disdain, but my pity. I let car after car in front of me, since I am far above petty arguments as to who gets to go first at thirty miles per hour. I also have a strong desire to show other drivers that I don't actually have a tiny penis, but none of my ideas for how to communicate that seem like they will go over well, such as taking out my penis, pointing to it, and yelling "See? I don't have a tiny penis!"

Being seen driving a Lamborghini, I assumed, would be most of the fun part of driving a Lamborghini. But it isn't. First of all, isn't the entire point of being seen in a Lamborghini to get two women for a threesome? But—and here is the car's one major design flaw—there are only two seats. So I'd have to meet two women at a club, take one home, drive back to the club, and take the second one home. By then, the effect of the Lamborghini would have worn off on the first one, so I'd have to take her for a quick drive somewhere, thus de-Lamborghini-sexing the second one. The math just doesn't work out.

Besides, women have as much interest in car engines as I did before I got in the Superleggera. When I ask Adam Carolla if women who don't know anything about cars really care about what men drive, he says they absolutely do. "A guy gets a nice house, but you can't go into a club and show chicks pictures of your house with an infinity pool. So you pull up to the club in a Ferrari and when you get out of your Ferrari you put on a Rolex, which lets people know you have a Ferrari, and the Ferrari lets them know you have a nice house," he explains. He argues that the women you'd attract this way are not gold diggers. "They're not like, 'I want his money.' They love the fact that the guy has drive, is self-assured, is his own man, and has confidence. And when you have all those things, guess what? They pay you." I'm guessing that back when Adam was a construction worker, he had a different theory.

One disappointing thing about driving a car that looks this cool is that you can't appreciate its beauty when you're in it. Sure, the interior is nice, but you can only appreciate a nice interior so much. I was at a Jay-Z concert at The Cosmopolitan hotel in Las Vegas for New Year's Eve and he ended the show by saying, "You lucky motherfuckers, you lucky sons of bitches, I wish I was you so I could see what was going on. That's some really arrogant shit to say but I swear I wish I was you tonight. I'm just being honest." I now empathize with the exquisite torture of being Jay-Z and never being able to see Jay-Z live in concert.

I pick up my cousin and take him to lunch in Beverly Hills, where we learn that when you valet a Lamborghini, they do not actually take it wherever they take valeted cars. There is a space for a Lamborghini right in front of every restaurant so everyone can see it. Unfortunately, the valet guy does not tell your hostess and waitress that you came in a Lamborghini, so they don't treat you especially well. And no one inside the restaurant knows. The whole special relationship is between you and the valet guy, who isn't really the person you're looking to impress.

After lunch, I tip the valet and drive away, feeling very cool until I realize that I tipped the valet my normal two dollars. As I entered my Lamborghini. Which he assumed I owned. I should have slipped him a twenty. I feel awful. And not because he parked my car right in front and watched over it. No, by getting a two-dollar tip from a Lamborghini driver, I had made him question the basic laws of the universe. He was standing there, staring at his two singles, worrying that either the spooky physics of quantum mechanics had expanded to make all actions unpredictable, or that rich people had become even bigger dicks. I vow never to go back to that restaurant, until I realize that he will never recognize me in my Mini Cooper. Or he'll figure I lost all my money, which will explain that two-dollar tip.

At home I pick up Laszlo and I put him in the passenger seat and drive him down the little dead end we live on, and he giggles just like I did. This car makes people happy. It is the first man thing I've done that I totally, instinctually enjoy.

My male friends are way more excited about the Lamborghini than my female friends. I had no idea so many of my guy friends, even the least manly ones, are into cars. And how creepily sexual car talk is. When I stopped by to see Adam Carolla at his giant garage, he asked his producer and high school friend Donny Mis-raje for some help finding motor oil for one of his Lamborghinis. "Donny, I'm changing my rear end fluid," he said. Then, after Donny pointed to a bottle: "The tranny gear fluid is the same as rear end fluid? I never realized that."

It didn't stop. There were rods, strokes, and lubed-up drive shafts. I asked Adam if these terms are due to the fact that men like to name things after their penises. "No," he said before presenting a man koan: "Why does the gayest guy in the Village People dress like a lumberjack?" I asked him to explain. "There's a certain point when you become so manly you actually become gay. The only guys who wear chaps are super-gay guys and super-straight guys. There's no regular guy saying, 'I drive a Ford Taurus and I just like to wear chaps once in a while.'"

This is something I've believed for a long time: Being gay is really manly. Take away all the coats of civilization, and homo-sexuality would be a testosterone fest. Gay couples would spend all day watching sports, barbecuing, fighting, and having sex. Like in ancient Greece. And, I believe, current Greece. I'm not saying all the man stuff I'm learning is sublimated sexual desire for other men. It's not that guys watch men in tight shiny pants tackle one another because they really want to be tackling them with their penises. It's just that if we weren't so uptight about our sexuality, guys would watch football together and, during the commercials, blow one another.

When men hang out, they're aware of this subtext: that we're all one blowjob away from being gay. And because the taboo against that is so strong, we make lame jokes—as I've done too many times in this book—in which we call ourselves, and one another, gay. We race to it, so we can harmlessly accuse ourselves of gayness, inocu-lating ourselves before anyone else can mock us with more of an edge. It's not a healthy way to handle this discomfort with physical and emotional intimacy. Women deal with it far better, mostly by making out with one another in front of men in bars.

I vow to stop this juvenilia. So I ask Alex Gregory, my friend who is most excited about the Lambo, if he wants to go on a late-night drive with me through the windy hills to Malibu and catch some dinner by the ocean—and I do not make any gay jokes, which is difficult. He's thrilled, not about my lack of gay jokes, but about riding in a Superleggera. When we get close to the ocean, we pull off in the hills just to look over the cliff at the water. It's an effort not to mock hold his hand, but I resist, and instead we have a long talk about fatherhood, marriage, monogamy, and pornography, and how much like we like three of them. We drive away, park in front of the restaurant, very uncoolly wiggle out of the impractically low seats, and drop off the keys with the impressed valet. Alex, who is a sitcom writer and *New Yorker* cartoonist, asks the family waiting for their car if they assume we are total dickheads because of our car. They do not. They assume we've made a lot of money in a tech IPO. This is not a very common occupation in Los Angeles. They did not think we were actors, producers, or drug dealers. Even in a Lamborghini, I am not cool.

This might be why no one I know, no matter how much money they have, will ever own a Lamborghini. It's too flashy, designed for athletes and Wall Street traders. My demographic can brag about spending ridiculous amounts of cash staying at the Post Ranch Inn, eating at the French Laundry, and traveling to Japan, but if any of us bought a Lamborghini the rest of us would just talk about how worried we were about him. All of my friends believe that the only reason a person would want something this fun would be to seek attention, reclaim youth, or long for power. As if those are bad things. There is nothing fun about being a liberal.

The next morning I wake up early to take a long drive before the traffic kicks in. Driving down Mulholland Drive on the ridge of the Hollywood Hills looking down on Los Angeles, I pass another Lambo, whose driver gives me a thumbs-up. I give the first non-ironic thumbs-up of my life. And it feels great. It's my first contact with the fun of manhood, the pure reckless thrill of being alive. I feel bad for the me of three days ago. That dude was a bummer.

I park the car outside my house, having failed to consider that not having a garage is a problem when you borrow a $237,600 car. My next-door neighbor, Adey Bennett, walks over to the car as I'm climbing out of it. Adey is well over six feet tall, in amazing shape, and a little scary. He walks with the slow, long steps of a cowboy. Cassandra and I are pretty sure he's either a deejay, a drug dealer, or—more likely—both. There were only families and older couples on our block until my neighbor moved away and rented his house to a group of four people in their early thirties. They have a loud dog, loud cars, loud music. Our only conversations with any of them have been asking them to turn something down.

I particularly don't know Adey, because he's mostly awake when I'm sleeping. When he is awake, he's either on his super-loud motorcycle, his regular-loud motorcycle, or his comparatively quiet monster truck, none of which you can talk over. The one thing I know about him is that he's really good-looking. That's because whenever a woman comes to our house, she says, "Who's that really good-looking black guy?" This includes whenever Cassandra comes to our house.

So I'm surprised that Adey is friendly. And mellow. And nice. He offers me his windshield-mount camera to record all the crazy driving he assumes I'm going to do while I have the car. Adey knows a lot about the Superleggera. And while I do not, just having it for three days is enough for him to feel comfortable talking to me about lots of things. I find out that Adey is not a deejay. He also doesn't sell drugs. He works at an ad agency, is designing a fashion line, races a supermoto bike, and calls women "females." I fear he is exactly what Cassandra was hoping the firefighters would

be like. We talk for a while, and I eventually check out his motorcycles in his garage and pretend to understand his descriptions of
them. But I legitimately do think they're cool, and if they have to
be loud to be cool, I can understand that now. Adey tells me that,
a couple of weeks ago, he got pulled over by cops after cutting a
guy off, which, we both agreed, is totally acceptable when you're
in a motorcycle. As he waited for the officer to walk over and give
him a ticket, Adey saw a slim opening ahead in the bumper-to-
bumper traffic, gunned his motorcycle, and took off, leading to a
five-minute chase in which he eventually lost the police. He then
ditched his bike for the night at a cool hotel bar, later having it
repainted to avoid detection. Apparently, I could have saved a lot
of time and just learned to be a man by hanging out on my block. I
had no idea I live in Hazzard County.

The next morning I wake up sad, because I have to return the
Lamborghini. There is so much we didn't do together, like catch
supervillains, evade cops by crossing state lines, and have that
threesome. I let Laszlo sit on my lap pretending to drive it and he
looks at me in a way that lets me know he is not disappointed with
the guy he got for his father.

I put him in the car seat in the back of my Mini Cooper and
Cassandra drives it, following me and the Lamborghini to the car
dealership, where I hand over the keys. I drive Laszlo and Cassandra back home in my Mini with the top down, using the sport-shift
option to accelerate a bit faster, though there's no jolt of rocket pro-
pulsion. Still, it's fun, and Laszlo is gap-toothed smiling wide.

Laszlo, to my surprise, doesn't ask where the car is the next
day, or the next week. The only person more disappointed than me
that the Superleggera is gone is Adey. But he's still interested in me
without my Lamborghini. Adey shows me videos he's shot, and
asks me for advice about getting articles about motorcycles into
publications. He emails me deals on used Lotus sports cars that he
thinks I should trade in my Mini Cooper for, and, once, a website

selling carbon-fiber baby seats that will allow me, apparently, to race these sports cars around a track with a baby riding shotgun. One of the items on The List is "No helicopters; no motorcycles," which I wrote after talking to friends who did emergency room rotations in med school. But now I think, just like Matt Nadel showed me, that maybe there's some way to harness this risk and make it worth enjoying.

Though not the way Adey does it. He sends me links to his YouTube channel where he takes turns on his motorcycle so sharp that he purposely drags his elbows against the road. I also enjoy short videos he's made of the asses of women who follow him from club-I've-never-heard-of to club-I've-never-heard-of. Of all the things I thought learning about cars would do, I did not expect that it would turn my scary next-door neighbor into a friend.

Adey is not only the first person I've met through a car, but also the friend I've made through Laszlo. Sure, I've met parents at the park or in a music class, but this is the first time that Laszlo pursued someone because he thought he was cool. Laszlo will yell "motorcycle" or "monster truck" and say "Adey" with this little smile when he hears his motorcycle coming up the street, and then Laszlo will grab my hand and lead me toward our front door. We'll go to Adey's garage to see his motorcycles and Adey, who has amazing patience for both kids and mechanical objects, will explain the parts that Laszlo points to. He's Laszlo's hero.

One day, as Laszlo and I stand with him in his garage, Adey starts talking about his Muay Thai training. This is very exiting because I know what Muay Thai is. It's a form of kickboxing that I have been reading about to prepare for my fight with Randy Couture. And my little bit of knowledge allows me to ask Adey some Muay Thai questions, which leads him to tell me he won't use his skills in street fights anymore. A little while ago, Adey got drunk and his friend got in a fight, so Adey stepped in and grabbed the other guy's head and repeatedly kneed him in the face. The morning after the fight, Adey woke up with blood all over his leg and a fair bit of regret, vowing to never let that happen again. I nod as if I understand how that must feel.

But what I'm really thinking is that I hope face kneeing isn't a major part of Randy Couture's fighting style. I am hoping he is more of a noogie and wedgie kind of fighter.

7
TAMING ANIMALS

Taking care of a dog seems maternal to me, but I'm learning that men can care about anything deeply—a car, a football team, a Scotch—as long as it's not a person. Having a dog is a basic, Jack London part of being a man. You take your dog hunting and keep spotted ones around the fire station. Owning a dog shows your mastery over animals. They protect your home. They are companions you don't have to talk to.

I, however, look at dog owners with the same disgust you would have if people kept goats in their homes. The entire point of a house is to keep nature out. People call in professionals to fumigate when they see a mouse, yet they purposely bring slobbering, shedding dogs into their beds.

I don't see how people love dogs and still eat meat. Just because they're cuter than cows? Cuteness is the warped ethical system resulting from a culture that deifies emotion. This is how much I don't love dogs: When Michael Vick was put in jail for running a dogfighting ring, I thought, *This guy goes to jail and Colonel Sanders gets statues of him placed all over the world?*

I get that we all want to be loved, but is it really love when you entrap an animal, provide its food, and physically control how many seconds it gets to socialize with its own species? If you think that's love, you also believe Mammy loved Scarlett O'Hara. I love Cassandra deeply, but if on our first date she told me that for our entire relationship I'd have to walk behind her and pick up her poop, I would have not have called the next day.

Yes, I am afraid of dogs. When people find this out, they ask me if I've ever been bitten by a dog. This is a stupid question. It's like asking me if I'm afraid of neo-Nazis because I got Holocausted. The reason I'm afraid of dogs is because they bite. They make this clear with their barking and growling and teeth baring and biting. If people did those things, I would assume they were neo-Nazis. My fear of dogs is completely logical: I am more afraid of dogs than squirrels but less than tigers. If dogs weren't scary, there wouldn't be so many mascots named after them. There is a reason that the University of Georgia teams are the Bulldogs and not the Fightin' Sheep.

Having grown up with a dog, Cassandra has been trying to convince me to get one since we met. I believe the entire reason she wanted a child was to train him to pester me to get a dog. Which is going to be easy since, unlike most kids under two who don't have a dog in the house, Laszlo is already unafraid of dogs, even ones that weigh three times as much as he does. I have a photo of him standing in a wide sun hat, smiling at the camera with his hand stretched up resting comfortably on a giant chow chow as if he were a nineteenth-century naturalist discovering a new species. We recently started sending him to a nursery school a few days a week and when the school bunny bit his finger, drawing blood, Laszlo bragged about his boo-boo and put his finger right back into that cage as if he were on *Baby Jackass*.

So after feeling the unexpected thrill of the Lamborghini and the peacefulness of camping, I am willing to try to get over my fear of dogs by taking care of one. In my house. For two weeks. If I can get over my fear of dogs, then Laszlo won't be embarrassed every time I get scared by a bark. And if he grows up to be not that bright and wants a dog, I might even be able to deal with having one.

I feel ready for this insane experiment because my adventures in manliness have given me confidence and reduced my uptightness. More than that, they've chiseled at my identity. Yes, much of my personality is immutable, possibly even genetic. But a lot of me was created in a sloppy rush of desperation: I wanted to be the academic, cynical, funny one and my role models didn't like sports, money, fast cars, or being outside, so I didn't, either. I didn't want to go hunting because then I would no longer be the urban intellectual who could say he never hunted. It's how I wasted four years— most of them in college—not drinking, because I defined myself as a non-drinker and didn't want my self-image muddled by the occasional beer. It's also how I spent six years with a mullet. Identity is so important that a man at the height of his hormonal surges will forgo nearly all opportunity for sex just to avoid being confused about who he is.

An even larger part of my identity was constructed more lazily, by copying whatever people around me happened to be doing. The real reason I don't hunt is because almost no one I've known has hunted, and I therefore assume it's for dumb hicks. I've limited myself in order to join a tribe, and wound up with attributes that are inauthentic. The truth is that I don't like dogs simply because we didn't have a dog when I grew up. Though I still think Jews who have dogs are trying too hard to assimilate. It's not like at the end of *Fiddler on the Roof* or the beginning of Elie Wiesel's *Night* anyone is crying about leaving behind his beloved schnauzer. It's not just because we're a traveling tribe. Gypsies and Irish Travelers seem to drag their dogs from country to country. The real reason Jews don't have dogs is that we're smart.

Cassandra is very excited about my plan to foster a dog for two weeks, hoping that she can prevent me from giving it back afterward. The dogs she wants, however, are not going to help my man project. She wants a dog that will fit in her handbag. And while her handbag is way too big for a handbag, it is too small for a pit bull cage. Though if I offered to buy her a Marc Jacobs bag big enough, she might go for a pit bull.

I also need a dog that won't eat Laszlo, which limits its manliness. So I'm going to get a small dog. Which means I will get made fun of both for having a small dog and for being afraid of that small dog. This is not going to go well.

But just as I've convinced many women, I tell myself that size doesn't matter. When Shawn Green told me about standing alone during batting practices in major-league parks hitting off the tee, I thought he was just telling me about the importance of focusing all your attention on one moment until all those complicated motions in a swing become as involuntary as breathing. But after I pictured him in the stadium hitting off that tiny tee as fans oohed over his teammates sending homers into the upper decks off pitches from a coach, I realized the most amazing thing was that Shawn had no interest in impressing anyone. He was a professional athlete whose goal was to impress himself. If a tiny dog is better for Laszlo, if it makes Cassandra happy, if it will help me get over my fears, then I don't care if it fits in a flowery pink teacup.

Though I had never noticed them before, every Sunday morning in Los Angeles street corners are taken over by dog adoption agencies. Dogs in cages are tended to by incredibly attractive women, sort of like booths at a trade show. Only, these women aren't being paid to be there. And they're all crazy.

People assume that women who are horribly abused by men become strippers and porn stars. It seems to me that, percentage-wise, more of them become animal lovers. Porn stars may separate sex and love, but animal chicks gave up on human love entirely. Forget peacocking and negging and all the complicated tricks that *The Game* taught guys about picking up women. My advice to guys looking for a short-term relationship with a hot crazy chick is to walk up to the most attractive woman at the bar and say, "Are you the woman from the dog rescue?" Even if she somehow has never been involved in animal rescue, she will not let you leave until she hears about all the good work you do saving abused dogs. The only downside is that while you're having sex, six dogs will be watching you.

One of these hot chicks, Kari Whitman, says she can find a dog that is perfect for me, Cassandra, and Laszlo. Kari's charity, Ace of Hearts, has saved more than two thousand dogs by giving them to good, loving people who are nothing like me. I am not at all surprised to find out Kari is an interior decorator who had her own reality show on WE called *Designer to the Stars: Kari Whitman*. I am even less surprised that she was a high school cheerleader and, under the name Kari Kennell, acted in movies such as *Chained Heat II* after appearing as *Playboy*'s Miss February 1988.

After her own dog, Ace, died, she started her charity. "Ace was my best friend, my boyfriend, my father. He filled so many voids in my life. I loved him so much," she says to me the first time I call her. "The men in LA are so bad that it's nice to put your energy into something else." I believe that a couch, a bottle of Pinot Grigio, and twenty minutes of *Old Yeller* would totally get me in her pants.

Kari, however, says that would never happen, since my fear of dogs makes me wimpy and undesirable. "I find it very attractive when a guy has a dog because it's a great test run for fatherhood. It's similar whether it's the baby screaming and crying or the dog peeing in the house," she says. Women who are attracted to guys because they clean up dog pee must be into some seriously kinky stuff.

"I think hot chicks are looking for hot guys who love dogs. It's Dating 101," Kari says. "We used to have a party after each dog adoption. It was *Peyton Place*. We were saving dogs and getting laid. You need to start your son off with dogs right away."

On Sunday, Cassandra, Laszlo, and I go to an Ace of Hearts adoption center in the parking lot of a Petco in West Hollywood, arriving a few minutes before they're officially ready. The place is lousy with hot chicks. Kari has gigantic breasts popping out of a pink tank top, and enormous sunglasses covering her face, which is surrounded by waves of blond hair. She and her hot assistants are putting little signs on the dogs' cages. They are all harried and uninterested in dealing with human beings. Even though I've emailed and talked on the phone with some of them, when I try to ask questions, they are formal and annoyed. Then they kneel in front of the cages and talk to the dogs in excited, high-pitched, loving voices.

Cassandra finds most of the dogs way too big and unhandbaggable. But we agree on Biggie Smalls, a small dachshund-terrier mix who has way too much energy for my liking, in that he is moving. Laszlo loves playing with him and gets caught up in his leash as Biggie Smalls runs around him. It all feels pleasantly American. Biggie Smalls is being fostered by a very nice young guy named Dimitri. He says it would be a great help if I took Biggie Smalls for two weeks since he is about to go on vacation and hasn't figured out where to leave him. One of Kari's assistants gives me a lot of paperwork to fill out—more than I had to fill out at the hospital when Laszlo was born. She is also going to come by in two days to inspect our house and, if it passes, drop Biggie Smalls off with a bed, food, and treats. At the maternity wing of the hospital, someone came by to tell Cassandra where her nipples were and wished us luck.

When no one shows up two days later, I call Kari's assistant, who tells me the board decided that transferring Biggie Smalls to my house for just two weeks would be too disruptive to his life. I want to remind this woman that Biggie Smalls is a dog. And that when the man in the yellow hat threw a bag over Curious George and transported him thousands of miles in a ship, George thrived so much he became famous. I also want to tell her that you don't need to hold a board meeting to make decisions of this level. But there is no convincing her. I believe that, for women who seek solace with animals after abusive relationships, all male voices are like the noises adults make in *Peanuts* cartoons. So while I say, "We'll take very good care of Biggie Smalls," she hears "raperaperaperaperape."

The next few Sundays, I drive from sidewalk adoption fair to sidewalk adoption fair, talking to hot chick after hot chick, some of whom starred in *The Exorcist* and some of whom are Richard Pryor's daughter. I pick out a dog, fill out forms, talk to someone over the phone afterward, send more forms, and never hear back. Offering to take care of a dog that's about to be euthanized is a hundred times harder than getting a guy you've never met to give you a hundred thousand dollars to gamble with.

Then I remember that the woman who cuts my hair, Nikki Terranova—herself a super-hot chick with long jet-black hair, rocker clothes, and a past that includes bad relationships—rescues lots of dogs. I'm well aware that at this point in my journey toward manhood I should no longer have my hair cut by a woman, no less one whose title I am entirely unsure of: Hair cutter? Stylist? Cosmetician? I should have a racist old male barber who tells jokes and strews his tables with copies of porn magazines I assumed folded decades ago like *Oui* and *Swank*. But it's hard to break my relationship with Nikki, even if I have to refer to her as "The Woman Who Cuts My Hair."

Nikki is involved with Animal Advocates Alliance and fills her Facebook page with pictures of dogs with captions such as "URGENT!! URGENT! This husky's LAST CHANCE AT SURVIVAL IS TOMORROW! Please where are all the HUSKY LOVERS?! Female, only 2 yrs old! I'M BEGGING FOR HER!" Cassandra often forwards me pictures of the most microscopic dog on Nikki's page, asking me if we can save it. It is as ineffective as trying to get me to adopt a pot-bellied pig by sending me photos of bacon.

Nikki knows where she can get me a dog, since there are six in her house right now. She has adopted scores of dogs about to be euthanized and found them homes. She's got an older English cocker spaniel named Montana who is mellow enough for me and Laszlo. Or at least Laszlo. Cassandra looks at photos of the black, long-eared, longhaired, sad-eyed dog and decides Montana is ugly and has no interest in keeping her past the two weeks of my experiment. Montana is perfect.

But I'm pretty nervous. I need to hang out with a dog and get some advice on what to do with it. So I call Shorty Rossi, who has a pit bull rescue group that is chronicled on a reality show called *Pit Boss*. It is becoming very difficult to meet someone in Los Angeles who has not had a reality show.

My man experiences have led me to believe in immersion therapy. I'm no longer afraid of camping, fire, Scotch, Warren Sapp, or gambling other people's money. So I figure that if I can hang out with a pit bull for an afternoon, maybe an old, partly deaf English cocker spaniel won't seem scary. I don't know much about pit bulls other than the fact that they are the deadliest animals on earth. When they bite you—and they will bite you—their jaws snap shut so tight, they will release only if you pry them open with a stick. I'm assuming Shorty owns a lot of sticks.

Shorty, who is four feet tall, runs a talent agency for little people actors. He is so intense about rescuing pit bulls that, at one point, he had twenty-five of them living in his house. He invites me over to his apartment to meet one of his pit bulls, whose name is Hercules. The labors this Hercules has accomplished include eating his way through the middle of a door to get out of a room. When Shorty bought an extra-thick door to prevent Hercules from tunneling through it, Hercules simply ate through the drywall next to the door and walked out of the room through the pit-bull-size hole he made. It takes Hercules less than a minute to eat an entire T-bone steak, including the bone. Of all the pit bulls Shorty has ever had,

Hercules is the most hostile around other dogs. "He doesn't want to be with anyone besides me and this other dog, Mussolini," Shorty tells me over the phone. I'm guessing Shorty's other pit bulls are named SEAL Team Six and Y Chromosome.

I drive over to Shorty's apartment, which isn't on the greatest block in Los Angeles. It's part of a stucco-covered eight-unit building, and two of the other people who live here also have pit bulls. I walk up a flight of outdoor stairs and am greeted by Shorty, who is wearing a black hat, a red button-down shirt, and shiny black pants. I join him on a very low couch, watching a TV on a shelf that sits just above the ground. When I ask where Hercules is, Shorty assures me that he's locked in his bedroom, which considering his history of door eating isn't at all comforting.

Shorty explains that I have nothing to worry about, that I have a better chance of winning the lottery than being bitten by a dog. He says I have a one in twenty-five million chance of being bitten by a dog, while one in twelve people are victims of a violent crime. These are shocking statistics due to the fact that they are not at all true. It would mean that only twelve Americans have been bitten by dogs. An American actually has a one in fifty chance of being bitten by a dog each year. The numbers are worse for men, and much worse for people who have pet dogs. While it's true that not many people are killed by dogs compared with humans, that's only because dogs don't have guns. If humans had to bite each other to death, the American homicide rate would be much closer to Japan's.

To bond, and buy some time, I ask how he got the name Shorty. It turns out this is a very dumb question, much as if he were to ask why my nickname is "Jewy." He was born Luigi Rossi, but he's been called Shorty since sixth grade; it even says it on his passport. He gravitated toward pit bulls from a young age. "Pit bulls are misunderstood. Little people are mostly considered to be circus freaks," Shorty says. "I understand these guys. They get a bad rap." When he asks why I'm afraid of dogs, I tell him I can't predict what animals will do—if they'll jump on me, bite, me, claw me, or, worse yet, lick me with their disgusting tongues. "But you can predict humans?" he asks.

"Yeah. I mean, not completely. But generally they don't just bite you. Or hump your leg."

"You don't know people. My attitude is you don't trust no one," he says. "I've been betrayed a lot. I have this defense up."

In high school Shorty, who is white, joined the Bloods street gang, whose members apparently are much more committed to racial and height diversity than most large organizations. Right after graduating, Shorty shot a guy in the stomach and was given twenty years for attempted murder. He served ten years, ten months, and ten days, some of it at Folsom State Prison.

I walk with Shorty to his bedroom door, which he opens slowly. Hercules calmly walks over to Shorty and I stand there, frozen, which is how I deal with fear. Shorty tells me to pat Hercules's head and scratch his butt. I do not want to scratch Hercules's butt. In fact, other than his mouth, his butt is the region I am most interested in staying away from. Besides, scratching his butt does not seem like a great way to introduce myself. It seems like a fourth- or fifth-date move. Luckily, it turns out that dog butts are located on their backs, so I touch that part. Then Hercules licks Shorty's face, which is disgusting. And Shorty thanks him for it. I have seen just about enough.

Shorty holds a tennis ball high in the air, relative to his size, which is not high enough to spare any part of me from Hercules's mouth when he jumps to get it. Hercules barks, which causes me to jump on Shorty's bed, which I feel bad about, though not bad enough to get down. When Hercules brings the ball back after Shorty throws it, Shorty tells me to remove it from Hercules's mouth. A mouth with jaws so strong you need a stick to pry it open. A mouth that ate through a door and then ate around a door. The mouth of a breed that got its name from being put in pits to fight actual bulls. I got my name from my maternal grandfather who designed men's dress shirts.

I put my hand on the damp ball and Hercules lets go. Forgetting everything Shawn Green taught me, I use all five fingers and throw it too hard and not at all in the right direction and instead of going down the hallway, it bounces off the door frame and back toward me. Which is where, I assume, Hercules is going to leap in his ball-induced madness. But Hercules keeps his cool, waits for the ball to land on the floor, picks it up, and brings it back to me. I have played ball with a pit bull. While I doubt that I won, it feels good.

Shorty brings me into the kitchen. His refrigerator, like the refrigerators of all great men, is empty except for beer and various mustards. Deep down, it seems, men believe there's always a chance that the hot dog vendor will stop by on his way home from the baseball stadium.

Reaching into a refrigerator drawer, Shorty hands me a small, square cookie that he calls a "treat." Despite my excellent work with the tennis ball, he is not giving it to me as a reward. I am to feed it to Hercules. From my hand. Upon Shorty's command, Hercules sits and I lower the cookie toward his mouth, and then drop it in panic. I expect Hercules to eat it from the ground and us to be done with this insane experiment. But Shorty tells Hercules to wait patiently while I pick it up, which is a little humiliating for both of us. I bring it toward Hercules's open, wet, sharp-toothed, T-bone-crushing, drywall-eating mouth, and kind of drop it in from an inch above. I do not believe Hercules finds it necessary to chew.

I drive home from Shorty's house thinking that I can handle taking care of a dog for two weeks. I'm getting a little bit of Shorty's confidence from doing all the stuff I've done. The failures I've experienced are making far less of an impression on me than my successes.

A few days before Nikki is going to drop the cocker spaniel off at my house, she sends an email that contains this sentence:

"Montana's food has to be cooked for her." I do not know what this means. I have to put dog food in the microwave? How did the dog communicate this demand for hot dog food? Did he bray soulfully whenever given room-temperature Alpo? Did he push his dog bowl toward the microwave with his nose and indicate a cooking time by tapping his paw?

Nikki explains that I need to actually cook Montana's food from scratch. When I ask some questions, like why the hell I have to cook food for a dog, Nikki emails me a rock-solid answer: "SHE WILL GET DIARRHEA." Should I not want to clean dog diarrhea, I have to make a blend of white rice, oats, carrots, celery, broccoli, pumpkin, and either steak or chicken. Luckily, Montana will accept leftovers so I can make this not-dog-food in large batches every few days. I know that dog breeds range greatly in size and temperament, but I find it strange that one dog can need freshly prepared midwestern casserole while another snacks on door.

Nikki rescued Montana from the Baldwin Park Animal Care Center, where she was on euthanasia row. She found her a home with a bunch of guys who lived together after graduating from the University of Oregon. These guys had to get rid of her a few months ago when their landlord wanted a five-hundred-dollar dog deposit and they didn't have the money. This doesn't make that much sense to me, but I figure if I ask more questions Nikki will just say "THEY HAD DIARRHEA." Diarrhea is a real conversation stopper.

Late in the afternoon, Nikki shows up with Montana and a bunch of dog stuff: a giant square pillow for her to sleep on, a water bowl, a food bowl, chicken jerky strips, and a Tupperware container full of her midwestern casserole. Nikki is talking quickly, giving me a lot of information, all of it confusing. The people at the shelter, for instance, told her that Montana is six, but Nikki thinks Montana is seven. I have no idea how Nikki can know this. I can't tell a forty-two- from a forty-nine-year-old human being, no less a dog. The only two ages I can guess for a dog are puppy and dead.

Nikki says I have to walk the dog four times a day. While I knew dogs go for walks, I just figured that was just a euphemism for taking them outside so they could relieve themselves. But apparently dogs really like to walk. So in addition to three short, evacuation-focused walks, Montana and I are going to go for one long, romantic stroll around the neighborhood, during which she may or may not pee and poop.

Nikki gives me the leash for the first dog walk of my life. Laszlo, who has already petted and dominated Montana, wants to come. So I pick up Laszlo with one arm and grab the leash with my other hand. Nikki tells me that the main rule of dog walking is to remember that I'm in charge, not Montana. Then she tells me that I should let Montana stop and smell things: Interrupting her while she's smelling something would be like interrupting a person when they are in the middle of reading a letter. This makes sense until we start our walk. Montana stops to smell everything. It's as if I tried to walk down a street paved with letters people wrote me. Much like when I walk while reading email on my phone.

I cannot believe the things Montana needs to stop and smell. These are things I would go to great efforts to avoid smelling. Nikki grabs the leash and tells me I need to yank her away from going into any burrs, which seems tricky since it requires knowing what burrs are.

Laszlo keeps pointing to spots he thinks Montana should pee, yelling "over there" and pointing to perfectly acceptable plots of grass. But Montana ignores him. After about four blocks, Montana finally finds a spot that she deems worthy of her urine. It looks a lot like all the other spots we walked by. I cannot believe how much time she spent on this decision. I base my outdoor urination location on whether I'm far enough from the road for people who see me to think I made an effort not to be seen. Montana's calculations involve sunlight, ground saturation levels, and the carbon dating of trace amounts of urine from other dogs. Where to pee is clearly

Montana's only creative outlet, and she's not going to mess up her chance to shine.

When Nikki leaves, Cassandra rubs Montana's head, looks in her sad eyes, and says, "She's kind of fat. She's got stinky breath. Hi, honey! She likes me!" This is apparently how Cassandra learned to talk to dogs in her small, white-trash town. She uses a really high voice, is affectionate, and insults her in ways that would impress Joan Crawford.

Shortly after Nikki leaves, Montana goes to sleep. This, it turns out, is Montana's main activity. I had no idea that dogs slept so much. I can't believe Nikki spends so much of her life worrying about dogs being put to sleep when they're pretty much doing that already.

At night, with the dog sitting on the pillow and Laszlo playing with toy cars, it feels quieter than I ever remember it being in this house, even before Laszlo was born. I put on Jim Croce's *Photographs & Memories: His Greatest Hits*, which I played on my Sony mono tape deck every night as I went to sleep as a little kid. Every time I've heard these sad songs as an adult, and thought about the fact that I chose to listen to them every single night, I got depressed, thinking about what a lonely kid I must have been, even though I don't remember being that way. But right now these songs don't sound depressing. They sound safe. They sound like I had a cozy, warm, happy childhood.

I didn't realize until right now that this—Laszlo, Cassandra, this house, sitting here on this couch—this is my life. I thought these were just people who signed in to join my adventures. Even Laszlo seemed less like my offspring than the wacky sitcom character who lives in the spare room downstairs and doesn't speak much English.

Everything feels slow, which I hate, only right now I don't. I thought having a dog and a kid would be slobber and barking and running back and forth. But it's calming. I feel something that's not just the absence of loneliness but something more tangible. Like anti-loneliness. It's that present-ness that Shawn Green and Matt Nadel, the day trader, both had. And I'm finally getting some of it, too.

Right before I go to bed, I wake Montana up and take her for a walk. I have no idea how this will go, but Montana doesn't seem worried at all. She bounds out of the house, and I hold her back with the leash. It's the first time I feel like I'm on the same team as an animal, instead of maneuvering around it.

About two blocks from our house, in a spot anyone would be impressed by, she defecates. I'm surprised to discover that picking up dog poop does not faze me, thanks to nearly two years of changing diapers. But this does surprise me: Dogs don't wipe. People focus on opposable thumbs, talking, and using tools as the main differences between humans and animals, but I'm going with wiping. I'd much rather have a roommate with only one thumb than a two-thumbed one who didn't wipe his ass. And now Montana is going to sit on my furniture with her unwiped ass. This is why you should not have animals in your house.

I return triumphant, excited to tell Cassandra about my fascinating dog observations, but she keeps interrupting before I get anything out.

"When I was walking him, he…"

"SHE!"

"Why does he poop at the…"

"SHE!"

"He just seems to…"

"SHE! SHE! SHE!"

I have no idea why Cassandra is so invested in the gender of this dog. How will it possibly affect my behavior toward it? Will I play more games with a male dog and quietly nod and say "I know" with a female dog? Am I supposed to know the gender of all animals? Am I supposed to look underneath dogs for dog penises and dog vaginas? Isn't there so much hair down there that I can't tell? I find it hard to tell human genders in 1970s porn close-ups. I don't expect animals to know my gender and I don't think I should have to know theirs. In fact, I don't even think I should have to assign genders to humans before they're old enough to have breasts. When I meet a new parent I go with "What a cute kid. How old is your cute kid?"

The next morning I wake up at seven, nervous with responsibility. I take care of Laszlo for the first two hours of every day, but now I have to walk Montana and make her food, too. Laszlo is still sleeping, so I slip on some sweatpants, find Montana and her unwiped butt on our couch, and wake her. Her ability to go from fully asleep to fully awake frightens me. Maybe this is why dogs sleep so much. I think they're doing it wrong.

She sits down so I can clip her leash onto her dorky harness, and she runs toward the door. Montana does not want to listen to me about where to walk. I don't blame her. I would not listen to someone who walked behind me, picked up my feces, and kept them in a bag. I am shocked she's willing to go out with me at all. I am pretty sure that when she barks at other dogs, she's saying, "This guy? Oh, he's just my personal chef. I know it's weird, but for some reason he's collecting all my poop. I think he just likes to know how his food was digested. He's pretty committed to this chef thing. He even insists on cooking my food from scratch."

After Montana poops, I bring her back and microwave some of her not-dog-food for her. Then Laszlo gets up and I heat up some oatmeal for him and wait until he poops before I change his diaper and put on his clothes. The first three hours of my day consisted of waiting for others to poop.

I don't know if it's the walking, the heating up of the not-dog-food, or the fact that even animals can sense my awesomeness, but Montana likes to be around me. For some reason all dogs like me. Even though I try to make it clear that I'm not at all interested.

They sense, I suppose, that I am good and pure and true and the kind of sucker who would cook food for them.

While I'm typing that afternoon, Montana sits next to my chair and looks up at me. I say hi and keep writing. Apparently, she's looking for more conversation, so I try asking her about how she's dealing with the transition to a new home. Nothing. She just keeps looking up at me.

When Cassandra walks into my office half an hour later, Montana is still looking up.

"What do you think she wants?" I ask.

"Pet her, you idiot!"

"But then I have to wash my hands again."

"Most people don't wash their hands every time they pet a dog."

"That's crazy."

I pet Montana, which goes well, though I think it would be healthier if she sought affection from her own species. I don't want her to get any weird ideas. She's supposed to be man's best friend and this seems like a little more than that. If I petted Mike Gorker, I don't think we'd still be friends. At least I hope not.

Later that afternoon I take Montana for a hike from our house into the Hollywood Hills. As soon as we get to the street, Montana is straining against the leash, so I start running with her. Sprinting. Her legs are galloping and it's kind of exhilarating. We're running at the same pace and it's more fun than running alone, which doesn't mean it's fun, just more fun than running alone. There must be scenes like this in *Old Yeller* or *Marley & Me* or *Travels with Charlie*, none of which I know anything about. But I bet they're just a bunch of montages like this followed by a scene where the owners cry about having to put the dog to sleep.

On the hike, other dog people stop and talk to me. I am part of the dog community, which I like because I like being part of any community. I'm smiling and holding Montana back while she barks at other dogs and I give the other owner a little apologetic shrug that says, *Dogs, right?* Then Montana stops to really smell this other dog's butt. This is not something I would do to another human being, and we are a species that wipes. It seems awkward to make small talk with the guy whose dog's butt is getting smelled out, but it seems more awkward not to. I'm not sure if we're supposed to pretend the butt smelling isn't going on or address it directly, like "Wow. It seems like your dog's butt smells fantastic. What do you do? Wipe it?"

I decide to tell the other guy—an older guy with two dogs—that I'm new at this dog thing and if the butt smelling goes on too long to just let me know. He tells me to relax and enjoy it. He tells me how much he loves his dogs and pulls out his wallet to show me a souvenir photo of him and his two dogs posing in front of the Hollywood Walk of Fame, only the stars names have all been changed to famous dogs like Benji, Lassie, and probably just Benji and Lassie. Looking to end this, I tell him my name and shake his hand. But his middle name is Noel, which is really close to Joel, which is enough for more conversation even though Montana has learned everything she needs to know about both of his dogs' butts.

Then Noel, whose first name I never learn, asks me for my birthday. Dog people, I'm guessing, are big gifters. But instead he pulls out his wallet again and unfolds a big chart. I'm not going anywhere for a while.

"You're a five. A five plus. A five of spades. And your number is tripled because you're a Leo. You must have had a lot of difficulty in your life," Noel says.

"No. Not at all. My life has been really easy."

It's clear by his expression that no one says this. That when you say to anyone that they must have had a tough life, they always respond with an outpouring of their soul. But even if he were a super-hot chick instead of a not-so-hot guy, I don't think I would have told him that my life was hard. It hasn't been. I have great parents, plenty of money, a career better than I dreamed of, a great wife, a sweet kid, no significant tragedies. It's a large part of why I haven't had to learn to be a man. There's been nothing to man against.

He asks for Cassandra's birthday. And then Laszlo's. I am now having difficulty in my life.

After I extricate myself from the numerologist, Montana and I run and hike for an hour. She's like a great personal trainer. Only when we get within a few blocks of our house does she tire out. She sits down in the shade, refusing to move. I fear I have broken the dog on my first full day. Eventually I drag her back home by the leash. But when I go to take her out at night, she just sits in front of the house refusing to move. Either something is physically wrong or she is just afraid I'm some kind of professional athlete who is going to want to do a late-night half-marathon. But I'm pretty sure even dogs can tell I'm not a professional athlete. I'm a little worried.

The next morning, though, Montana is back to her sprinting self. But Cassandra decides that Montana needs a haircut right away, to reduce both my sneezing and the dog's smell. I walk down the street to Tailwashers, where the walls are decorated with paintings of dogs getting manicures and dogs with their hair in rollers. It turns out that Tailwashers is not a place you just walk in and get a dog haircut. I have to make an appointment, and the earliest one is three days later. And they'll need to see forms from the vet to show she's got her shots. This is what I would need if I were traveling to Haiti. To get a haircut all I need is hair.

Three days later I drop Montana off at 10:30 AM. She is not done with her appointment until 3 PM. I am given a four-page "Health Report Card" in which I am informed that Montana has heavy tartar covering her teeth, healthy gums, good pads, and weight management that "looks great." Her anal glands were "checked, not needed." I am pretty sure that I've never had my own anal glands checked. As I wait for Montana to come out from the back of

Tailwashers, I angrily Wikipedia "anal glands" and discover I don't have any. Thank God. Anal glands lube up the dog's anus when he poops and, more importantly, secrete a dark-colored, foul-smelling liquid that is unique to each dog in the way that I suppose each rotting egg smells different from every other rotting egg. This is what dogs are running up to one another to smell. I'm telling you this not to disgust you but make you realize exactly how insane it is to let these beasts inside your home. And because anal glands get impacted a lot, you're supposed to bring your dog relief by massaging the outside of her ass until she releases her excess anal gland juice from her butthole. Again, if Cassandra laid this out as part of her needs on our first date, I'd still be single. I pay Tailwashers seventy-eight dollars, which is way more than Nikki charges me for a haircut but way less than you'd have to pay me to check anal glands.

Montana comes out looking like a newer, younger dog. Apparently, I judge the age of a dog by the length of its hair. She also has a big, yellow, contest-winning-type bow on her collar that somehow does not bother her, so I leave it on. This dog experiment might be making me feel manlier, but it is not making me look manlier.

In fact, when Cassandra and I take her on another hike, Montana causes me to suddenly sprint and then quickly stop so she can smell something. Cassandra looks at me with disgust and tells me I'm not "master of my dog." I'm less concerned about this than the fact that I'm not "master of my wife."

Besides the mastering, Cassandra is also constantly telling me to pet the dog. I like Montana—or at least I like that she doesn't bark, lets Laszlo do things to her face that seem unpleasant, and has a lot of enthusiasm for walking—but I'm not dying to touch her. She's a dog, not a pet stripper.

"Most people can't keep their hands off a dog. It's like seeing a baby and wanting to kiss it. They just see a dog and want to touch it," Cassandra explains.

"Do most people see a cow and want to touch it?"

"Have you ever touched a cow?"

"No."

"They're not soft. They're bristly."

"Are dogs the softest animals?"

"You're not getting this."

I force myself to give Montana friendly, guy-like pats and even rub her belly once when she rolls over and clearly wants it rubbed. Which feels weird. I don't love the petting. But I've come to enjoy the walks. It's like finally getting those little forced breaks that smokers get. Being outside makes me feel better. I get to see my neighborhood in the morning and late at night, up the hilly roads in the moonlight, finally enjoying the stillness that is precisely why I wanted to live here. I run into my neighbors, who have dogs, and we talk. And not about dogs. Or numerology. I feel more connected to where I live. Montana has showed me how stupid it is to be indoors. In return, I want to show her how stupid it is for her to sleep indoors.

The only thing I don't like, besides the poop, is that whenever we pass another house with a dog, they get into this aggressive barking showdown that makes me jump. Montana never barks at home, but outside she becomes a totally different dog, ten times more active and alert. The moment we get out the door she has what Shorty told me is called "game." Montana strains against her leash, looking to fight whatever dog she sees, even though most of them are to her what a sumo wrestler is to me. It's as if she's completely unaware while she's barking at a golden retriever across the street, staring it down, that she has no chance of winning this intimidation contest because is wearing a giant yellow bow on her collar.

On our hikes Montana's aggression is even worse because a lot of owners don't leash their dogs. I am sure Montana is about to get in a fight with this other dog when the owner comes rushing over. *Great*, I think, *now I'm going to have to fight him*. Having a dog,

I fear, is like having a drunk friend. Worse yet, he isn't going to be scared to fight me since I'm a guy with a dog with a giant yellow bow on her collar.

But instead he says, "If your dog bit my dogs, that would be okay because my dogs aren't on a leash." Why is he telling me this? Is he just super into the intricacies of dog law? Is this his way of feeling me out for his dogfighting ring? Are his own dogs aware of this rule and would have just let Montana bite them, barking, *Yeah, you got us on a technicality. We're not leashed. Bite away*? No. Despite his deep belief in the Geneva Dog Conventions, it would have been dog disaster, with blood and anal gland fluid everywhere. By the time I get home I realize that this was his way of saying "sorry." I know I'm working off a small sample size, and that nearly 40 percent of Americans have a dog in their home, but what with this guy, the numerology nut, Kari, and Shorty, dog people seem weird.

And I'm not entirely sure that Laszlo is one of them. Sure, he likes Montana and asks about her a lot, but he's becoming more and more threatened by her. Emotionally. Not only are they the same size, but my relationship with Montana is pretty similar to the one I have with Laszlo. I feed them, take care of their bathroom needs, rub their bellies, and talk super-slowly to them. My time walking Montana is time away from Laszlo. So I'm not surprised at his reaction when I ask him: "Do you want to keep the dog?"

"No."

"Do you want to send her away?"

"Yes."

"Do you want another dog?"

"No."

I'm with Laszlo, but I do like having Montana around much more than I thought I would. In general, I like having more activity. I'd like a second child to provide that activity, but Cassandra isn't up for it. She says it's because when she was pregnant she got a thyroid problem, anemia, sciatica, swollen ankles, and problematic breathing, but I tell her that I'm pretty sure it's because she hates Laszlo. I'm not very good at sweet-talking my wife into having more kids.

But even though Laszlo is wary of Montana's place in our home, I like watching him interact with her. I wish I could see him do that with a sibling. I need to get Cassandra really drunk and take advantage of her, and by "take advantage" I mean bring in a doctor to extract her IUD right before I have sex with her. I'm going to need a lot of The Macallan.

Late at night, after nearly two weeks of living in our house, Montana leaves a big puddle on our bedroom's wooden floor. I'm on my knees mopping it up with wood cleaner, just hours after cleaning up the poop that Laszlo—who was running around naked with a Potty Pirate hat full of Potty Pirate stickers from his Potty Pirate accomplishments—dumped on the floor upstairs. And I don't really care. It's not just that experience has callused me to things I used to girlishly recoil from. It's that now that I know about anal glands, this doesn't seem so gross by comparison.

The peeing, in fact, was great, since it convinces Cassandra, who was apparently secretly considering keeping Montana, that the dog has to go. So when I get a reporting assignment in Atlanta a few days later, Cassandra says she isn't going to take care of Montana for me while I'm gone. I call Nikki. She'll pick her up the day before I leave.

I cook Montana the final batch of not-dog-food I will ever make. I throw a bunch of beef broth into the rice instead of water even though that's not part of the recipe. My desire for her to like her food is strong enough to make me risk DIARRHEA. But I still feel distant from Montana. In fact, I feel a little gross touching her food with my hands, even though there is nothing dog-food-like about it. I just can't get over the human/animal division. It's also why I don't really like a lot of Disney cartoons. There's a part of me that thinks Mickey Mouse should be lured to a seven-foot-tall glue trap and held under Splash Mountain.

When Nikki shows up, I worry that Montana won't want to leave my excellent cooking and long-distance running ability, but she bounds straight into Nikki's car. Neither Laszlo nor I cry. We rub Montana's head, say good-bye, and pose for pictures but don't seem to feel anything. It's not horribly emotional, like when we gave the Lamborghini back. Having Montana around was nicer than I imagined, but I never broke through the interspecies thing where I thought she was different from other dogs. For Laszlo, I think he just doesn't form a lot of attachments yet. He doesn't ask about me the entire time I'm in Atlanta. He hasn't even brought up the Lamborghini.

Even though I didn't fall in love with Montana, I do see why people keep animals in their house, and it's for the exact same reasons I thought they were crazy for doing it. It's not that dogs are so great that they make up for all the disgusting stuff. The disgusting stuff is the greatness. Montana reminded me that I'm an animal, too, with a daily cycle of eating, sleeping, and going to the bathroom that makes up more of my life than my complicated thoughts, most of which are about eating, sleeping, and going to the bathroom. I, too, need to walk and run and be outside and have my belly rubbed and even tussle every so often.

I liked seeing how kind Laszlo could be. A few weeks after Montana leaves, as I take Laszlo's clothes off for his bath, I see an ant on the floor. I point it out to Laszlo and he gets very interested, getting a toy car right near it, driving it toward the ant. Then I tell Laszlo to be gentle because the ant is very small. And Laszlo gets his face right next to the ant and gives him a kiss, though he is smart enough to do one of those Hollywood air kisses and not actually wind up with ant lips.

Kissing ants doesn't sound manly, but it is. Laszlo is fearless and gentle, which is what I'm learning to be. I think fearlessness helps make people gentle. With each task I've completed, I've become a little less fearful and a little calmer. I could kiss an ant. Or have a dog, if it comes to that. But, honestly, I'd rather kiss an ant. At least you don't have to cook it dinner afterward.

Just a week after Montana left our house, she got adopted by a really nice woman a few blocks from me. Nikki posts photos on Facebook of the two of them cuddling on her beautiful outdoor furniture. They sleep in a bed together and she's always sending Nikki emails about what an amazing companion Montana is and how she brightens her life. It's a happy ending. Though the woman has cancer. But still, Montana-wise, a happy ending.

8

BUILDING SHELTER

Having Montana around made me realize that while this might just be a house to me, it's Laszlo's home. I like it here, but I don't feel the desperate connection I had to my childhood home. My parents sold that place right after I graduated from college, and, about once a week, I still dream about it. When I drove by the house with my mom a few years ago, I was too afraid to stop by and bother the family living there, but she walked right up to the door. The back-yard was clear-cut, the family room blocked off with glass doors etched with dolphins, my room pinkened with *Playboy* logos for the daughter. Which made the dreams much creepier.

The men I've met so far on my man journey did things them-selves and took pride in the results. Herbie loved that firehouse, rebuilding parts of it himself. He loved that place partly because of that work. I want to love Laszlo's house as much as I loved the one that now looks like the set of a reality show about people who own a Greek diner. I want to stop inhabiting a world that other people laid out for me like a cloak over a puddle. I want to build it myself. And I want to do it, someday, with Laszlo.

If I am going to learn how to fix stuff around the house, the best person to learn from is Cassandra's dad, Ken. Because I will not even have to ask him. I'll just need to stop avoiding him.

If Cassandra had a different father, or better yet no father, it would solve a lot of my problems. And not just because women with no dads are willing to do anything in bed. It's because Ken Barry has given her unrealistic expectations of masculinity. He's six foot five, 1950s-handsome, has the biggest hands I've ever seen, and rarely talks. He rebuilt their entire Victorian house without any help, and when he visits us he not only fixes everything that's broken but finds things that are totally fine and fixes them, too.

The first time Ken came to our house in Los Angeles, he asked me for some tool and was shocked that I didn't have that tool. And some other tool. It turned out that the manliest tool I owned was a crème brûlée torch. So Ken took me to Home Depot, where he kept grabbing things from the shelves, telling me how much I needed them, and putting them in my cart. Though many of them had different names, such as "pruner" and "lopper," they were simply scissors of varying enormity. In an effort to get out of there quickly, I paid $250 and have never used anything we bought. Regular scissors continue to suffice for all my projects, which consist of cutting out the names of plumbers, electricians, handymen, and gardeners.

Until I met Cassandra, I assumed that fixing stuff in your house was a pre-industrial activity abandoned around the same time people stopped sewing their own clothes and canning their own food. Both of which Cassandra's mom does. If one of those *Lost*-like time machine shifts sent us all to the eighteenth century, it would take Cassandra's parents months to notice.

Fixing my house seems as misguided as filling my own cavities, making my own microchips, or imagining my own sexual fantasies without porn. But while getting your computer fixed is completely acceptable man behavior, calling a handyman to patch up your walls is not. Fixing your own house, Ken explains to me, is about being able to handle your everyday problems instead of paying some other man to bail you out every time a pipe leaks, a curtain needs to be hung, or that thing that holds the other thing up isn't being held up anymore by another thing. I have a lot of terms to learn.

And I'm psyched to learn them. Until now, I'd never thought of self-reliance as literally being reliant on myself. I thought it was just about making money and connections. So more like relying on other people. Ken, however, grew up assuming he'd have to do a lot himself. His dad—a man I know only by the name he asked Cassandra to call him, "Big Daddy"—was a steamfitter, a job that sounds like it should have disappeared when gasoline was discovered. When Ken was seventeen, Big Daddy told him he'd have to start paying rent, so he moved out on his own and got a job laying cement, then later as a carpenter. When I was seventeen, my parents sat down and figured out a monthly budget of how much to give me while they were paying for my insanely expensive college three thousand miles away. My mom included, in her calculations, a line item for dry cleaning. I still haven't used up the dry-cleaning allotment.

Ken bought the house Cassandra grew up in for five thousand dollars in 1974, without telling his wife, Hope, about the purchase. It takes a certain kind of manliness to choose the town and house you're going to spend your life in without consulting your wife. And a far greater manliness to get away with it. Though they were hippies, and still do lots of hippie stuff, Ken and Hope have a very traditional relationship, in that he does stuff and she doesn't like it, and then they don't talk about it. My marriage is more about me asking Cassandra if she's sure she's okay with something that we overdiscussed and agreed upon. Ken could have a harem and his life would still work. You add any third party to our marriage— a visiting parent, a nanny, a provocative *Wall Street Journal* article— and nothing gets done.

The Victorian house that Ken bought is in Hoosick Falls, New York, a town that has been deteriorating since its heyday, which was in 1890. Ever since the Walter A. Wood Mowing and Reaping Machine Company—then the largest farm machine factory in the world—shut down, so did Hoosick Falls. Once, while walking down Hoosick Falls's main street, I asked Cassandra what all the boarded-up shops used to be when she was growing up. "Boarded-up shops," she answered.

Ken's plan in 1974 was to spend a year or two fixing the house, flip it for a profit, and buy a home in a town that perhaps went bust in the early twentieth century. Ken has been fixing up the Hoosick Falls house for thirty-seven years. It is really nice, but most of Cassandra's childhood photos were shot in rooms with bedsheets for doors and Sheetrock walls that she was allowed to draw on. Even in the 1970s, this wasn't okay. Having finally finished the Hoosick Falls house, Ken has decided to expand his real estate empire. Six years ago he bought a house in Dundee, New York, a town that never even had a heyday. Ken spent twenty-four thousand dollars on the house and, I'm pretty sure, got screwed. His idea was to let Cassandra's brother, Ian, a winemaker nearby in the Finger Lakes, live there and fix it up just like Ken did in Hoosick Falls. But when Ian decided to live with his future wife, Tricia, who had been spoiled by a life of doors and walls, they bought their own house. That's when Cassandra's youngest brother, Brian, moved in.

Brian has not done much with the house. That's because in a lot of ways, Brian and I are very much alike. Especially if I had remained single and my tastes hadn't changed since I was fifteen. Brian likes to watch movies over and over, play video games, and go to concerts. The main difference between Brian and me, besides the fact that he's blond and six foot five, is that he has the man quality of needing to know everything about a subject and then tell you everything about it. The other manly quality about Brian is that he refuses to eat things that aren't meat or potatoes. He also refuses to eat meat and potatoes with sauce on them. He won't wear shirts with buttons on them, since that would be putting on airs. Another difference between Brian and me is that, having worked as a handyman at a condo and grown up with Ken as a father, Brian can fix anything. He freely chooses not to do it. I have a lot of respect for Brian.

Now that Ken is getting more serious about quitting his job designing and selling video camera covers, he's spending weekends driving four and a half hours each way to Dundee to fix Brian's house, which is actually just his own house. Once it's fixed, he plans to flip it and use the profits of the sale to build a brand-new house on a nearby vineyard he bought. Then he and Hope will move into the new house, and he'll start building the winery's tasting room. This, judging by history, will take Ken, now sixty, approximately 120 years. Ken is the only person I know who has get-rich-slow schemes. Brian, as you can imagine, is not too worried about getting kicked out of his house anytime soon.

When I call to offer to spend three days helping with the Dundee house, Ken gets way too excited. I explain that I want to learn a little bit about everything so I can do basic repairs around my house: fixing leaky pipes, patching holes, hanging curtain rods, putting in light fixtures, unsticking doors. But I can tell that all Ken hears is "Free labor!" Although he's never called my cell before, a few weeks before the trip he calls to tell me about this trailer he bought that attaches to his car. It's called a Prowler, and he's going to park it in the backyard of the Dundee house and sleep in it for much of the summer. As he describes the Prowler and its shower, sink, hot plate, and bunk beds, it becomes clear that he thinks I should sleep in this trailer with him, so we can wake up and start working right away. I think this is a bad idea for many reasons, all of them having to do with me sleeping in a trailer.

Cassandra is looking forward to the trip, not so much because she believes I will learn useful skills, but because she thinks it will be funny to see me go crazy with frustration dealing with her dad and brothers. "You don't do long, slow projects. You're always whipping off these things in your head, super-quick," Cassandra says. "Their whole MO is tangible, physical manifestations that take years. You are going to be like, 'Come on. Let's just get this done. Why aren't you guys hiring a bunch of Mexicans?'"

"Have you seen your father do a project?" I ask. "Mexicans getting paid by the hour would be like, 'Come on. Let's just get this done.'"

As I'm getting more afraid, Ken is getting more excited. He's sending me emails with photos of his Prowler, which looks like the thing behind the door on *Let's Make a Deal* when you lost. To distract Ken from talk of staying in his Prowler, I ask him what I should wear to work on the house. He tells me to bring boots with steel toes. I am getting sick of being told what the toes of my boots should be made of. Still, I guess if I want to keep doing man stuff, I need to get a pair of boots. I figure I'll buy them at a store near Dundee called Famous Brands Outlet. I had been there once before with Cassandra's family, all of whom spent hours looking at boots and jackets made by Carhartt, Dunham, Woolrich, and Keen, while I walked around, saying, "This brand is famous?" All of this clothing was surprisingly expensive. I couldn't figure out how men justified spending this much on clothes until I noticed that no one in the store referred to any of the clothes as "clothes." It was "gear." Boots were "gear." Jackets were "gear." Things that actually were gear, like backpacks and tents, were also "gear." Men have no separate word for clothing.

Ken is a lot more comfortable outdoors than I am. A few weeks earlier, when Cassandra and I had taken him and Hope, along with my mother and her husband, up to a house in Napa for a long weekend, Ken caught a frog and brought it in the house. Ken, to reiterate, is sixty years old. An hour later, when Ken's eyes started to burn and he couldn't figure out why, Hope asked, "Did you wash your hands after touching that frog?" That is a sentence Cassandra has never said to me. It is, I believe, a sentence no one has ever said to anyone besides Tom Sawyer.

I tell Ken that Cassandra, Laszlo, and I will be declining the invitation to stay in the Prowler and will instead spend three days at a bed-and-breakfast. Shortly after we check in, we go to survey the Dundee house. It is a cozy, eight-hundred-square-foot house that might cause people who walk in to say, "I think I'll go some-where else to smoke my crack." The porch is missing planks; the windows are boarded up. Instead of using the popular pipe system, the kitchen sink drains into a bucket. The bucket probably does not need to be emptied often, since it is unlikely there is much kitchen activity, due to the fact that all the pots and pans are scattered about the house collecting rainwater from roof leaks. One part of the kitchen wall is just exposed boards with some kind of foam squirted in between to keep the wind out. The entry room has been abandoned and the door replaced with a bedsheet in the style made popular in 1970s homes owned by Ken Barry. The kitchen is packed with stacked boxes. The upstairs—which has the sink, toilet, and shower—has no walls at all, only wood beams and two-by-fours signifying where a ceiling and walls might go if one were the pam-pered kind of person who needed a ceiling and walls. From what I could tell, Brian owns only eight things: a TV, DVDs, video games, mustard, barbecue sauce, beer, a fork, and swords. These are, I believe, the man essentials for entertaining.

Less than sixty seconds after walking into the house, Ken notices a broken light fixture hanging from the hallway ceiling and fixes it. In sixty seconds. This is a project I would have talked about for weeks before calling an electrician. There are live wires and he touches them with his bare hands without turning the fuse—or even the light switch—off. I am seriously worried about the next few days.

The next morning Ken picks me up in his Ford F-250

four-by-four, a limo-length, Hummer-high white truck he uses to pick up groceries; a car that is impossible to park and makes him insanely happy. Even happier than his other pickup truck, a Ford F-150. He looks down at my sneakers, worried about their lack of steel reinforcement.

"Just be careful of any nails," he says. This is not reassuring. When I ask him if my jeans are okay, he says that jeans are great for construction work. In fact, he has a whole jeans system: He buys new jeans to wear to his office; when those jeans get beat up, he uses them for chores around the house; when they get too ugly for that, he wears them for messy work like roofing; when they get really ragged, they're used for tar and cement work. My jeans system is similar: Cassandra buys me a pair; I wear them every day until she tells me they're out of style; she puts them in a garbage bag; she takes them somewhere where they are given away to people who probably use them for tar and cement work.

When we get to the Dundee house, Ken and I unload an enormous number of tools, each of which he cleaned and repainted in his excitement about the weekend. It is the cutest man thing I have ever seen. Feeling like I need to show some enthusiasm over the tools, I ask Ken what each of them does. I am not really listening until he says that some are tools for fixing tools. When I ask if he has any tools to fix the tools that fix tools, he looks at me like I am an idiot.

Ken tells me we're going to start by tearing the roof off the house and putting a new one on. This seems like a pretty big task to fit in before teaching me how to hang pictures and unstick sticky things. I ask how long putting up a new roof will take. Ken thinks for a while, obviously sensing my implication that this one task will take up too much of our three days, keeping me from learning the more practical skills I want to use around my house. "Probably two years," he says. Then he proceeds to lean the ladder against the roof.

Which does not go well. I know this because Ken yells, "God-damn it!" Ken got the ladder—the one we'll use all three days to go up to and down from the roof—from the winery where Brian works. The winery was willing to part with this ladder largely because it is broken.

After Ken fixes the ladder, which I distrust, Ken looks for old rotting bits of wood that are still sort of part of the porch. I do not think this wood would make the kind of roof I'd be proud of. Ken tells me to go up the ladder of death and stand on the roof itself. The crappy, leaky roof that needs to be replaced.

"Will this roof support us?" I ask.

"We don't know, really. If you fall, just relax and enjoy the ride."

As I nervously crouch on all fours on the very front part of the roof, Ken bounds up the ladder of death. He instructs me to nail random-size pieces of rotten wood into other random-size pieces of rotten wood. Eventually, I realize that we aren't building a roof at all. We are building a platform to stand on while we build a roof. It is a roof to work on a roof, kind of like tools that work on tools. This does not seem like a good use of our time, compared with fixing the house. Which also doesn't seem like a good use of our time.

In the middle of building this not-roof, Ken decides that a tree needs pruning. So he grabs a chain saw and holds it over his head, leaning off the roof and wildly chopping at a branch just out of his reach, looking like a crazed serial killer of trees. After he cuts down a few branches, he climbs onto the tree itself. While holding the chain saw. Though I have not read the OSHA brochure on jumping off a roof into a tree while holding a chain saw, I am pretty sure his method is not safe. I express this by pleading for him to stop, which he does, reluctantly.

Standing on the roof, I look back fondly on my earlier, carefree, not-standing-on-a-roof years. I had not appreciated how unsloped the ground was, and how a misstep would not cause instant death. Unlike Ken, everything I do on the roof takes about twenty times longer than it would if I were not standing on a roof.

Once we finish the scaffolding, Ken tells me to go over to the very top of the roof, and then walk over to the other side, proceeding to the very bottom of the roof—which is technically called "the most dangerous part of the roof"—in order to nail down two enormous pieces of plastic covering. When I finish, Ken tells me the plastic will protect the roof in case it rains tonight. We'll remove it in the morning.

"We're doing this for one night? Even though this roof has been uncovered like this for years?" I ask.

"That's what men do," Ken says.

"Where's the risk analysis?"

"Risk analysis is for pussies."

I do not put that on The List.

It is still early in the afternoon, so Ken and I drive to a diner in the town next door. I get a burger, and Ken gets a steak sandwich and bean soup, which seems like a much manlier meal. We both get pie, which is the only acceptable man dessert. You never see truckers order a coffee and a lavender crème brûlée. Pie is acceptable because it is two pieces of bread with fruit in the middle. It's the dessert that's closest to being a sandwich.

Over our fruit sandwiches, Ken tells me that I'm doing well on the project. What he says, specifically, is "I actually didn't think you'd be able to hammer a nail." And: "You had some good safety tips."

Ken is less worried about my performance than the fact that the project is bigger than he anticipated. Way bigger. He's pretty sure the entire roof is rotted and that we're going to have to completely replace it.

"Here I am stuck with a house in a town I don't even like," he says. "This is one of the biggest mistakes I've made in a while."

"What was the biggest mistake before this?" I ask.

"The backhoe might be."

When Ken bought the backhoe, I asked him what he was going

to do with a backhoe, which was my way of asking what a backhoe was. Ken listed a number of ambitious projects for his piece of excavating equipment consisting of a digging bucket on the end of a two-part articulated arm. Projects such as moving trees, digging up holes for foundations, scooping out trenches for trellises, and creating ponds. What he didn't list was: fixing a backhoe. Which is the only thing he's done with the backhoe.

It's not as if Ken didn't have life experiences that would have led him to believe the backhoe project would have turned out like this. In 1964, when he was in high school, Ken bought an aunt's 1949 Dodge Coronet so he could rebuild it. He is forty-eight years into this project. It was parked on his lawn for all of Cassandra's childhood. Now Ken pays a guy $110 a year to keep it in a barn a few towns away. After he fixes the Dundee house and builds a tasting room on the vineyard, he's going to bring the car out there and really get to working on it. By then it will be worth a lot of money as an antique from the pre-flying-car era.

It's not that I'm a pessimist and Ken's an optimist. It's more that Ken underestimates the difficulty of projects and I overestimate them. I've avoided having an intern because all I can think about is being responsible for remembering another person's birthday. Starting a winery—the paperwork alone—sounds like a hassle. I picture agriculture, bottling, sales, marketing, liquor licenses. Ken sees: Winery!

He's got an entirely different sense of time than I do. He not only repairs things, but sketches and paints as well. On business trips, he is usually approached by at least one hooker. I have never been propositioned by a hooker, even when I've interviewed hookers. At first I thought it was because Ken is going to salesmen hotels and salesmen restaurants. But he got solicited near the elevator at the Hard Rock Hotel in Las Vegas. I've been to the Hard Rock many times, and I had trouble getting restaurant hostesses' attention. Then I figured out that whereas I walk quickly, looking like I know where I'm headed even though I don't, Ken is always point-ing out foliage, wildlife, and architecture. Ken gets approached by hookers because at every moment of his life he looks like he's wait-ing for a hooker.

After pie, Ken and I go to a small hardware store. That hard-ware store is called Knapp & Schlappi. For thirty minutes, Ken walks around Knapp & Schlappi, picking up stuff and examining it: tools, nails, screws, stuff meant for cars. When I ask what he's looking for, Ken says, "I've just never been here before." To Ken, every hardware store is somehow different, like a record store, and there might be a rare European bootleg wrench he's spent years searching for.

Ken tries to talk me out of buying a pair of work gloves since grabbing fistfuls of fiberglass insulation, he insists, isn't that pain-ful. I decide not to trust the man who swings chain saws from trees. After I buy the gloves, we go outside to look at two-by-four planks of wood. We look at a lot of them. As you would imagine, they all look the same.

"Why are we looking at them?" I ask.

"To see if it's good wood," he says.

"You can tell?"

He picks up a two-by-four with disdain. "I wouldn't use that for firewood," he says.

For the record, Knapp & Schlappi, that is Ken's opinion and not mine. I think your wood is very wood-like.

We head upstairs in the Dundee house, where amid the peel-ing insulation and pans to collect water, there are already a bunch of two-by-fours. The house, it turns out, is full of PVC pipe, two-by-fours, and rolls of insulation that previous owners bought in failed attempts to fix the house, which was built in 1904. The house is like some Edgar Allan Poe short story, with ghosts of ama-teur carpenters warning us of our fate.

Since we've finished all the pre-roofing, I ask Ken to teach me some practical home repair work. Which to him means: Free labor! I don't know if I'll ever have to remove insulation from walls, but now I know how: You grab it. We peel the soaked, mottled pink insulation from the wall straight onto Ken's skin. Then he uses his ungloved hands to direct me to gather the insulation and rotted wood and throw it out the second-floor window. I did not know you could do this. Throwing things out a window is incredibly fun. In no time at all, we scatter a huge pile of rotted wood by the side of the house. It is not far from another pile of wood created when Ken had demo'ed the back porch. That pile is festooned with two tires, a hubcap, and many metal window frames. This is right near the Prowler that Ken parked in the backyard. Along with his pickup truck. All of this sort of killed the vibe the next-door neighbor was going for, with his manicured lawn, trampoline, wood deck, aboveground pool, and no piles of garbage. I always assumed that houses turned white-trashy due to a horrible tragedy, such as alcoholism, depression, unemployment, or a physical handicap. No. A house turns white-trashy when someone decides to rebuild it himself.

I ask Ken again for some home repair tips, and he takes me into the basement to show me how to fix pipes. This sounds like the kind of thing I might actually do. The basement is tiny, but Ken plans to dig the dirt one and a half feet deeper so it has enough ceiling space to be a fully operational workroom. Otherwise, he says, it will be "wasted space." I try to explain to Ken that this is not Tokyo's Ginza district. This is Dundee. It's all wasted space. But Ken insists on his plan to dig out the basement. "There's no material. It's just exercise," he says. I am pretty sure that Ken thinks the Puritans were lazy.

I thought Ken was just clueless, taking on projects without thinking them through. But that's not it. Ken knows this house isn't going to make him any money. He knows he's never going to live here. He's doing this because he sees something ugly that he can turn into something beautiful. It is, structurally, a great old house. That's what Ken sees, not value or practicality. He sees beauty everywhere; when he drives his eyes are never fully on the road as he points out animals and unusual trees so far in the distance I can't even see them. Ken went to Pratt for architecture and quit the profession after being asked to make too many strip malls. He has a tiny studio where he paints landscapes and portraits. He's a perfectionist who is proud of every project he does. Just like those firefighters want to run into fires because that's what they're trained to do, Ken wants to fix hopeless houses. It's value he can add to the world.

I grew up in a suburban world of disposable everything. It's a sloppy way to live. I could use a little of Ken's respect for his tools, his house, his work. But not too much. Ken is insane.

It's surprisingly easy to remove pipes with a pipe wrench. Pipes are just giant screws. I screw pipe caps on with my bare hands in a way that both feels manly and makes me sure they will be blown off from water pressure shortly. We redirect the water so it goes straight from the washing machine to the lawn. "It's not exactly code, but the amount of times Brian does wash, I think we'll be all right," Ken says.

While we are trying to figure out which pipes go where, and which size each of them is, and how to loosen the rusted ones, childhood images flood back. I remember doing home repair projects with my dad. He did try to teach me all of this stuff, after all. I just forgot. There was a big red metal vise attached to a workbench in our dark basement. And there was a saw, and nails and hammers and a frustrated dad talking to himself, and me asking questions and him not wanting to answer questions because he was concentrating and me bored, bored, bored. I remember how tense it felt while he tried things that didn't work, and how every so often my dad would ask me to bring him a tool like a utility blade and I'd go look for something that looked like it had a blade and some sort of utility. I'd slowly sift through this big box of tools, hoping it would use up time before I'd have to stand next to him again and feel that tension. Which is precisely how this feels now. It is only 5 PM. Time has not moved this slowly for me since high school. High school shop class.

We finish up and head over to meet Cassandra's family at her other brother's house, which is a much, much nicer home than the Dundee house Ian was supposed to live in, and not just because it has a roof. It also has a bathroom with a door on it. Ian isn't home yet, leaving vast minutes of unplanned free time. Ken spies some fallen branches on the lawn, gets the chain saw from his truck, and shows me how to chop firewood. I am enjoying slicing through the log, hunks falling off in front of me, when Ian comes home and asks why I'm not wearing goggles. I could easily get a woodchip in my eye. Ken never mentioned goggles, or woodchip eye. I wonder what else he hasn't mentioned. Is there some kind of giant net you're supposed to put around a house when you go on the roof? Roof helmets? How unsafe is this madman? Answering my question, Ian reveals a huge scar on his leg he received when he was sixteen and working with his dad and a chain saw.

Unlike Brian and Ken, Ian is a red-cheeked, husky, smiley, soft, sweet man. He doesn't talk, either, but I think that's just what all super-white men are like. I once spent part of an Easter with Cassandra's extended family without talking to see if anyone else would. After several minutes of silence, Cassandra's aunt asked her mom if she got some casserole dish she left in front of their house a few months earlier. "Yes," Hope said loudly. "Thanks for that." Then we went back to eating ham in silence for ten minutes until I couldn't take it anymore and started to try to get Big Daddy to say racist stuff.

Though Ian will wear buttons on his shirt, he mostly wears gear. So I'm a little surprised when everyone suggests I change into one of Ian's concert T-shirts for dinner. My non-concert T-shirt has gotten so disgusting, it is less presentable than a concert T-shirt. But I want to keep it on, so I can go out filthy and sweat-stained and people will see how hard I worked and treat me with respect and fear. Also so I won't have to be seen in a Phish shirt. But everyone insists, so I put it on. I am also upset that my right forearm is sore from hammering. Despite years of my insistence to the contrary, it seems that masturbation really isn't great exercise.

The next morning, after a breakfast that our innkeepers insist Ken and I eat, we don't get to the Dundee house until ten thirty. Ken may have had a point about sleeping in the Prowler. But after knocking on the door three times, we realize that Brian is still sleeping. While he gets ready, we kill some time on the porch waiting. I ask Ken about a rusted-up metal slot attached to the railing.

"What's this for? Opening beer bottles?" I ask.

"A flag."

There's a lot of mystery in the world when you've only ever lived in blue states.

We knock some more, since, it turns out, Brian went back to sleep. We get him up again, and thirty minutes later he joins us. Ian couldn't get off work, so he isn't coming. Brian's friend had promised to come in return for some extra flooring Ken had given him months ago when the prospect of roof work was months away. So he doesn't show, either. Other people are more aware of Ken's practice of exploiting his labor force than I am. The only home repair I'm going to be learning today is more roofing.

The three of us climb the ladder of death, onto the scaffolding of death, where we take a closer look at the roof of death. Though I'm not yet an expert, I do know that a roof should not be growing grass. That's more of a ground thing. We grab at the tar paper, which peels right off. As do the wood shingles. And the plywood. All of which we throw onto the ground.

Beneath those layers are just some wood beams. That's it. I cannot believe that this is all there is to a roof. It's just a couple of layers

of stuff, nailed together. The difference between indoors and outdoors isn't as dramatic as I assumed. It's what I observed when I was
in that tent with the Boy Scouts. Only that tent was made better.

We haven't removed much of the roof when Ken's mumbling
really kicks in. "Holy crap. Here we are. No turning back," he says.
A few minutes later: "I don't know. Crazy stuff."

It turns out that the phrase *tear the roof off* implies far more
excitement and fun than the task actually offers. It's actually a
lot of pulling and pushing and sweating the roof off. Plus, either
there isn't a standard operating procedure for de-roofing, or Ken
skimmed that part of the manual. His first plan is to build more
stuff. He wants to go inside and crisscross two-by-fours on the
wood beams just under the roof we are removing. Then—from
inside the house—he wants to lie on the two-by-fours, point his
legs at the roof, and kick really hard, hoping to bust a hole into
the roof. Really. This is his plan: to kick the roof off the top of the
house. Unable to talk him out of this, I go in the house and watch
him lie down and kick. This does not work.

Ken comes up with a second idea: going outside, standing on
the roof with a circular saw, and cutting holes in it. This seems
like a recipe for roofeye. But then I come up with a brilliant plan,
based on songs of yore I heard in the 1980s: bash the roof in with a
sledgehammer. Thanks to the obviousness of my genius, and a lack
of extension cord for the circular saw, we go with my idea. Which
totally works. I am slamming a sledgehammer through a roof—
wood cracking, splinters flying, me repeating over and over how
this is my idea. Then, without warning, I notice Ken's foot shoot up
through the roof from underneath. His hands appear on both sides
of this hole, ripping it open, climbing through it like the Incredible
Hulk. I hope one day to own a painting of this.

We stand on those two-by-fours on the ceiling inside the house,
our heads popping up through the roof, swinging the sledgehammer down and throwing wood and tar and shingle on the grass next

to that poor bastard's pool. At one thirty the ladyfolk and childrenfolk come by with a picnic and Ken says, "Man, I could use a cold beer right about now," in a way that contains absolutely no irony at all.

After lunch, we tear the entire roof off and throw all the debris onto the backyard, which is now more like backdebris. Afterward, at the bed-and-breakfast, I shower and wood comes off my body. Brian spends the night sleeping in a roofless house under the stars, which makes me even angrier about nailing down that plastic sheet the day before.

The third day, it turns out, will also involve nothing but roofing. Ken wakes up super-early to drive many towns over to buy lumber from someplace other than Knapp & Schlappi. Ian, Brian, and I stand on those unstable two-by-fours on the top floor with our heads sticking out, and nail new two-by-fours onto the crossbeams to make a new roof. I get to wear a nail apron, which is definitely the manliest form of apron, but still not all that manly. I am less afraid of heights than just two days ago. Instead of slowly crawling around on the roof, I am walking at the speed of a mime fighting a windstorm on a roof that's on the moon.

At noon Cassandra comes to pick me up so we can make our flight, and I am not sad to abandon my crew mid-project. When I see photos weeks later of the finished roof—or at least the finished front half of the roof, since the back half will have to wait until at least the following summer—I don't feel a sense of accomplishment. Even if I loved carpentry and felt I made a real contribution, I don't think I'd be proud of any roof that protected a house that crappy.

Back at home about a month later, when the plastic lever you press to get drinking water from the refrigerator snaps off, I go online and look at the schematics, order a part, use a magnetic screwdriver to take out tiny screws, and install it. A month after that, I screw off a pipe under our bathroom sink to clean out the hair that is blocking it. I replace the tank fill valve in our toilet. I climb a ladder to my roof and brush off the leaves, except for the ones on this particularly steep corner. My house is no longer a black box; it is a slapped-together mess of old and new wood, pipes and wires, and it can handle a few holes I might put in it, which can always be patched up. Not only is it cheaper and quicker to do these jobs than calling a guy to come in, but, just like Ken said, it does feel good. Mostly because Cassandra keeps telling me how sexy it is. She definitely has daddy issues.

But I still don't enjoy fixing things. And not because my dad ruined home repairs when I sensed he wasn't having a good time. If that were true, I wouldn't like cooking, working, or listening to other people. No, this is who I am genetically: a guy who doesn't like the nuts and bolts of guy stuff, unlike my son. Which is depressing. Because it means that every step forward in being a man is going to be difficult and unnatural.

I don't want to be frozen into the person I've become. I want to learn to measure self-worth in accomplishment instead of effete cleverness. But from what I've gathered from seeing movies with scenes about Alcoholics Anonymous, changing your nature requires constant work, a sponsor, and bad coffee. I don't even like good coffee. I've been dicking around on the edges of manhood, taking care of a cute dog, riding in the back of a fire truck, playing catch with a Major League Baseball player. I haven't been becoming a man. I've been becoming a Make-A-Wish Foundation kid. The problem is that I don't want to change badly enough to quit my job and become a carpenter's assistant. I just want to change a little bit, which might actually be less likely than changing completely.

I'm in the backyard with Laszlo as he happily waters plants, himself, and me, wondering if this journey really is necessary anyway. So far, being a dad hasn't once required being a man. It's required what I'm doing at this moment right now: just being present, staying calm as Laszlo soaks things that really shouldn't be soaked, making him feel important and understood. I hug him and his garden hose against their joint will, soaking us all, and Laszlo starts to sneeze wildly. He sneezes all the time, since he's afflicted with the same pathetic hay fever allergies I have. But this sneezing doesn't stop. It's one continuous fit. His face turns splotchy and red. I pull up his shirt and see hives spreading over his entire body.

I pick him up and run to Cassandra, who tells me she had given him a bunch of mixed nuts for the first time. Which she thought was fine, because he's had almond butter since he was old enough to eat. I cannot get angry about this due to the fact that right before Laszlo was born, I wrote a column in the *Los Angeles Times* titled "Nut Allergies—A Yuppie Invention" in which I argued that parents greatly exaggerate their kids' allergies.

We are about to call the doctor when Laszlo starts shrieking and pulling at his eyes. We drive him to the hospital, trying to calmly tell him to stay awake as his eyelids start to puff over his eyeballs. We stop the car in front of the emergency room entrance, step out of the car, and he vomits slightly more than he's cumulatively eaten in his whole life.

After that, Laszlo starts to breathe normally. The emergency room doctor gives him some Benadryl, teaches us how to use an EpiPen, and tells us that Laszlo has a severe allergy to nuts. What she is also saying is that Laszlo isn't such a badass. He might love cars and tools, but he can be destroyed by a single pistachio. Sure, there's an outside chance that he could turn it into a cool kryptonite thing, but it doesn't sound manly when you pause in negotiations with Lex Luthor to ask the waiter if they use peanut oil in a dish.

Back at home, I move all the nuts to super-high shelves and realize: Laszlo has been fronting for some time. All his talk about cars and dogs may just be talk. As a baby, when an actual garbage truck came down the street, with its backup noises and low rumble, Laszlo would drop his spoon, abandon his bowl of yogurt, cry, and run to my arms. Leaf blowers caused this as well. When a toy lights up or makes noises unexpectedly, we still have to leave the room; if this happens when we're at another kid's house, Laszlo immediately gets his shoes and takes them to the front door. He is so cautious that he did not walk until seventeen months—about seven months late—even though I'm pretty sure he knew how, due to the fact that he has not once truly fallen when walking. We are the only parents I know who did not need to babyproof our house. The one time Laszlo crawled toward an electrical outlet was to hand me a plastic safety plug that had fallen out. He gets upset when his hands are dirty. When we're at the playground and kids grab toys from Laszlo, his strategy is to cry. It is not an effective strategy.

Sure, Laszlo is all man on the inside—an obsession with cars, a desire to figure out how things work, a fearlessness of animals and the ocean. But he's surrounded by a thick candy shell of wimpiness. He begs to go the playground, where he climbs everything bravely. But as soon as we drive up to the playground, he yells, "No kids!" If there are a lot of kids, he'll demand to go home rather than risk them grabbing his toys. At music class, while other kids run around and sing and bang instruments, he snuggles deeply into my lap. His favorite activity that doesn't involve cars is drawing.

I feel a great relief. I don't have to learn some kind of cartoon version of old-fashioned masculinity. My son is just like me. Maybe even wimpier. He's not going to want to camp, hunt, or fight. To father this kid I certainly don't have to learn to fix a roof. And I definitely don't have to fight Randy Couture. So I decide to change my plans. The rest of my path will be filled with the skills of new manhood. Skills he can actually use. And that I can, too. I will wear a suit every day, mix cocktails at night, learn how to appreciate classical music. Laszlo is into art, which I know nothing about, so maybe I can take a sketching class. Which also sounds boring, but at least instead of staring at Ken when I'm bored, I'll be staring at a naked female model.

I'm feeling pretty good about redefining my manquest when I talk to my friend Mike Gorker. He's got a daughter just a few months older than Laszlo, and he tells me that he worries all the time that she will turn out like we were—too shy. He doesn't want her to stand in the corner at high school parties like we did. He doesn't want her to not go to sleepaway camp, like we didn't. Though he feels bad about saying it, he tells me that he's relieved she's a girl, since shyness is far worse in a boy. He's right. The first girl I asked out was when I was twenty-two. My pickup line was, "Do you go on dates?" I fear that's where Laszlo is heading, only it will be worse because he'll then mumble something dorky to her about the different parts of a car engine.

I don't want him to be afraid like I am, never asking the guy at the kids' shoe store for the balloon, never making the networking calls for his career, never once asking for a raise. He seems even more delicate than I am: tall with big hands, but super-skinny with tiny rock-star bones. He is happiest sitting alone and drawing or building tracks for his trains. He's a perfect combination of the meekest parts of me and Cassandra. Before he was born, I wrote on The List: "Say yes immediately. You can always back out later." But already, when anyone offers him anything, he says no, even though most of the time, after thinking about it for a few seconds, he comes back and says yes. His instinct is to avoid experiences.

Maybe it's not my fault. Maybe there's nothing I can do. Maybe he just randomly got meek genes. But I do know this for sure: When I'm in a situation where I don't know what to do, I stand in the exact same position as my dad does. I've got to stand the way I want Laszlo to stand.

I started this project because I was afraid I wouldn't be able to do all the things my son would want to try. But now I have to change because I'm about to raise a boy who doesn't want to play at other boys' houses because it could mean going into the woods, jumping ramps on dirt bikes, or playing with a lizard, which all boys seem to think is an okay pet even though it is clearly a lizard. I am about to watch someone be me again. And I am not going to let that happen.

9
PROVIDING FOOD

I spend three weeks trying to figure out a better way to become a man than these oversimplified, overengineered little challenges when the solution finally becomes clear. What I need to do should have been obvious after I drank The Macallan and found the lack of rage at the bottom of my masculinity: I need to destroy stuff. I've made a huge mistake—and one only a guy who didn't understand men would make. I skipped the starting point. Once I experience the thrill of exploding, shooting, and demolishing, all my other man skills will fall into place. By understanding violence, I'll appreciate the efforts to control that wildness: building shelters, putting out fires, escaping in a fast car, taming a dog, stopping a linebacker from tackling the quarterback. Before boys sign up to be Boy Scouts and protect nature, they fry a few insects with a magnifying glass.

The two poles of male behavior are construction and destruction. The best man day in the world would involve building a bridge and then blowing up that bridge. Which is why you can't make a better man movie than *The Bridge on the River Kwai*, unless you make *Two Bridges on the River Kwai*.

My roofing trip with Ken proved that I have no predilection toward building. But maybe I'm really talented at demolition. That's an equally important part of being a man. Action movies are all about exploding buildings, crashing cars, and killing guys. No one is sitting down for two hours to watch superheroes bang out car dents.

Before Laszlo learned to stack blocks, he mastered the art of making me construct huge block towers so he could crawl over, swing his arm, knock them down, and laugh with glee. At the time, I felt like I was teaching him how to be a terrorist. But now I see that I was teaching him how to establish dominance.

So now that I've enjoyed the process of creating life, it's time for me to kill. The problem is that I'm not so into death. I never watch action movies, horror movies, or movies about old people—just to be safe. But I will never know what half of masculinity is all about if I don't go hunting. If I can pull a trigger, then I'll know that somewhere so deep down even The Macallan couldn't find it, there's a masculine instinct to dominate.

The best man to teach me how to hunt is Matt Stedina. Matt runs his own fishing and hunting tour company, Vermont Trout Bum, and annually qualifies to be one of the sixteen people competing in ESPN2's *Field & Stream Total Outdoorsman Challenge*. He is incredibly manly—quietly confident and unafraid. He is also Bizzy's husband. Bizzy is the only reason my parents didn't think I was gay. From kindergarten until fifth grade, I was obsessed with Bizzy. Not with her shoes or clothes, but in a totally non-gay way in which my stomach hurt when I was around her, and I put a star next to her photo in every class picture. Though, I now realize, that seems pretty gay, too.

I spent most of first-grade recess asking my friend Heather Wishman to find out which boy Bizzy liked. When Heather reported back that it wasn't me, I asked Heather to find out the top two boys Bizzy liked. We went at this daily, until I made the top ten. There were only twenty kids in our class. And half were girls. I was ecstatic.

Bizzy was not only the prettiest girl in our kindergarten class, but the smartest, which meant Bizzy and I got to be in our own reading group, which was, technically, the only reading group. Despite her name, Bizzy was also the most sophisticated kid in our school—the only person I knew whose parents traveled to Europe and drank wine. She was an excellent skier. By the time she was eight, she somehow knew how to banter. Bizzy was so musically talented that while we were still in elementary school, she played her viola in a concert at Lincoln Center with the New York Philharmonic. When I finally got Bizzy to come over to my house to play in second grade, she understood how much it meant to me and didn't cancel even though she was sick. Within an hour of being in my room, she barfed on my blue carpet. I treasured that stain for years in a way that would impress Monica Lewinsky.

By the time we got to high school, Bizzy was too cool to consider dating me. We started hanging out over the summers in college, however, and then a bit more after college. Finally, we made out at a New York bar called the Village Idiot and it was nice. But only nice. It turns out that eighteen years is a lot of buildup for a kiss, and passion gets muted when you're doing something partly to impress your five-year-old self. Plus, you sacrifice a little romance in exchange for making out at a place called the Village Idiot.

I understood why things didn't work out between us when I met Matt. He's so unfathomably manly that when I ask him to take me hunting, he instantly agrees to go into the deep woods with an armed, completely inexperienced marksman who spent a good chunk of his life pining for his wife.

Matt suggests we go turkey hunting. Which bums me out. I want to shoot deer or moose or bears or mastodon. No one sounds manly talking about shooting a turkey. It's a half step up from telling people you shot a chicken. But Matt assures me that turkey hunting is the most dangerous, challenging, and proactive type of hunting. Plus it's the only thing you're allowed to hunt in the spring in Vermont.

To hunt turkey, however, I need a hunting license. Which you can't just buy. You have to take a course. This seems outrageous. I just want to go on one hunting trip while being supervised by an officially licensed guide. I have to sit through a course for that? What kind of nanny state do we live in? I am only five minutes into planning my hunting trip, and I have already shifted further right than the National Rifle Association.

The class is ten hours long, usually given over two days. But I saw in someone's blog posting that if you take an online test, you can just show up for the last four hours of class. So I go to the website of the International Hunter Education Association and begin my studies. The first page, and all the remaining pages, are largely about how natural hunting is. These are the first words of the test: "So you're interested in hunting? That's natural! Hunting is a natural activity for humans." Hunters, I keep being told, love animals and conservation and conserving animals: "Hunting has nothing to do with violence or aggression. Almost every hunter will tell you they love animals. Yet, hunters kill animals. How do you explain that? It's a little like farming or gardening." This makes sense to me, if vegetables screamed, and if, instead of digging them up from the ground, we shot vegetables in their heads.

The only animal to get its own section is the turkey. Because turkey hunting is indeed insanely dangerous. "Think of this—in no other hunting activity do hunters dress in full camouflage and hide, then make the exact sounds of the quarry they hunt," my test explains. I do think of this. I think of this a lot. The plan is that I'm going to try really hard to pretend I'm a turkey while I'm in the woods with people whose goal is to shoot a turkey? Then I'm going to have to tell a doctor that I got shot because I made turkey noises while hiding right near turkey hunters? I am pretty sure my insurance will not cover that.

I am not deep into the quiz when it mentions snipes. I laugh knowingly: Snipes are a fake species of birds used in a classic hazing ritual I had just performed in a racially fraught situation with underprivileged Boy Scouts. But it turns out snipes are in fact real wading birds, with a long, slender bill and cryptic plumage. Now I don't know whom to trust. Are the Boy Scouts incapable of lying, so they had to use a real bird name to trick kids? Was the whole hazing routine a trick on me to insert factual errors into my book? I stop thinking about this one page later, when the test informs me that people hunt squirrels.

I skim the rest of the quiz, not because I'm busy or because I'm disgusted by wild-squirrel eating, but because I discover that you can just take the multiple-choice quizzes at the end of the chapter over and over until you get them right.

A few weeks later, I show up at the Redondo Rod and Gun Club at twelve thirty for the last four hours of a ten-hour class. Inside a tiny suburban house, fourteen people sit around a conference table. None of the fourteen is particularly tough looking. In fact, nine of them are teenage boys. One is asleep. Two are with their dads. The walls are covered with mounted animals: three deer, two bass, two rams, and maybe one goat-type thing. There is a glass case filled with trophies and celebratory coffee mugs. On top, various bullets and guns sit out in the open. If I had read the online test, I'm pretty sure it would have said not to do this.

The guy leading the class, Leo Zamboni, is everything I want in a hunting safety instructor. He is heavy and short, with a gray goatee, and wears green shorts, a green polo shirt, a gold chain, white socks, moccasins, and a cap that reads CALIFORNIA HUNTER EDUCATION INSTRUCTOR. He punctuates the required information with real-life stories, each manlier than the next: "The last pig

I shot, I shot it through the heart and then I shot it in the shoulder. And it still ran a hundred feet. It didn't know it was dead." While camping, he fought an intruding bear with his bare hands. On another occasion, when a bear reared up on its hind legs, Leo threw a box of wine in its face. He tells us this bear had bad breath. I thought that was a little judgmental since Leo's breath wasn't likely to have been that great if he was drinking from a box of wine.

Leo instructs us, when hunting big game, to "rip out their lungs." He calls people who don't know what they are doing "yay-hoos." Leo intimidates me enough that I do not even giggle when he uses, in rapid succession, the following terms: *ramrod, nipple, ball discharger*, and *cock fletching*.

Explaining why full-metal-jacket bullets—which are less likely to kill because they don't expand upon impact—are used in the military, but not in hunting, Leo says, "When you wound one soldier, it takes two other soldiers to take care of him, so I've taken three out of the fight." This causes the kid who had been sleeping to ask Leo if he had ever shot a man. Leo looks at him hard.

"I only shot three people," Leo says.

"Did they die?" sleepy kid asks.

"They died. That's the purpose. You shoot at me, you're going to die. I don't have no regrets. I'd rather be judged by twelve than carried by six." Then Leo goes back to talking about the importance of thinning animal populations for the long-term health of the ecosystem.

A couple of hours later, Leo hands out the test we need to pass to get our hunting license. Then he takes mine back, explaining that I'll get a special test since I already took the online one. I joke that it must be a harder test. Leo says it is indeed much harder, since I didn't sit through all ten hours of the course and the state of California needs to make sure I didn't just skim through the online version in thirty minutes. Which is exactly what I did. This doesn't worry me since I am amazing at multiple-choice tests. Then I look down. Unlike everyone else's test, mine has a bunch of blank lines that I have to fill in with words. Or numbers. Or maybe drawings.

If I don't pass this test, I'll have to reschedule my trip, and Matt gets busy later in the season when people are permitted to hunt animals that aren't so humiliating to kill. I start to sweat. I'm always among the first people done with any test, and yet two-thirds of my classmates have dropped theirs off on Leo's desk, and I am not halfway done. I am still making guesses when the sleeping kid—who not long ago asked Leo what the "rod" in "rod and gun" meant, and also has a jar of almond bath salts in front him—hands in his test. I have no idea what to fill in for "the amount of a given species you're allowed to kill." I put some words together in my mind—*game, limit, bag, whack, knock off, ice, rub out*—and string them together. I am screwed.

Somehow I get an eighty-eight. Sure, Leo gives me "game limit" for "bag limit," but I really did know all the parts of the bullet. I am, as far as the state is concerned, ready to go out into a field with a loaded gun and kill an animal.

Thing is, I'm not. When I get back home and slip my hunter education certification card into my wallet, I wonder what I'll do when I have to pull the trigger. When we had mice in our New York apartment, I freaked out and closed all the kitchen doors to trap them there, my heart beating double time. My plan was to give them the kitchen and just use the rest of the apartment. It was Manhattan, after all. How much cooking were we really doing? But Cassandra got glue traps and a few hours later, put on gloves, picked up the traps they were scrambling to get out of, and dunked them in the toilet until they stopped breathing.

Looking into another living being's eyes and killing it seems to require a toughness I don't have. It's not that I have a deep affection for other living creatures. The only time I'm interested in an animal is if it's on my plate. I think it's insane that so many of the books I'm reading to Laszlo are about animals. Why are farm animals so crucial to his early education? The vast majority of Americans haven't lived on a farm for more than a century. I should be reading him books about the cute little sounds that Chinese businessmen make.

But when Laszlo was finally old enough to eat chunks of real, non-babyized food, I couldn't bring myself to give him meat. Cassandra thought my moral equivocations were lame and that Laszlo could use the protein, so I made some extra Dover sole and let her put some on his high chair. He loved it, looking civilized even though he ate it with his hands. I vowed to give him only fish that aren't factory-farmed and, I believe, are as stupid as fish. But the next day I gave him leftover short ribs I cooked for a dinner party. He shoved them into his mouth, his face a grease-smeared, savage smile. If it's possible to look manly in a bib, Laszlo did it. I have no doubt that despite his overall wimpiness, he loves meat so much that if you gave Laszlo a baby gun, he could kill a turkey. I also have little doubt that somewhere in America you can buy a baby gun.

I felt bad about giving Laszlo that steak, and all the subsequent steak—which is his favorite food—because while I may not feel any empathy for animals, I've always thought that eating meat is immoral. It's not the first thing I'll be sent to hell for, but entering Laszlo into an easy program of murder without his knowledge felt wrong. So does killing this turkey. It seems even more wrong than eating a turkey sandwich, since I'll be enjoying both the meat and the murder. Or, more likely, grossed out by the meat and freaked out by the murder. Still, it's murder for entertainment.

Before I fly back east, Matt sends me a helpful email saying, "You may use a shotgun of mine if you don't want to carry a firearm onto the plane. Can be tricky these days." I read that email ten times before deciding that he isn't kidding. I find bringing the tiny toothpaste container my dentist gives me onto a plane to be tricky these days.

My flight lands and I drive to Bizzy's house in Stockbridge, which is an hour from the closest city if Vermont had a closest city. Bizzy's been inviting me up to Vermont, where her parents had a vacation home, since high school. But I never thought about just how crazy it was for a girl who grew up on classical music, wine, and European vacations to move to such a remote place.

I drive uphill on a dirt road and then down a long driveway, where Bizzy's two adorable kids are riding bikes. Her daughter looks just like Bizzy did at her age, and I remember that shy, excited feeling I had when I first met her mom. Bizzy, who also looks a lot like she did when we first met, is standing with a guy named Matt, who is a friend of Matt's. Matt2 is in the army, and he thinks he remembers me from Matt1's "hootenanny," which was his bachelor party where everyone got drunk and shot guns at stuff. I inform Matt2 that, while I was at the wedding, I had not hootenannied.

Bizzy lives in a huge, beautiful log cabin house, the extension of which Matt built. With logs from his own backyard. That he chopped down himself. The vaulted-ceiling living room has three mounted deer heads on the wall. He killed one deer with a rifle, one with a muzzle loader, and one with a bow and arrow. There are three more mounted deer antlers, from deer that I assume he killed just by looking at them. Matt walks in wearing a baseball uniform from the league he pitches in and dominates, since he also pitched for his college team.

It'll get dark soon, and Matt wants me to get a few practice shots in before I aim at a turkey that he'll be standing right near. So he takes me practice shooting at his friend's property, which apparently is okay with his friend. If I had something called "a property," I don't think I'd tell all my friends to come whenever they want and shoot there. In fact, no shooting would probably be pretty high on my list of property rules.

I do not like carrying a gun. Especially when it has a bullet in it. It feels scary, like a loaded gun. I sit against a tree, push the shotgun into my shoulder, and aim at an empty box of bullets twenty feet away. I'm afraid the recoil will cause the back of the gun to hit me in the eye, giving a bruise called "raccoon eye" that other hunters will make fun of. I would not be afraid of this if Matt hadn't told me about it. I would very much like Matt to stop telling me all the awful things that might happen.

I pull the trigger. It doesn't hurt at all. It's exciting and empowering. I want to do it again.

Which I will have to. Because I have totally missed the target. This, Matt explains, is largely due to the fact that when I pulled the trigger I closed my eyes. My second shot, though, I keep at least one eye open and blow that empty box away like it slept with my empty box wife.

Driving back to the house, Matt tells me the worst part of hunting is bringing the dead animal to a weigh-in station at a post office or gas station, as required by law. "Non-hunters and antis are forced to see it, and they don't want to and I don't want them to. I've gone with my son and we've killed a deer and are having the time of our lives and they don't want to see that," he says. He'd loved hunting with his own dad growing up in Shinglehouse, Pennsylvania, where they went after turkeys all the time. I'm surprised his dad was into turkey hunting, since when Matt was two his dad got shot by a friend while turkey hunting. This would have probably turned me off the sport.

Like me, Matt didn't bother with the Boy Scouts, but for completely different reasons. "That's more for people who don't live it," Matt says. "I kind of did it all with my dad. We hunted. We camped. We fished. You ever see one of those MY KID BEAT UP YOUR BOY SCOUT bumper stickers?" Matt grew up in a town where even the bumper stickers were tough.

Back in his kitchen, in front of Bizzy and his kids, Matt shows me the skills that won him the turkey-calling competition in the *Total Outdoorsman Challenge*. He takes a small latex semicircle from a tiny box, cups it to his mouth, and makes a sound exactly like a turkey. No one laughs. There is a man impersonating a turkey, and they are nodding appreciatively, acting like he's banging out the *Goldberg Variations* on a piano. Matt has his head tilted, his eyes rolled back, and his hand over his outstretched neck like he's Charlie Parker. "That sounds really hot right now," he says. "Hear the way that one is rolling over?"

These, he explains, are mating calls. There's lots of different female flirts Matt can play on his reed. In all of them he's trying to sound like an attractive, sexually liberated female turkey, so a turned-on male turkey will approach us, at which point we can shoot him in the head. It turns out that to kill turkeys you have to know an incredible amount about turkey sex. Their mating ritual starts at 4 AM, turkey happy hour. At that time, we might not even need to use the calls to trick them into letting us know where they are. "Most turkeys gobble on their own because they want to get laid in the morning," Matt says.

"Who doesn't?" asks Bizzy.

"Later in the morning, their pecker hurts. They don't want to play," Matt says.

Apparently, a male turkey spends his spring morning banging a bunch of female turkeys until his turkey penis hurts. Sometime before that happens, Matt and I will hide in the woods and pretend we're a hot, desperate female turkey. We will do this by making sounds a lot like a rusty trumpet played underwater which, apparently, is what a slutty turkey sounds like. So, not that different from a very drunk woman.

Matt shows me one sharp, ugly sound called "cutting," which we'll need when we want to pretend we're a tough female turkey ready to fight other hens trying to seduce away the turkey of our desire. "That's a hen saying, *Fuck you, you cunt, that's my fucking man*. The gobbler loves it. He's like, *Those bitches are fighting over me*," Matt explains. "It's so much like dealing with a woman."

Matt does his best horny female turkey sound, moving his head like a turkey as he plays his latex reed, his face red from exertion. "You need to put energy into your call," he says. Then he does a quieter call. "He might gobble at that, but is his dick hard? No." Matt plays an even softer, unattractive, whiny yelp. "That means, *I'm not sucking your dick and you're taking me to dinner*." During this, Bizzy prepares a seared tuna topped with white bean puree, olive tapenade, and roasted cherry tomatoes in orange chili oil.

"You know more about turkey sex than I do about human sex," I tell Matt.

"I do," he says.

After dinner, Matt leaves to get camouflage gear from his friend so I can borrow it. That friend's name is Grizz. "Grizz gets so excited when he shoots a turkey, he vomits," Matt says. I wonder if extreme excitement is why Bizzy barfed on my carpet in second grade.

When Matt gets back, he shows me a video on YouTube of one of his friends shooting his first turkey. The guy looks so happy. I do not imagine I will be able to produce that kind of a smile for Matt when I kill an animal. I, however, might be able to match Grizz vomit for vomit.

We head to bed since we're waking up at 4 AM. Is each man event going to start even earlier, until eventually we're starting things the day before? Why do men like to wake up early? And how do they then wind up at strip clubs? Do men never sleep?

In bed my stomach cramps up. When I was a kid, this happened all the time, whenever I got anxious. Every year until high school I'd spend the day before the first day of school holding my stomach. The summer before my sister was born, the pain was so debilitating

a doctor ordered me to drink barium and have an upper gastroin-
testinal series to find out if I had ulcers. It's gotten far better largely
due to forcing myself to meet new people and go to new places as a
reporter, but still, it happens. It hasn't been this bad in years.

At 4:15 AM I am somehow in Matt's driveway. We go into his dirty
GMC truck, since his identical, but clean GMC truck is reserved for
formal occasions. This is the brilliance of masculine thinking. When
women like things, they dry clean them and hang them in obscure
downstairs closets no one uses. Men don't clean things. If we want to
keep something in good shape, we buy an extra one.

In the truck Matt is chewing tobacco, practicing his turkey
calls, and blasting country music. I feel less like I am going hunting
than like I am on a Disney World ride about going hunting. Matt
drinks a chocolate Slim-Fast, which apparently is the breakfast of
hunters. I need all my concentration to breathe at this time of the
morning and he is somehow simultaneously driving, drinking a
Slim-Fast, and chewing tobacco. Matt offers me a chocolate Slim-
Fast, which I decline, mostly because it is a chocolate Slim-Fast.
When I draw my knees to my chest and clutch both sides of the
seat, Matt explains that he is driving fast in the exact middle of a
two-way road because at four fifteen you don't have to worry about
other cars, but you do have to worry about animals darting from
the sides of the road.

Matt informs me that we can shoot only adult male turkeys. I
do not believe, given the lack of light, my inexperience, and my ner-
vousness, that I will be able to spot a fully grown turkey penis. I'm
still not entirely sure Montana was a female dog. But Matt tells me
that male turkeys are easy to identify, since they're the only ones
that gobble and have that weird red wattle thing on their necks.
When the turkey gets excited, the wattle gets flushed with blood,
thereby enlarging and turning red. Turkeys are as subtle in their
sexuality as people in Miami.

Besides, Matt assures me that we'll have plenty of time to distinguish between turkey genders, since he is going to use his seductive calls to slowly draw out a turkey until he is only a few feet away. I ask Matt if he ever has trouble pulling the trigger. "Sometimes it's hard to shoot them," he says. "It's hard for me to catch trout. You don't want to hurt their mouth. But how do you capture the beauty of a wild trout without catching them and taking a picture? They're meant to be caught." I remember this answer from my test.

We arrive at an enormous piece of land owned by some guy Matt knows. Matt has "tied one up" for me—tracked one particular turkey's habits and whereabouts so we can use that information to shoot him in the head. We walk silently through the dark woods until Matt signals to stop, and puts down a plastic male turkey. I had no idea Matt was carrying a plastic male turkey. Or that you could buy a plastic male turkey. Matt's plastic turkey looks like a jake, a young male turkey. Adult alpha males, the ones we want to kill, like to approach a jake so they can beat him up and humiliate him; then the alpha turkey forces the jake to watch as he has sex with all the female turkeys. I am starting to feel much better about shooting a turkey. Turkeys are assholes.

Male turkeys will fall for our lame-looking plastic replica even though they're smart and see almost 360 degrees around them. They just can't smell much. "If turkeys could smell, they'd rule the world," Matt says. I'm not convinced that sharpened olfactory senses would get them a permanent seat on the Security Council, but I will buy that it might stop them from being farmed for meat no one enjoys that much.

In the woods Matt hears so much more than I can—deer steps, owl squawks, squirrel whatever-sound-it-is-squirrels-supposedly-make. Matt asks if I hear particular things and I tell him I do even though I do not. The sun rises and it's really pretty, but still, it's cold and we're in the middle of nowhere and I'm starting to consider drinking a Slim-Fast. I am starting to see why the Boy Scouts sleep close to their cars.

The tied-up turkey apparently figures out Matt's plan, because he never shows up. After an hour and a half we head back to the truck. On our way to the next turkey-hunting spot, we see a huge male turkey by the side of the road, his feathers fanned out wide. There are about six female turkeys around him, and more are crossing the road to go have sex with him. He is the Fonzie of turkeys. There is a jake standing ten feet away, not having sex with anyone. I spent college as that jake. We pull over and Matt starts making calls out the window. The alpha male turkey starts to walk our way. Even though he's got a pile of turkey pussy right there. Matt's call is that hot.

I slowly move to get out of the truck with my gun. Matt is horrified. He orders me to get back in the truck. I ask Matt when we're going to shoot this turkey. Matt looks at me like I'm a bloodthirsty psychopath, hellbent on random turkey murder.

"That's not the game," Matt says.

The game has a lot of rules and codes, but basically, you have to get a turkey to come to you—not you to it—before you shoot him. Killing a turkey you come across by chance is extremely un-sportsman-like, it turns out. The only honorable way to hunt turkey is to hide behind a tree and make weird noises to fool him into thinking you're a female turkey who wants to have sex with him; then you shoot his head off. I do not think the turkeys are aware of the rules of this game.

Instead of killing this turkey in an un-sportsman-like manner, which would have allowed us to go home, we drive to the Coolidge State Forest. We barely enter the woods when Matt halts me by putting his arm across my chest. A deer is right in front of us. For ten minutes, we look at a deer right in front of us. Matt is enthralled at every stomp and snort. I feel like I am watching a ten-minute-long

YouTube video of a deer. Also, I am a tiny bit scared of being this close to a deer.

After the deer takes off, Matt says he's afraid the deer told the forest about our presence. Also, he thinks the jays and squirrels have given us away. I wonder if Matt believes the animals sing joyful Disney songs when we're not here.

We head deeper into the woods anyway. Matt hears the faint sounds of a turkey and points to a tree for me to sit against. He sits against one in back of me and starts making very sexy turkey calls, which bring the turkey closer. About twenty minutes into this, Matt whispers that it's okay if I take a nap. I feel awful that Matt can tell how boring I find this. I also feel awful that Matt thinks it's okay for a person to fall asleep with a loaded gun on his lap.

My eyes, however, do start to close. Luckily, I get to stop my battle with sleep because Matt heard the turkey change directions, requiring us to move deeper into the forest. We go up a hill and down another one to get on the other side of him. Matt sets up the plastic jake, makes a few sexy sounds, and the turkey gets close enough that Matt can tell that he's a big turkey, about twenty pounds, and already has hens near him that he either is going to have sex with, just had sex with, or is having sex with right now. I am surprised that turkey sex is the one forest noise Matt can't make out.

After another hour the sounds start to fade. "He's being a dick," Matt says. I think we're the dicks for wanting to shoot him in the head, but I suppose everything comes down to perspective. I believe that Matt is so into the game that he is not thinking of himself as a hunter; he's thinking of himself as a hot female turkey who is being snubbed. So, in a way, the turkey is totally being a dick.

We move farther into the forest, and the turkey sounds get louder. We stop and each lean against a tree, side by side. The turkey gets so close I can hear his feathers puffing out, and it sounds like a car starting in the distance. Matt is scratching at the ground with a stick and making very loud clucking noises. He is displaying a passion that, if I were a turkey, would make me fall deeply in love with him.

Matt motions for me to take the safety off my gun and put my finger on the trigger. I take my gloved hand and shield the barrel's reflection. My body is perfectly still. The noises are getting so loud, if I move my head I will definitely see the turkey.

I don't know if I'll be able to pull the trigger. Not because I'm panicked. It's the opposite. This is the most intense adrenaline-filled moment of a hunt, right before the kill, and instead of being absolutely present like an athlete at the buzzer I am thinking of when I was a kid, when my parents would bribe me with an extra hour of TV if I would go over to a friend's house to play. And he'd want to go play in the woods, which just meant looking around the woods, and I got sad, bored, and lonely. Even if it was my own backyard. My backyard was big and densely wooded; my parents purposely bought that house so I'd have that big space to play in. Most boys would have spent every afternoon there, inventing games involving wars and explorers and war explorers. In high school I realized I'd never even once bothered to find out where my yard ended. So I finally did. It took about three minutes. It ended at a Little League field. I'm sure that just beyond was a rifle range, a saloon, and a Roman Colosseum.

While my parents tried to engage me in the centuries-old tradition of sending soft suburban Jews into the wilderness for the summer, I refused to sleep away from home. So Camp Riverbend, the day camp I went to until I aged out of it, was able to teach me only canoeing and archery, which don't come up much in the real world. If they ever build a time machine, the first trip I'll make is to seventeenth-century America, where Pocahontas will think I'm a stud.

Meanwhile, Matt spends November 13 to 28 in the woods for

white-tailed deer season—his favorite time of year. He spends his days sitting in a tree, usually never seeing a deer. "The highlight of the day is holding out on the Snickers bar and then the turkey sandwich," Matt had told me. "I think about whatever I can to stay sane. It's a battle of the brain. It's an art to sit there motionless for eight hours."

I am too dependent on stimulation for this. I have lost the battle of the brain today, suffering from a mix of overconcentration and understimulation that in junior high in New Jersey I defined as "mall tired."

It turns out that you have to really care about animals to want to kill one. Matt, who is scratching the ground and making turkey noises behind me, wants to know what it feels like to be a turkey. He wants to know what they eat, how they have sex, what they're thinking. I admire it. I've made my world small so I can control it. Matt made himself part of a bigger, older world. He understands how, stripped of the subtext of politeness and civility, all of us humans are really just animals maneuvering to get what we need. We do the same things these turkeys do when we're horny, when we're hungry, when we're hunted.

But I don't have that appreciation of the details of raw nature. I was interested to learn that turkeys are mean, raping, fighting bastards, but I would have preferred to get that information via a *New Yorker* article. I don't need to be part of their world. Their world bores me. I suspect it would bore me even if I were a turkey.

If I don't kill this turkey it will be due to a lack of focus, not morality. I no longer have a problem with hunting. Killing is wrong, but shooting this turkey, which will not die of old age but instead meet some kind of violent death in these woods anyway— and really does seem like a frat-boy jerk—is far less wrong than eating a turkey sandwich made from a bird trapped for its entire short life in a windowless shed with his beak cut off. There is much less suffering here. And far more honesty. I have, thousands of times, indirectly paid someone to kill an animal for me so I did not have to confront the death I caused. Compared with what I've done, this is humane. I will not have trouble pulling this trigger. If I were ever drafted and sent to war, and that war happened to be against turkeys, I would perform admirably.

But as sure as I feel that I've got a turkey killer somewhere inside me, I'll never know until I see that turkey fall. I can make out the separate gobbles and clucks of the male and the one female turkey still with him. My finger is on the trigger and one eye is shut, hoping I can keep calm and wait long enough to spot the male before I shoot. I want to do this. Not just so I can go home. But so I know I can kill.

"They busted us. Oh no. We're busted," Matt whispers. I have no idea how he can tell, but he is sure the hen accompanying our turkey warned him about us. I put my safety back on and peel back the mesh camo veil. We've lost the game.

Matt is really bummed. I am, too, and not just because if we don't kill anything, there was no need to have taken that hunter safety course. But because I didn't find out if I definitely could pull that trigger, or how I'd feel after.

On the way back to the truck, Matt consoles himself by looking for shed antlers by the sides of trees where he found some in the past. I ask Matt what exactly people do with antlers. "I just hold them and jerk off to them," he says, expressing his deep love of deer. Then he gets wistful. "These deer are ghosts. I never see these things. It makes it a little easier to go to bed knowing they exist."

We drive to a few more places until noon, when turkey hunting legally ends, but we wind up with a fairly typical turkey-hunting experience in that we never even really see one. None of Matt's turkey-hunting friends even heard a gobble that day.

I can tell that Matt is more disappointed than I am, that he understands the feeling I missed out on more than I can. I don't want him to feel this way after all he's done for me. So I tell Matt that I still want to provide my own lunch, convincing him to show me the other half of his business: being a fishing guide. At the river I put on some rubber boots and Matt picks out an intricately sewn plastic ball from a big box of intricately sewn plastic balls. Matt sewed all these plastic balls himself, and they're really pretty, which is even more impressive since they also look like insects, which are not at all pretty. Matt pushes one onto the hook and flings the line like a lasso.

Matt is so emotionally connected to the animal world he even empathizes with the flies, which he points out are mating everywhere. Two right in front of us get eaten by a trout mid-coitus. "It's a short, brutal life," Matt says. And for a moment, I understand how much wisdom you can gain by understanding how nature works. And then I go back to realizing that they're flies.

I am much happier than when we were hunting. It's beautiful: the river rushing and the birds overhead. The darkness and sullenness of the forest are gone. We can chat and not wear camo nets over our faces. Casting a rod isn't much of an activity, but it's a 1970s European disco compared with sitting against a tree not shooting a gun.

The river is so clear, I can see tiny brook trout swimming yards away. I land two on my hook, but they escape when I yank at the line. I hand Matt the rod, and in a few minutes he reels in three tiny, shiny brook trout with pink spots, puts them in a plastic bag, and we walk up to his camp.

Matt mentioned his camp earlier, and I pictured a piece of land where men put up tents, either in groups of two or with their wives. That is not at all what a camp is. A camp is a cabin that a group of men spend days in together. They're like little frat houses, only girls never come over. So like frat houses with no purpose.

Matt's camp, which he's been coming to since 1995, is called Camp Jimmy Dean, though they all call it GINUH, which stands for God, It's Nice Up Here. The cabin is owned by Johnny, who is in his eighties. And the guys who use it—Sapshak, Whitey, Grizz, Bert, Hiram, and RB—are all far older than Matt. That's because hunting, much like the Boy Scouts, is becoming less popular. Between 1996 and 2006 the number of Americans who hunt went down 10 percent, and the number of people who fish dropped 15 percent. The number of people named Whitey is also down significantly.

While I can kind of almost see spending a day sitting in a tree, I cannot see sleeping in this cabin. It's not that I'm prissy. When Cassandra is away, I will eat expired food, throw dirty tissues on the floor, go the gym, and sleep unshowered in my post-workout muck. I have never felt that any bed, pullout couch, futon, or cot was uncomfortable. Yet this place disgusts me. If the animals of the forest broke in looking for revenge, they would decide that the humans who slept here were not safe to eat. The cabin smells of mouse shit, which I instantly know even though I've never smelled mouse shit. It is one big room with bunk beds, but blocking the kitchen area are two garbage cans overflowing with nothing but Molson Ice bottles. The walls are filled with photos of the guys posing with dead deer. Under one shelf is a row of turkey beards nailed to the wall, like a mad turkey dictator was trying to intimidate his turkey subjects. Turkey beards are long, black, straggly clumps of hair that look like they've been scalped from the soul patches of members of a ZZ Top cover band. When I comment on how ugly they are, Matt looks at me like I'm insane. "No," he says. "They're beautiful." The wall near the sink is decorated with the whitetail edition of this year's Racks Calendar, in which each month has a photo of a woman in a bikini holding a rack of deer antlers. The measurements given are not of the women, but of the deer antlers.

There is a bumper sticker on the wall that reads: YES ON I PRESERVE MARRIAGE, and another that says, I'M NOT A FUDGE PACKER, I'M A TRUE VERMONTER. There's also a cartoon in which a deer sodomizing a man says, "Here's your deer sausage, motherfucker!" It is not specifically homophobic but, due to the look on the hunter's face, does imply that anal penetration is undesirable. I guess I'd be defensive about my sexuality if I were constantly leaving my wife to go into the middle of the woods, drink cases of Molson Ice, and sleep on bunk beds with dudes.

This is not what I pictured when I thought about stealing Laszlo and taking him to a cabin. The cabin in my mind looked a lot of more like a Las Vegas hotel room. This is anti-Vegas. When you're hanging out here, you're really just hanging out. I do not like my male friends nearly enough to spend even one night with them here. When women aren't around, my energy dissipates, though it does not make me so lethargic that I can't get up to throw away at least one beer bottle.

After touring the cabin, we head back to Matt's truck, pick up his son from day care, and head back to Matt's huge, beautiful house. Matt dips the trout in cornmeal and sautés them in butter with some fiddlehead ferns he foraged. They are truly delicious, but it's uncomfortable in the house. I don't know if it's just been a long day, or if coming home empty from a hunt is always a downer, or if this is just normal afternoon man silence, or if Matt—who insisted I'd get the high that everyone gets their first time hunting whether we killed a turkey or not—senses that I didn't completely appreciate it. All I know is that it's not a good idea to stay until Bizzy comes home from work. I really am the master of anti-male-bonding.

I want to thank Matt for exposing his identity to me, and tell him that his ability to infiltrate animal society is fascinating, but I can't figure out a way to say it that doesn't sound like, "You're a giant hick." I consider explaining that it's me, that I'm just not interested in anything for more than a few hours, especially when it involves not talking, but that also sounds like, "You're a giant hick." I go with "I better get going."

Driving away from Bizzy's, feeling more free inside my car every mile I go, I get mad at myself for not getting more into the hunt. My brain turned off, maybe from fear, maybe from the unfamiliar, maybe because brains don't turn on until 9 AM. Maybe it's because my aggression just isn't there. Or maybe it's because I don't have Ken and Shawn's patience. But I fear it's because hunting requires a male comfort with loneliness that is even more frightening to me than killing. If I'm going to be a man, I'm going to have to find an entirely different part of myself. One that somehow, someway, can stop talking.

Because that's part of the problem I've been having. It's not so much that I'm uncomfortable with physical discomfort: I'm uncomfortable with mental discomfort. I got bored working on a house with Ken; I got bored in the woods with Matt. I need those ticking stock numbers on Matt Nadel's screen to distract me. I'm not still and quiet and manly like Wiggles, Captain Buzz, and Shawn Green. I'm full of nervous boyish chatter and worries about what other people are thinking. I feel farther away from being a man than when I started. And I started sleeping near my car at a Boy Scout camping trip.

I'm back at home in the middle of the afternoon when Cassandra walks in the door, shaking and about to cry. She'd been driving her Prius home, up our curvy, dead-end street, when some neighbor driving his SUV too fast the other way almost hit her. As they were facing each other post-near-miss, the guy—a neighbor—gave her the middle finger. Cassandra jumped out of her car, leaving Laszlo strapped to a baby seat in the back, and was about to ask the guy what he meant by the middle finger, even though she must have known he meant "fuck you." She got halfway to his car when he got out, got two inches from her face, and screamed at her for honking at him. She was afraid he was going to hit her.

I hug Cassandra while she cries. Then I warn Cassandra that it's dangerous to get out of your car to confront crazy drivers in Los Angeles, especially when our baby is there. This, while having its merits in practicality, does not comfort a woman as much as going over to her tormentor's house and kneeing him in the face. Which I did not even think of doing.

After she calms down, I leave for a television pitch meeting with two male producers, which consists less of me telling them my great ideas, and more of them yelling at me for being such a pussy. I need to go over to that guy's house, they insist, and I need to do it right away. I tell them that this sounds like a really unpleasant way to spend my afternoon. One of them tells me he keeps a collapsible metal baton in his car at all times, and buys videos about how to do horrible things to other human beings with a collapsible metal baton. These are network sitcom producers. If network sitcom producers keep collapsible metal batons in their cars, what does a guy who screams at new moms for using their horns to warn of an impending accident keep in his house?

I get home dreading what I have to do. When I ask Cassandra where the guy lives, she says she doesn't know. I figure this is because no one really wants to help a guy who looks forlorn about kicking some ass. Still, I have to do this. So I go to email a neighbor to ask if she knows where this guy lives, but Cassandra pleads with me not to escalate things and let this maniac know where we live, thus making her scared to be in our own house. I like this reasoning a lot. Too much.

I never go to the guy's house. In fact, when Cassandra and I see him in his truck a couple of months later, I wave hello at him, and he waves back. I don't know if he senses the ironic, faux friendliness of my wave, which is really more of a middle finger, but I think he does.

I don't even have the fantasy of going to his house and beating him up and dragging him by his lapel to my house so Cassandra can hear him grovel an apology that includes how intimidating and sexy I am. My fantasy is that Cassandra forgets this ever happened.

I know I should have gone over there. I know that even if it had provoked him, it would have made Cassandra feel loved and protected. I would have been exactly the kind of man I want Laszlo to pattern himself after, and not the one who fears confrontation when it's necessary.

But now it's way too late. I'd have to spend five pre-confrontation minutes trying to jog his memory about, you know, this time when you were backing up and there was this Prius and you both got out and yelled, you remember, right?

Months later, Cassandra's friend emails her that a registered sex offender lives on our block. It's that guy. He went to jail for "rape by force or fear," "sexual battery," and "oral copulation by force or fear." In his petition hearing, a psychiatrist diagnosed him with "anti-social personality disorder" and "atypical paraphilia with sadistic features." This should make me more sorry I didn't take him on, to protect Cassandra and Laszlo from a real danger. But it does the opposite. I feel like I protected them by not riling up a psychopath. This was not a guy I was going to turn around with a conversation, even if it included some face kneeing. He has most likely been face kneed many times, by far better face kneers. My confronting him would not have made a positive difference even if he were just a typical paraphiliac. But I still feel awful.

It turns out the guy doesn't live on our block anymore. He was just renting a neighbor's guesthouse and moved away a while ago, probably shortly after I waved to him.

I've gone half a life without anything horrible happening partly because I avoid people who do horrible things. Once again, things worked out as well as they possibly could in this situation. I don't regret not going over there. I have a far bigger problem: I regret that, after all this effort to become a man, I don't regret not going over there.

10
DEFENDING MY COUNTRY

Since making myself a man has failed miserably, I'm going to let someone else do it for me: the U.S. government. Asking the government to do what I should do myself seems a little liberal and wimpy, but apparently when you join the military they ask for stuff in return. So I'm going to get rid of all my choice, all my ego, all my pussyish risk analysis, and get the military to force me to fight. I want to use the military as rehab for being addicted to wimping out.

There's a certain type of man I'm most afraid of: the kind who is trained to kill people. If I can survive even a few days of basic training with a troop of military recruits without quitting, then my chance of not crying when I get in the ring with Randy Couture will be much higher. Because I don't feel ready. This may be because my pre-fight regimen has consisted of trading stocks, walking dogs, and watching football on TV. This is not the stuff of *Rocky* training montages. You cannot blast "Eye of the Tiger" over a guy picking up dog poop.

When I ask the Department of Defense if I can be a soldier for a few days, I am surprised that someone not only gets back to me, but has each branch of the military compete to make me the most exciting offer. I am particularly surprised since a few years ago I wrote a column for the *Los Angeles Times* with the first sentence "I don't support the troops." I was trying to say that it's hypocritical to claim you're against the wars in Iraq and Afghanistan but support the people fighting it. But those subtleties were obscured by the sentence "I don't support the troops." The week that column was published, I learned, mostly through political talk shows and death threats, that America very much supports the troops.

I've been vaguely anti-military my whole life. Part of it is just growing up in a liberal New York suburb. When I asked Warren Sapp why he never thought about joining the military even though his uncle and lots of kids in his town did, he said it was because, as a good student and athlete, he had other options. As did I. "You didn't think about it. It wasn't on your radar. It was for the poor kids," Sapp said. And it wasn't just off my radar, like it was for my friends. It was on my radar as something to actively avoid. In third grade Tommy Reynolds and I wrote a little satirical newspaper that I got my dad to make copies of so we could hand it to the rest of the class. In it, I wrote a parody of the army's television commercial, replacing "It's a great place to start" with "It's a great place to end." To me, all militaries throughout history were the tools of powerful people who tricked the less powerful into risking their lives. And I was not a boy interested in being a hero for myself or anyone else. I've never liked action movies. I sort of liked *Star Wars*, but my favorite character was C-3PO, the gay British interpreter robot whose sole purpose was to build tension by warning the other characters not to do whatever dangerous, heroic thing they were about to do, and then blame them as soon as things went poorly. He said things that seemed very wise to me, such as "Surrender is a perfectly acceptable alternative in extreme circumstances!" When I played Dungeons & Dragons, I was never a fighter or an assassin; I was always a magic-user. Even in my fantasy life, I was a nerd.

The marines offer to have me spend three days trying out some of the marine boot camp challenges on their base. Even better, the army will let me spend three days joining an army troop as they go through boot camp—training, eating, and sleeping with them. I am also considering an offer from the navy, when I get an email from a three-star general in the army trying to win me over. "The Navy? I thought this was about doing something manly? You do know they go on boats, right?" writes General Mark Hertling. "Will keep the offer open, if you come to the conclusion that you really want to test yourself. :)" The only thing more shocking than getting an email from a three-star general is getting an email from a three-star general with an emoticon in it. I am very tempted by the army offer since there's a chance I might be able to survive three days in a branch of the service that uses emoticons. Better yet, if I do survive three days of army boot camp, General Hertling wants me to fire a live round from a tank. The army has never let a civilian do this, since it normally takes weeks of training and carries special dangers, like losing a finger or destroying a village. I am not at all sure this is a good idea. I am desperately afraid the air force is going to offer to let me drop bombs on Iran. Because I have trouble making decisions, and even more trouble saying no to people who have been trained to kill, I say yes to both the marines and the army. I don't even bother returning the navy's call.

I'm going to start by trying to complete a bunch of marine boot camp activities, ending with The Reaper. This is the giant hill at the end of a nine-mile hike that recruits at the base in San Diego climb at the end of The Crucible, the most difficult part of any of the military branches' boot camps. The Crucible consists of fifty-four hours of horrifying exercises and challenges, including being shoved into a room filled with tear gas. During this they get only three meals and almost no sleep. I'm just doing the hike, ending with The Reaper, the part that every marine spends his thirteen weeks of boot camp being told to fear.

I arrive at 0730 at Marine Corps Recruit Depot San Diego, which was built in 1919 and looks like a gorgeous college campus, right near the ocean. I walk to an old Spanish building to meet Sergeant Wayne Edmiston, who is thirty-four and looks like a less threatening, goofier Matt Damon. He's got an easy nervous laugh, but huge arms. He's been in Iraq twice, videotaping the war as a marine journalist.

I assumed there were styles I could choose from when getting a marine recruit haircut. It's not that I thought I could bring in photos from magazines of my favorite actors. I just thought there were maybe four options, like a high and tight, and like a low and tight, and maybe a buzz and a 1 or a 2. So maybe five types. But recruits get all their hair completely shaved off. It goes straight from the clippers into a plastic pipe that sucks all the hair into the garbage. The barbers aren't marines, just old Italian and Mexican guys. They charge four dollars. Still, it was the best haircut I've ever gotten. It took less than three minutes and, better still, I know absolutely nothing about the man who shaved my head: not his name, his troubled relationships, or his work with dog adoption agencies. Without any hair, I feel connected to my body, like it's a useful tool that doesn't need ornamentation. Suddenly, hair seems as feminine as jewelry.

Sergeant Edmiston brings me to the indoor pool, which, along with the firing range, is the only low-stress environment at the Marine Corps Recruit Depot. As it instructs on the sign outside this building, there's no yelling, no rushing. Recruits look at these two places as a break in their thirteen weeks of basic training. So I am pretty shocked when, right after walking into the pool area, a drill instructor takes me to the locker room and screams at me to get naked RIGHT NOW! Then he leads me to the bathroom and screams at me to piss in the urinal. When I do, he stands close and counts down from thirty, as fast as he can. Not having yet been given the military secrets of super-fast urination, my stream is still going strong when he gets to zero. So he starts counting down again, this time from ten. I am not sure what to do. Should I stop mid-piss? And shouldn't I be commended for being able to piss at all with a guy yelling at me? When my stream finally stops, he screams at me to walk quickly through a corridor where sprinklers on the wall spray me with cold water. Which is a little Holocausty for my taste.

I'd always wondered how drill instructors yell ridiculous things in recruits' ears and no one cracks up. That mystery has been solved. Even though I know these guys are just playing a part and I'm not a real recruit and I can leave at any time, the yelling is still real, and it is really stressful. It's like I'm at the world's best haunted house.

Wet, cold, and more than a little uncomfortable about being naked while everyone else is dressed, I'm relieved when my drill instructor screams at me to put on desert-camouflage pants, a long-sleeved shirt, and tan boots. This seems like untraditional swimming gear, but this definitely feels like one of those "save all your questions for the end" situations. Before I can get my wet feet into the boots, my drill instructor screams at me to MOVE ON! My shoes are untied, my shirt unbuttoned, and he screams at me to keep moving and BUTTON YOUR BLOUSE! This is the brilliant drill instructor stuff I've been hoping for: emasculating me by referring to my clothes in female terminology. But by the fourth time he says "blouse," I realize that the marines actually call their shirts "blouses." And their pants "trousers." Instead of swim trunks, the sergeants running the pool are wearing those linerless, abbreviated 1950s gym teacher shorts made out of heavy tan cotton. And a belt. To swim in. During warfare. Against enemies who are probably wearing something more Nike. Since the corps was founded two hundred years ago, the marines have not changed anything they didn't absolutely have to. Plus, you confuse the enemy when you swim up to the shore dressed like their grandfather.

I fumble with my buttons as I speed walk to the pool and am screamed at to shout YES SIR! a lot. Which is weird, because the giant sign I was forced to read specified that this is a quiet area where yelling is not permitted. Generally, I'm a sign-listener more than a people-listener, but in this case I decide to go the other way. So in the pool area I scream YES SIR!, walk to the shallow end of the pool, cross my arms in front of me, put a boot out, and step, falling into the pool. The water is treated with a lot of chlorine, which I haven't smelled in a while. Everyone in LA has saline in their pools since chlorine is a little harsh on your skin. I decide to also hold this comment for the questions-at-the-end period.

I am not a strong swimmer. I could never figure out that alternating-side-breath thing, or the pushing-the-water-with-your-arms thing. Basically, the swimming thing. If I were forced to choose a military branch, I would choose a land-based one. Luckily, my drill instructor screams that I am not allowed to put my head all the way in the water, which means I have to do a sloppy doggy paddle, which is my chosen method of swimming. After doggy paddling half a length, I get a quick lesson on how to blow up my blouse and trousers to make floating devices. I climb a fifteen-foot-ladder, cross my arms, and step off the diving board; there isn't time for my usual fear of heights, since it is superseded by my fear of angering a man who thinks I urinate lazily. I tread water for four minutes, without needing to resort to any blouse-blowing tricks. I swim to the end of the pool and…that's it. I passed Combat Water Survival 4th Class—enough to be a marine. This is ridiculous. They can't let people be marines who can only do what I just did. I can't swim properly. If I had to fight someone in the water, I would die in minutes.

Since I did so well, I am sent to qualify for 3rd Class. Though I don't feel like I'm really being given a choice in this, I have to say YES SIR! when I'm asked if I want to keep going. I am pretty sure I didn't say it loud enough, because the drill instructor answers my YES SIR! with OPEN YOUR DISGUSTING MOUTH! I am also screamed at for touching my DISGUSTING FACE. It is a DISGUSTING HABIT that can lead to DISEASE. I knew from the moment he told me to take my clothes off that this guy cared about me.

I get a lot more gear to put on top of my soaking clothes: a Kevlar vest, a Kevlar helmet, a backpack full of something heavy, and a fake plastic rifle. I haven't fastened any of it right, so everything is dangling from my body, but I am screamed at to MOVE! anyway. I look a bit un-put-together, like I am heading home at 8 AM from some kind of army walk of shame. Swimming in all this gear seems ridiculous. As soon as I step into the pool, two drill instructors yell at me to KEEP MY MUZZLE DOWN! I remember from hunter safety class that I should never let my muzzle get wet. But they insist I should. I believe that if Leo Zamboni were here, being screamed at by these guys, he would submerge his muzzle, too.

All I have to do is walk the first half of the length of the pool, and then do this doggy paddle/breaststroke for another quarter and swim the rest. I jump back in, do a little more swimming, and that's it: I am now 3rd Class—an overqualified swimmer for the marines. I am losing a lot of faith in our military. For 2nd Class, I swim some more and then grab my drill instructor by the collar and tow him halfway down the pool until we can both stand. Even though I'm thirty-nine and afraid of the water, I would be in the top 10 percent of my recruiting class for swimming. I am qualified, swimming-wise, to be an officer. We should really stop invading other countries.

Sergeant Edmiston brings me to Duncan Hall, which is where actual, post-boot-camp Marines eat. It's a lot like a college dorm, and the buffet—which costs $4.50—isn't any worse. Though I was hoping the marines hadn't discovered my column about not supporting the troops, it's a very high-tech organization with access to Google. Sergeant Edmiston says, over surprisingly good goulash, that he is sympathetic to my opinion, which is very generous, particularly since, right this moment, he is supporting the journalists. The reason Sergeant Edmiston joined the marines is to make our country strong enough to prevent it from being attacked. "I think of all Americans like they're my wife and daughter," he says. "I have sympathy for people who can't protect themselves." I have never heard patriotism explained quite that way: that the feelings you have for the people you love can be extended out to people you don't know. Edmiston says, in fact, that as a citizen of a powerful nation, he feels a responsibility to those in trouble throughout the world. He is somehow making my lack of patriotism seem selfish.

Midway through our conversation, we see Gunnery Sergeant Andrew Cox, who had been in charge of my pool training. He's a blond, smiley, thirty-three-year-old who is much, much less intimidating now, even though he's out of that embarrassing 1950s swimsuit. He hates the outfits, too, especially since he has to wear them in swimming competitions, and the only speed they're built for is the speed of getting made fun of. I ask Sergeant Cox why he joined the marines, and I am not prepared for the answer. It's not to serve his country, or for the discipline, or to protect others. It's for the good time. "You get paid to go out and do everything you wanted to do as a kid," he says. Which is surprising, because I have yet to see a bunch of recruits playing ColecoVision, watching MTV, and getting to third base with Heather Locklear. But Sergeant Cox had a much more Boy Scout idea of what was fun, and now he's not just building forts, but living in them.

Sergeant Cox asks me to guess what his job in the marines is when he isn't a drill instructor. I am not particularly familiar with marine jobs. All I can think of is "killing people from close by" and "killing people from far away." He smiles, leans forward, and whispers that he's the drum major for the base's band, which, judging by the way he presented the information, is just as embarrassing as being the drum major anywhere else. Knowing he's a drum major makes me feel comfortable asking him something that's been bothering me the whole time he was screaming: Did he feel bad while he was scaring me? "Inside, to be honest, I might feel bad when I'm yelling at recruits. But it's not my role to make them feel better," he says.

That is someone else's role. Every recruit has three drill instructors. One is called a "daddy." He's a little older, and after every trying physical activity, he tells recruits an inspiring story, runs discussions about values, and gives evaluations. The experienced drill instructor, or "J," encourages recruits during activities. The third hat, or "Heavy," wears a green belt and this huge-brimmed green ranger hat, like Yogi Bear's friend, but he wears it low, almost over his eyes, and even though he's dressed like a giant Boy Scout, the fact that he's not self-conscious about his outfit makes him even scarier. The Heavy has this truly frightening, robotic, frog voice within days of boot camp, due to his constant screaming. His job is to cause stress, hate, and discontent. When decorated marines who have fought in wars see their Heavy years later, they still get afraid.

The sergeant in charge of this base's physical training is a thirty-two-year-old eighth-grade dropout who insists, despite looking a lot like Alex Rodriguez if he'd taken even more steroids, that he's a Jewish guy from New Jersey. There seem to be a lot of Jews in the world of manliness. We just don't hear about them because we Jews in the media never go places where we could meet them.

Like a lot of military guys who serve overseas, Jewish Alex Rodriguez would rather I didn't use his name, since he believes it makes him more vulnerable to an Internet-using enemy. But I think the real reason is that, particularly for enlisted men who didn't go to college and aren't high up in the organizational chart, they have been taught that ego and attention are undignified. It takes me a while to even process this. They are the last people in America who don't want to be famous. These guys don't even know the number of Facebook friends they have because *most of them don't even have Facebook friends.*

Jewish Alex Rodriguez thinks I'll do fine on the obstacle course, since the recruits, who are able to do it, are mostly "kids who played more video games than football." When I ask him the big difference between men a generation ago and men today, he says, "Hard-soled shoes. These kids have never worn dress shoes or work boots." This is a great metaphor for what so many men have been telling me: Technology has made men soft and sloppy.

But that's not what he means. He means that the only difference he can possibly think of is footwear choices. He quotes Chesty Puller: "Old breed? New breed? There's not a damn bit of difference so long as it's the Marine breed." The marines have always turned boys into men. By the time you're done with boot camp, you're just as manly as your marine dad and your marine grandfather.

I hear a lot about Chesty Puller while I'm with the marines. Despite having a 1960s stripper name, Lewis Burwell "Chesty" Puller was the most decorated marine in history. He said things such as, "They're on our left, they're on our right, they're in front of us, they're behind us...they can't get away this time." Most Chesty Puller stories involve him getting shot and not noticing. They also involve disliking superiors. He is the marines' action hero.

When I ask the eighth-grade-dropout sergeant why he joined the marines, he quotes the end of the Saint Crispin's Day speech from *Henry V*, when the king rallies his troops:

> We few, we happy few, we band of brothers;
> For he to-day that sheds his blood with me
> Shall be my brother; be he ne'er so vile,
> This day shall gentle his condition:
> And gentlemen in England now a-bed
> Shall think themselves accursed they were not here,
> And hold their manhoods cheap whiles any speaks
> That fought with us upon Saint Crispin's day.

Though he likes the marines and the man they turned him into, he feels he was tricked by his recruiters into believing his life would be boring if he didn't experience war, just like Henry V tricked his troops. But he's glad that he joined, partly because it bonded him with his distant, abusive father, who had been in the military.

I can't believe that soldiers are allowed to say whatever they want to reporters: whether they approve of the war in Iraq, if they think their recruiter tricked them, what they don't like about boot camp. It's not just confidence; it's dedication to democracy and the free speech that goes with it. No other organization I've seen is like this. If I got a mid-level General Electric employee to tell me that GE refrigerators kind of suck, he'd be fired. It's a weird sort of freedom the military gives its soldiers: You may not be allowed to piss for as long as you'd like, but you can say anything.

Jewish Alex Rodriguez, however, doesn't like to talk to non-military people about what he did in combat. It requires too much explanation and, more importantly, too much uneducated judging, both positive and negative. But he does tell me that he captured a bunch of Iraqis and held them as prisoners, right after a firefight in which he killed one of their brothers. Months before that, the sergeant had lost his own brother in a car accident. I ask how he dealt with killing someone and then facing his brother, and he says the marines reinforce the fact that your actions saved the lives of your fellow soldiers. "As soon as you get back they pat you on the back and say, 'Because you did this, we accomplished this.' It's constantly reinforced from everyone."

On his desk, hiding under the book *1776* by David McCullough, the sergeant has a brochure for the San Diego Symphony. He says he doesn't broadcast his interest in classical music, but he doesn't hide it, either. He had just been at the pool and saw two marines watching YouTube clips from the musical *Wicked*. I am feeling more and more like I can be a marine.

I also see a skydiving booklet. Jewish Alex Rodriguez skydives because he's afraid of heights. Which, oddly, is why I don't sky-dive. "Irrational fear drives me insane," he says. Your odds of getting hurt skydiving are low, and you have to train your body to understand that. He's infuriated by a relative who's afraid of snakes and yelled at one of her students for putting a book about snakes on her desk. She would not make a good marine. Or probably a good teacher.

The obstacle course is very low-tech: a little metal, a couple of ropes, and a lot of logs. I get over and under the logs in decent time, but the rope, man, the rope. It's the same braided rope that those tiny boys slithered up in elementary school, and no matter how many times the sergeant shows me how to wrap my legs around it, I am too weak and confused to climb it. I fear that if I can't do this, I have no chance of getting up The Reaper. But Jewish Alex Rodriguez tells me that about 20 percent of recruits have the same problem and are given remedial rope climbing instruction until they get up. I fear I would be part of the 20 percent of the 20 percent who still can't climb it.

Falling off a rope over and over can build a pretty mean thirst, especially since I haven't had any water since lunch. The sergeant hands me an official marines water bottle that says, PAIN IS WEAKNESS LEAVING THE BODY. I am pretty sure that "Pain is an important signal your body is giving to immediately stop whatever it is you're doing." I drink a lot, remembering a lesson given to me by comedian Rob Riggle, whom I called for advice before I left. Riggle served as a marine lieutenant colonel in Liberia, Kosovo, and Afghanistan. He said that while The Crucible was the most difficult thing he'd ever done, boot camp is designed to help you succeed. All I needed to do was remember to drink water. "You don't want to be a heat casualty. They'll pull your pants down and put a thermometer up your butt. It's called a silver bullet. Then they throw you in a baby pool full of ice water," he said. This seemed very male: to take advantage of a man who passes out by drawing balls on his forehead or shoving things up his butt and putting him in a baby pool. "No," Riggle said. "It's not a fraternity hazing situation. It's a safety issue."

Riggle also told me that as difficult as it was, he's very glad he served. "On some level every man wants to know if he can hack it. How he would do under fire. Will he cut and run? Will he be so horrified he'll freeze? Will he be able to function? I was proud of myself. When I found myself in dangerous situations, everything faded away. The training from three years ago came back." Not only does he feel like he is capable of more than he thought; he feels safe in any situation. Which sounds to me like one of the best parts of being a man.

Looking to bond with Jewish Alex Rodriguez and Sergeant Edmiston, I make a joke about the silver bullet as I down a quart of water.

"No man wants that," Jewish Alex Rodriguez says.

"Some men do," I said.

"I don't think so. When two men love each other it's a little different."

I had pathetically tried to bond through homophobia yet again, and I had finally been called on it. In fact, unlike all the other man situations, the military avoids homophobic comments. They also avoid calling people curse words. Drill instructors can curse, but they're not supposed to directly call recruits any R-rated term, like a *dumb fuck* or a *useless motherfucker*. They can, however, scream in your face to piss faster. Apparently, politicians were horrified by the cursing, and outlawed it. The rule leads to some incredibly creative, horrifying insults, calling recruits "maggots" and "puke" and, in my particular case, telling them they "climb obstacles like old people fuck."

At the end of the day, I run the bayonet course. Tinny speakers blast the sounds of men being shot as they land in Normandy in the opening scene from *Saving Private Ryan*. I am told to scream as loud as I can while I hide behind logs, crawl under barbed wire, and, at the end, poke my fake bayonet blades into headless dummies dressed, oddly, in marine uniforms.

For the first time today I think: *This is not cool.* This is the job: Learning to murder people. They are not trying to hide this fact. Every exercise, every drill is explicitly designed to train you how to efficiently kill human beings. Not in a difficult-to-correlate way such as by doing accounting for Coca-Cola or marketing for Philip Morris, but directly, in a bayonet-through-the-throat way. Killing other people, for me, is a deal breaker in employment options. If *Time* magazine had said that they were going to give me my own column and an expense account I could abuse on dinners with Cassandra, but I'd have to kill some dudes I didn't know who had never done anything to me, I would have gone to law school.

The next day I wake up at 0530 at the hotel, and drive to the base to join a two-and-a-half-mile run with a bunch of marines, as we carry thirty-pound pig eggs—which are just a bunch of sand wrapped in red duct tape. The armed services spend about a third of all our tax money, but apparently it's not used for equipment, or for coming up with good names for their equipment. After the run, a sergeant whose chest, I'm sure, is bigger than Chesty Puller's, takes me to the confidence course. He asks Sergeant Edmiston if "medical is coming so we can start." Sergeant Edmiston says not to worry, that he's cleared me to use the marine ambulance. They are not starting me off with a lot of confidence.

There are eleven structures, all made out of logs and rope, and they have names such as "The Tough One," "Dirty Name," and "The Arm Stretcher." None, unfortunately, is named "Clever Word Play Game." In the very first one, The Dirty Name, I have to run up to a log five feet above the ground, grab it, pull myself up, stand on it, and then jump up to a log four feet higher. I take a running leap at the first log, grab it, slam my pelvis against it, try to push myself up, and fall onto the dirt, writhing in pain. The sergeants stand behind me, suggesting I jump up and rest my belt buckle against the log as I do a little pushup to raise myself. I am not wearing a belt. They tell me to picture myself wearing a belt. I take another running leap, slam my pelvis into the log, picture myself wearing a belt, flip over the log, and land face-first in the dirt, writhing in pain. The sergeants look disgusted. I do it again, this time really picturing the belt. I jump, slam pelvis, wrap around log, and then slide off into the dirt. Soon, they are going to tell me to stop, that I've shown excellent effort. But no. It's pelvis, dirt; pelvis, dirt; pelvis, dirt. My face is filthy, my pelvis so bruised I couldn't even get a job doing gay S&M porn. I ask to move on. They look at me like I'm too pathetic to even waste their time. I look at them like they could have loaned me their belts.

I assume the other obstacles are going to be even worse, but I manage to climb The Stairway to Heaven, a thirty-foot-high series of logs, simply by not looking down. Still, I accomplish very little else, falling off the steeply angled monkey bars over and over. The sergeants stand to the side, telling me to start at the beginning every time I fall. As my arms get weaker and weaker, and I fall off the bars of this supposed confidence booster sooner and sooner, I wonder if I should even try The Reaper. I wonder if even the military can fix me, or if it's twenty years too late to be starting this.

The last challenge, The Slide for Life, requires climbing up a huge ladder and then getting to the bottom via a thick rope angled at forty-five degrees, over a pool of water. The two sergeants assure me that it's not hard and I won't fall into the water. So I don't empty my pockets. I cross my legs around the rope and lie under it, pulling myself toward the bottom while upside down. Which is going surprisingly well. I am pretty sure I look very cool, like Spider-Man or a cat burglar or at least a plumber. But when the sergeants yell to flip over, I cannot figure out how to do that, and hang from the rope. My monkey-barred arms give out. I fall into the water. As do my phone, my wallet, and my notebook. The ink runs over my notes so badly that I am unable to detail all my failures on the obstacle course. Rest assured: Many other shameful things happened.

But I am, for the first time that day, happy. The water is cool and relaxing, and under the water you cannot hear the yelling. There are, though, some negatives to falling in the water. My phone is destroyed and my squishy shoes are going to make running difficult in the Combat Fitness Test. In fact, this might not be the optimal time to test my combat fitness. The confidence course, the obstacle course—those are group activities in basic training. You keep doing them until you master them, and your fellow recruits help you through them. Combat Fitness is the test you have to pass at the end of boot camp, alone, after thirteen weeks of daily training, to become a marine. And to get promoted once you are a marine. It is not for wet, out-of-shape thirty-nine-year-old journalists who have worked out today more than they have, cumulatively, in the last two months.

I figure we're going to abandon the test due to my being soaked, but two more sergeants arrive who are known to be fitness freaks—and that's by other marines. These are not men who are willing to acknowledge that soaked sneakers are a handicap in timed sprints. I begin by running half a mile on a track, my shoes sloshing, my brain making sure to reserve energy for whatever comes next. Somehow, I do it well under the time limit. I cannot believe how much man stuff I can do. That the hardest part has been getting myself to do it.

I have to do shoulder presses with a thirty-pound ammo can for two minutes, and even with my exhausted arms, I pass the minimum at minute one. Finally, there is this difficult obstacle course where I do push-ups, crawl with my face on the ground, run between cones, throw a fake grenade, and drag a sergeant my size as I weave between cones. I am exhausted, I am wet, I am very bad at throwing a grenade, and I finish well under the maximum time allowed. Although I can't climb a rope and haven't conquered any of the challenges a recruit would face, and am not sure I could deal with any of the yelling, at least on a purely physical fitness basis I am qualified to be a marine who has finished basic training. Without even doing basic training. Or even doing regular-person training by using my gym membership.

I leave the base and drive to a bar where I sit alone and have a burger and the first beer I've ever enjoyed in my life. It actually makes me feel better, like Gatorade. I can understand why Ken wanted one on the roof: Other men's lives are so much more challenging than mine that they enjoy beer.

Back at the hotel, I take off my shirt and get into the shower. There are massive bruises all over my chest, stomach, biceps, and forearms from unsuccessful encounters with logs. For the first time in my life, I have blisters on my fingers. I am even prouder of this than John Lennon was.

I try to go to sleep at 1830, which does not work due to the fact that it is 1830. But I have to wake up at 2345 to attempt to climb The Reaper. I have learned over and over that man stuff requires waking up early, but waking up the day before the day seems like it's breaking some basic rule in the space-time continuum that might erase important historical events such as my sleep.

I get two hours of sleep and drive an hour north to Camp Pendleton, where recruits do The Crucible as the last part of boot camp. At 0200 I join them at their very last task: the nine-mile hike that ends with The Reaper. If the marines can't make me get up this hill with all their war-tested screaming and shaming, I don't know if anything can toughen me up.

Against the night sky, the recruits are a sickly-looking long, moonlit shadow of helmets and guns lined up a mountain, divided in groups with each leader holding a troop flag, like a cross between the Boy Scouts and that statue of Iwo Jima. Their backpacks are weighted down with almost seventy-five pounds of gear, whereas mine has just one thirty-pound pig egg, but it's sitting right in the center of the bottom of my pack, digging into my shoulders painfully. There is not one smile the entire hike. These recruits have not had enough alone time to masturbate in thirteen weeks, and I can feel the tension. They could take out the enemy with their ejaculate.

Ahead of me, the tired, hungry recruits stumble like wounded soldiers. Some are physically pushed onward by their fellow recruits. Some hold guns for others. People fall constantly. One recruit breaks his ankle, which means he'll probably have to redo all fifty-four hours of The Crucible. A drill instructor yells the two least manly directives I'd ever heard: "POWER WALK! FIX YOUR BLOUSE NOW!" I cannot take the backpack digging into my shoulders any longer so, despite Sergeant Edmiston's disappointment, I wimp out and remove the pig egg from my backpack, completely lightening my load. Which makes too much of a difference. I'm no longer hiking. Now I'm just walking.

The Reaper is indeed pretty steep, but mostly these sleep-and-food-deprived recruits have been psyched out for thirteen weeks about it—and, like a metal hanger up the sleeve after a ghost story, they see what they've been told more than what is actually in front of them. A thirty-nine-year-old chaplain does the hike with every recruiting class, and he challenges me to run up the hill. Since I wimped out and got rid of my pig egg earlier, I take him up on it. While running, I hear First Lieutenant Olson yell from the peak, "Joel is a stud." I'm not. I'm a fraud. I should have kept that pig egg.

We reach the top just as the sun rises, which is timed just as perfectly for every recruiting class. Everyone goes to a truck filled with juice and green apples, and they look like Boy Scouts, so young and eager for instruction. They are light-headed with relief, talking for the first time, the near end of boot camp transforming their Heavies into near human beings. The drill instructors make recruits read aloud from several plaques on top of The Reaper. At the sign for Major General Merritt Edson, the plaque recounts how in World War II he received a Medal of Honor for leading eight hundred Marines to withstand an attack of more than twenty-five hundred Japanese at Guadalcanal. During this, 256 of his marines died. The drill instructor gives the lesson behind the story: "Shit happens. Marines come and marines go. But we have a mission."

It isn't all that inspiring, and neither is the part of the Major General Edson story that's not on the plaque. When he was fifty-eight and living in Washington, DC, as the executive director of the National Rifle Association, Edson went into his garage, turned on his car, and killed himself with carbon monoxide poisoning. Being this kind of a man has a price.

At the end of the hike, right before the ceremony in which they'll become actual marines, the recruits are ordered to piss in the forest. This is because in the past, recruits wet their pants during the ceremony. Marine procedure is changed only when something goes wrong. I cannot believe something hasn't gone wrong with those canvas bathing suits yet.

At the ceremony, I sit on some bleachers while tinny *M*A*S*H* speakers play all the hits: Toby Keith's "Courtesy of the Red, White & Blue (The Angry American)," Lee Greenwood's "God Bless the USA," George M. Cohan's "You're a Grand Old Flag," and a John Philip Sousa song I've never heard, though I basically have because they are all the same. The recruits have their backs to the bleachers, so no one can see their faces. Because this is a private moment. When their Heavy hands them the eagle, globe, and anchor emblem that signifies that they're official marines, he gets real close. It's the first time the recruit has heard this drill instructor use a quiet voice, and the Heavy leans into the recruit's ear and croakily whispers a moment when he was proud of him, a moment the recruit probably didn't even think the instructor noticed. When a man who has been yelling at you to eat and shower and piss FASTER! for thirteen weeks shows he cared all along, and you haven't slept much in fifty-four hours, odds are you are going to cry. Which, even from the back, I can see they are.

After the ceremony, the recruits go to the cafeteria to eat a Warrior's Breakfast, which consists of steak, eggs, donuts, waffles, cake, and other foodstuffs that will then come right out of them since they haven't really eaten in fifty-four hours. I ask the new marines what parts of boot camp will change them, and one says he never called anyone "sir" or "ma'am" before, but now that he has, he's not going to stop. I decide to try not to stop, either. It feels awkward, but it also feels respectful, not just of the ma'ams but of myself.

In between forkfuls of eggs, Private Irvin Aguirre, nineteen, tells me he joined the marines, like most of the guys he met, for the discipline. "I was just partying all the time. I would drink a lot," he says. "I used to work with drugs. Not take them. Just sell them. I almost got killed." Right after almost being shot, he signed up for the marines.

The week before Private Aguirre flew from El Paso to San Diego for boot camp, his house was surrounded by police. Not for drugs. His parents had been living in the United States for more than twenty years, but they weren't legal residents, and someone—he doesn't know who—reported them. His mom and dad were sent back to Juarez, which is controlled by drug gangs and is more dangerous than Iraq or Afghanistan. U.S. military aren't even allowed to visit there on vacation. Two of Private Aguirre's cousins and an uncle have already been killed there. His brothers, just thirteen and fourteen, moved in with his aunt. Private Aguirre's income from the military is going to have to support them. "That's what kept me going. My ankle was swollen, but I had to man up. Take responsibility. It just comes to you."

Though I have not been up for fifty-four hours, I cry. Sergeant Edmiston tells Private Aguirre that as soon as he gets home to El

Paso, he has to put on his uniform and go to the office of his U.S. representative and tell that representative to bring his parents home.

Private Aguirre says, "Yes, sir."

Back at home, I am much more interested in news about the war. It doesn't feel nearly as distant, and not just because I finally met some men in the military. I touch my fuzzy head and think that, if I were absolutely forced to be in Afghanistan, I could vaguely imagine doing what they're doing after thirteen weeks of boot camp. The marines made me feel that a little bit of suffering isn't a big deal; I could almost see how, in some situations, pain might indeed be weakness leaving the body. I feel that if I committed myself to the goal, I could run a marathon. I could get a tattoo. I could fight Randy Couture. I could do lots of things I have no interest in doing.

But I faced only physical tests. And I did them alone. I want to see if I can do something much harder: submerge my ego. I may be bad at suffering, but I'm really bad at joining a group. I need to make sarcastic comments, rebel, feel special. I cannot do what Warren Sapp told me was so great about football: sacrificing yourself for the team's goal. But if Warren Sapp, a man who puts his family crest on everything he owns, can stop thinking about himself, maybe I can, too. So I'm going to join an army troop at boot camp without telling them I'm not a real recruit, and see if I can not only make it through the challenges they face, but also fit in. I am counting on this shaved-head thing to make me look young enough to make this convincing.

In addition to bunking with the troops, I will also fire a tank, which was a major part of General Hertling's sales pitch in trying to get me to visit the army over the other military branches. General Hertling is extremely excited about having me fire a tank, which the army has never let any journalist do. In fact, civilians haven't been allowed to touch any powerful equipment since 2001, when a sportswriter and a CEO were allowed to operate controls while the USS *Greenville* submarine showed off a super-fast surfacing maneuver off the coast of Oahu. When it reached the surface, the sub's rudder sliced a Japanese fishing boat in half, killing nine crew members, four of whom were high school students. Secretary of Defense Donald Rumsfeld made a rule about not allowing civilians to do stupid stuff like that anymore, but Rumsfeld is gone and General Hertling wants me to fire a tank. Politically, I am much more aligned with General Hertling's "let civilians do stupid stuff" philosophy. But personally, I am nervous about the tank. I don't want to accidentally destroy anything. I closed my eyes the first time I fired Matt's shotgun. I don't know what I'll do if I'm trapped in a claustrophobic tank, dealing with complicated tools in a stressful situation. I know the army doesn't want me to get injured, but, historically, making sure no one gets hurt isn't the top concern of any military.

I get a briefing of what I'll be doing at boot camp, from Major Chris Mugavero. During our phone conversation, I tell him that I'm worried about firing the tank, and am not sure that doing it is really necessary for my goal of experiencing boot camp, since no one fires a tank at boot camp. He says the only thing I need to be worried about in firing a tank is being disappointed by everything in my life after that. "You'll never want to shoot anything again after this. It will all seem like bullshit to you," he says. "It's the best thing ever."

"What should I do right after I finish shooting it?" I ask.

"You'll want to be with a woman," he says.

I get the feeling he means even more than I normally want to be with a woman. This is the first time I have ever understood the connection between pillaging and raping.

Not everyone in the army can be a tanker. When you enlist in the military you have to take a multiple-choice test called the Armed Services Vocational Aptitude Battery (ASVAB). The better your score, the more jobs you can choose from. I have always been very good at multiple-choice tests and am working very hard right now not to tell you what I got on the SATs, though it does seem relevant to the story. So a 1480 out of 1600.

But the ASVAB is like the man SATs. I take a practice version online, and even the basic math questions are put in man terms:

Stan bought a monster truck for $2,000 down and payments of $450 a month for five years. What's the total cost of the monster truck?

But it isn't just man math and man vocabulary. There are sections on "electronics," "mechanical comprehension," "automotive and shop," and "assembling objects." There are questions such as "How many diodes should you expect in a bridge rectifier?," "Radar can operate at frequencies as high as…," and "The safest way to make a hole in sheet metal is…" There is no space to write the answer: "Not to make a hole in sheet metal."

I do not do well. I get 93 percent right in paragraph comprehension, but 68 correct in auto and shop and just 40 in electronics. This is nowhere near as good as a 1480 on the SATs, which is the score I got.

I am not surprised that I'm not fit for the army. When the United States invaded Iraq in 2003, Jim Kelly, the editor of *Time* magazine, stopped me in the hall and asked if I wanted to be embedded. I thought Jim was hitting on me. When I finally asked him what "embedded" meant, he and a bunch of other editors laughed at the punch line to their perfect joke. I do not think Jim tousled my hair, but it felt like he tousled my hair. I was determined to show him up and get embedded. Then he finally told me what embedded meant and I tousled my own hair.

Despite my 70 in technical comprehension, a three-star general had already promised to let me fire a tank. So I fly to Louisville, Kentucky, to go to Fort Knox, where I check in at the hotel on the base, which costs only fifty dollars and has no taxes at all, thus making it the best hotel I've ever stayed in. But I am nervous and have jet lag and can't fall asleep until nearly 0200. Which is a problem, because I have to wake up at 0445.

I put on army recruit workout clothes, and at exactly 0500 Major Mugavero, the man who told me I'm going to want to be with a woman after I fire the tank, picks me up. He drives me to a building where I join a group of almost two hundred new recruits who showed up late the night before and haven't gone to sleep at all. Then Major Mugavero leaves, and I'm on my own. We line up outside the Copple Reception Center and are led individually into a small, closed room with a garbage chute where we are given the opportunity to throw out our "amnesty" items. Among the many things listed that we cannot have at boot camp are three that make me think the sign hasn't been updated in quite some time: snuff, coke spoons, and blackjacks.

After disposing of our snuff, coke spoons, and blackjacks, we sit in a classroom with little high school desks. The guy next to me is wearing socks and boat shoes. I am not sure how you decide to go to boot camp in boat shoes, but if for some reason I really do have to enlist, he's going to be my goofy army sidekick.

There are nearly two hours of human resource lectures about payment schedules, insurance for dependents, and superior complaint procedures. Guys falling asleep are sent to stand in the back against the wall, and pretty soon the wall is lined with bodies. We get a lecture from Captain Iams about how awesome the U.S. Army is and how, due to some technicalities that are hard to follow, we're undefeated.

We are taught to say "yes, sir" and "yes, Drill Sergeant." We're also supposed to say "Hooah" a lot, which means "yes," "macho," "cool," "awesome," and "I don't know what to say." It's "shalom" for men.

The tone seems more mellow and reasonable than the marines. Captain Iams says: "This is not the Boy Scouts. If you wanted to sell Girl Scout cookies, you should have stayed at home." What he's saying is that this is Man Scouts, and if I struggled to get my first Boy Scout badge just a year ago, I am probably not ready for this. Though possibly more so than the guy in boat shoes.

Captain Iams tells us that the army doesn't permit horseplay. Which I think is a very fair army rule, though not one I would have expected him to have to tell us. He says we are allowed to have cell phones, at certain times. This is shocking. Aren't they supposed to read your letters and black out the interesting parts? My phone gets confiscated for security reasons every time I go to a movie screening, but the army is letting people update their Facebook pages with "These M16s sure do jam a lot!"

We should never, Captain Iams says, be separated from our "battle buddy," a concept that works a lot like the kindergarten "buddy" system except with the word *battle* in front of it. I assume no soldier actually ever refers to someone else as a "battle buddy" other than in the sentence "Dude, I can't believe that captain guy wanted me to call you a battle buddy."

Captain Iams gives us the "Moment of Truth" where we can walk outside and tell him anything we hid from our recruiter: a police record, medical problems, psychological history. No one takes him up on his offer. Which he repeats. Ten people walk out. He repeats the offer again. Three more people leave.

I look around at my fellow recruits, who are eighteen, zit-ridden, and nervous. "Why you looking around, little warrior? You should be studying," says Sergeant Viranti, pointing to the booklet I've been given.

"Yes, sir," I say.

"I am not a sir."

"Yes, Drill Sergeant."

We line up against a wall, silently waiting to get a haircut, which I don't really need because I just got my marines haircut. Before my dad reported for boot camp, he got his head shaved too, so they'd know he was prepared. I don't feel like my head stubble is giving me that same advantage. I still have to go the barbershop, where whatever I've got left on my head is Flowbee'd away in seconds.

Afterward, I'm called a "special little warrior" and taken out of the group to a separate room to meet Captain Michael Fritz, a handsome, tall man who wears an army beret in a way that makes it seem okay to wear a beret. He does not shake my hand and welcome me to the army and talk about horseplay. He silently points me toward two drill sergeants, neither of whom wants me to reveal his real name since they serve overseas and don't want the enemy to know anything about them. One, whom I'll call Sergeant Feldman, looks like a buffed-out Corey Feldman, and the other, whom I'll call Sergeant Richie, is black and mustachioed but otherwise looks nothing like Lionel Richie, but that's what you get when you don't let a writer use your real name.

Sergeant Feldman and Sergeant Richie are very intense, handing me a lot of complicated pieces of sand-colored-camouflage army uniform, telling me to put them on in specific, complicated ways, and pointing me to a room behind a closed door to change. The army, it seems, is less comfortable with nudity than the marines. I am thirty seconds into putting all this complicated gear on when Sergeant Richie yells, "It should not be taking this long to put boots on!" When I come out, he's disgusted at how I'm not standing at attention. And how sloppy my bootlaces are. And the angle of my cap. And the fact that I can't get Captain and Sergeant and Sir straight. I am criticized for twenty things and I can't fix one fast enough before the next is pointed out. I can't even dress myself properly. Sergeant Richie says all this in an unsmiling, inhuman way that feels like we're about to fight. The other two men are also not just unsympathetic, but hostile. I cannot believe how stressful it is to be this powerless. I am already sweating through my gear.

We walk to a van in silence and Sergeant Richie orders me to eat a Meal Ready to Eat—these vacuum-sealed boxes of food that will last three years, can withstand temperatures of 120 degrees, and are unharmed when dropped out of a helicopter at a hundred feet. I am not at all hungry, but I am too scared not to do what I'm told, so I eat this cold, goopy chicken fajita that I don't have time to heat up with the technology that involves a chemical brilliantly designed to create a smell that makes you not want to eat. I stand in the ninety-degree heat next to a bunch of tanks while the soldiers who work with them tell me how powerful they are. But I can't listen. I'm trying too hard to remember which ones to call Sir, which to call Drill Sergeant, which to call Captain, and to stand at attention, and it starts to get bright, like I'm staring directly at that sun, which must be right in my face because all I can see is white and I get this dizzy feeling that I'm sure will pass...

I am sitting against a tree trunk. I do not remember deciding to do this. I don't know why I was ordered to do this, or if I'm doing it correctly.

I'm told that I did not sit down by a tree. I fainted. I fainted and was caught and put down here. I have never fainted in my life. I have been in the army for three hours and I have not done any physical activity, and I have fainted. I am not simply as fragile as I was as a kid. I've grown even more brittle from a too-soft life. I am humiliated. I cannot figure out why these men standing above me are not urinating on me.

They do something similar. The sergeants throw cold water over my head and down my shirt and give me Pedialyte, which, I know from recent experience, is what you give infants when they're sick. They bring me inside to a room with a fan and I can't stop shivering. Then I remember my talk with Rob Riggle: the silver bullet. I scan the room in panic for a baby pool and an anal thermometer. Luckily, I don't see them.

I keep apologizing for the fainting, but they tell me not to feel bad, that I'd locked my knees, which causes lots of soldiers to faint. But I know that's not it. It was the stress. I was freaking out. I am thirty-nine, I signed up to be a fake soldier for three days, and I couldn't handle it for three hours.

One thought does penetrate my humiliation: My dad might actually be a psycho. My dad volunteered in the National Guard when he was twenty-four, during the Vietnam War, right after getting a letter telling him to report to his army recruiter because he was being drafted. After basic training, when he was training to be an artilleryman, he got in a fight with his sergeant. He was writing a letter home to his parents and his sergeant grabbed it and started reading it out loud, making fun of it. So my dad grabbed it back, the sergeant pushed my dad, and my dad punched the sergeant in the face. This part of the story always seemed a bit extreme to me, since it involved punching someone in the face. But now that I've met sergeants, and fainted around sergeants, I realize this was full-on psychotic. No one I talked to has ever heard of a private punching a sergeant. Punching a sergeant in the face is as insane as being a Soviet citizen in a May Day parade and punching Joseph Stalin in the face.

"I felt I was superior to all these sergeants who were yelling at people. They were misfits, basically," my dad told me. "I would laugh. It was funny to me. These were a bunch of low-life hillbillies yelling at me to eat fast. Yeah, I'm going to eat fast. You know when there's a real threat and when there's a bunch of guys trying to act tough. You didn't have a bunch of Harvard graduates yelling at you." This is where my father and I see life differently. If a bunch of Harvard grads were yelling at me to eat faster, I wouldn't be scared. Harvard grads, for the most part, are not known as a face-hitting bunch. They're more likely to mock me years later in a brief reference on *The Simpsons*. Low-life hillbillies, however, are face hitters.

My dad was given Article 15 from the Uniform Code of Military Justice, in which he had to sign a piece of paper and let his commander decide his fate, which is typically fourteen days of punishment and restrictions, and a loss of one week of pay. But my dad refused to sign the paper. Which meant he'd get a court-martial trial. "I said, 'Fine. Court-martial me.' I knew I could make a monkey of these guys on the stand."

They didn't want to deal with the hassle of a court-martial, so instead the drill sergeant just made my dad spend his nights moving sand from one pile to another with a spoon for a week. Which my dad pretended to like. "When the guys would sit down to rest, I would stand. Because I wanted to give it to the sergeants. They would hand me water, I would say that I didn't need water. They would call me 'New Yorker,' which was code for 'Jew.' They had images in their mind I wanted to change."

Whatever my dad accomplished in fixing Jewish stereotypes within the U.S. Army, I had just destroyed. I hear the sergeants talking about bringing me to the hospital, which is what they would do if I were a real recruit who fainted. Apparently, after I fainted, I failed to answer some basic questions. Which I do not remember, but might have been about electronics or auto and shop, which would explain why I didn't answer them. They are going to scrap the entire plan of having me do boot camp, and just have me watch the recruits. I can't let them do this. After giving up on making myself a man, I can't fail on letting other people make me one. I'll never be able to tell Laszlo he can do anything, that he can overcome his genetic weakness. Because it will mean he can't. I know that according to the briefing I got this morning, no one has ever taken on the U.S. military and won, but I'm going to try.

So even though I am nauseated and dizzy and shivering, I insist I'm fine. I can run five miles right now, I tell them, even though I know I can't. But I will if I have to. I try to look as tough as a man can while sipping Pedialyte through a tiny straw.

After medics take my blood pressure, Captain Fritz looks in my eyes, which want to open doll-wide to beg him to let me stay, but I force them cowboy tight.

Captain Fritz decides I can try boot camp, but says that

Sergeant Feldman and Sergeant Richie are going to drop the drill sergeant act. Which, to be honest, is more than okay with me. In fact, my main advice to recruits is to faint as soon as you possibly can. Just find a sunny spot, lock your knees, start thinking about how hard this is going to be, and the next thing you know it's all Pedialyte and fans and people worrying about you.

Once the sergeants drop the drilling, I am able to get to know them as people instead of as mean robots that think I suck at everything. I can now see that Sergeant Feldman, who had scared me so much, is five foot seven. Meanness adds four to five inches to your height. Even though he looks older than me, he's only twenty-seven. "I feel older than a lot of people, sadly. I refer to my soldiers as kids," he says. He's served in Iraq three times, and is going back in another month, and can't wait. "By the second time, it's more exciting than terrifying," he says. "Everything here is pretty flat after being there." He's not sure what he's going to do when the wars are over. "I'll feel a little displaced," he says.

I correctly guess the kind of kid that Sergeant Feldman was: an Eagle Scout who was a social outcast in high school, sitting in the back of the room reading Jane's military manuals and *Soldier of Fortune* magazine. "I was one of those guys who thought that pulling a trigger would make me a man," he says. "I was surprised how easy it was. But I found out there were guys who wanted to shoot people just to shoot people and that disgusted me."

I am not in the mood for lunch. I am in the mood for drinking Pedialyte and having my mom turn the television to *The Price Is Right*. It is over ninety degrees, and I am wearing a T-shirt, a thick long-sleeved shirt over it, long pants, boots, and a cap. Sweat pours down my face. I'm just trying to stay upright. At the chow hall I join a group of new recruits in a snaking line against the wall. Ten seconds later Sergeant Feldman looks at a recruit in the middle of the room: "Why are you looking at me? If you're looking at me, you're done eating!" I follow the recruit in front of me to a bench at a long table. There is a tiny bit of quiet talking among the recruits, which makes the place seem much more human than the marines' chow hall. I silently eat and watch the guy next to me start his meal with chocolate cake and finish it with two more pieces of chocolate cake. He is clearly a little excited to be away from home. Eventually the chocolate-cake eater leaves, and I finish. One of the recruits stops me and points to the chocolate-cake eater's tray, which he left behind. "That's your battle buddy's tray right there," he says. I cannot believe he is really using the term *battle buddy*. I quietly pick up the two trays and put them away.

After lunch Sergeant Feldman is eager to show me the huge murals recruits paint on their barracks walls. They are the kind of art that you don't see anymore now that 1980s heavy-metal records aren't made. Skeletons ride horses, carry scythes, plant tattered flags, stand on piles of dead bodies, and hold up severed heads. Fire rages below from devils' pitchforks. I don't see one mural of a unicorn prancing through flowers, though I think that would make you the most badass platoon of all.

Back in the van, we drive by a movie theater on the base, which is showing *Ramona and Beezus*, the poster for which has a little girl leaving finger-paint hands on her older sister's shirt. This does not seem like hooah material. The sergeants and Captain Fritz, however, tell me that they have to walk out of movies that have violent scenes since they bring back memories from Iraq. If Ramona beats the crap out of Beezus for getting paint on her shirt, a lot of M16s might go off in the theater.

Sergeant Richie has been to Iraq three times and Afghanistan once. When he's back at home, he gets night sweats and sometimes starts kicking his wife violently in his sleep. When he does, she has to get out of the bed and call him "Sergeant Richie" to wake him up. If she uses his first name, or ever touches him while he's sleeping, he'll attack her. Still, he's pissed about being stuck at Fort Knox another few months, teaching drill sergeant training school instead of going overseas. "You get used to some crazy shit. You build up a tolerance. After a while, they're shooting at you and you're just annoyed. You're like, 'Are you kidding me? After what happened last time to you? Are you kidding me?'"

Unlike Captain Fritz and Sergeant Feldman, Sergeant Richie wasn't an Eagle Scout. He was in a gang in Los Angeles and eventually got caught breaking and entering. He chose the army over jail. It's hard to imagine that he was that guy. It's not that the army softened him up, but it did smooth him out. So much so that when I ask him if he had to shoot anyone overseas, he politely informs me that I should never ask a soldier if he's shot anyone.

What Sergeant Richie will tell me is that it is harder commanding other people to shoot than to do it yourself. He was in charge of a checkpoint in Iraq, and locals would drive up after curfew, sometimes not stopping even when they were waved down. Iraqis, who felt like we hated their freedom, liked to test the Americans. Sergeant Richie had to decide if they were driving a car bomb into his base or if they were just civilians who weren't into following directions. One time, he was torn about whether to order his men to shoot at a car speeding toward them, refusing their commands to stop or even slow down. It could easily have been a suicide bomber. Or a carful of armed insurgents. It turned out to be a father rushing his daughter to the hospital. "I'll be honest with you, brother: 90 percent of us don't do it for country or flag," he says. "We do it for the rush. Same reason people ride motorcycles. It's addictive."

I join a platoon near the end of their thirteen weeks of basic training. The sergeants tell the recruits that I got sick at the end of my training and had to leave my troop and finish with them. We're about to do the obstacle course, which, I'm not surprised to discover, consists of a lot of logs. The sergeants demonstrate how to run each obstacle: First the sergeant does it the right way, and then he does it the wrong way, which involves lots of tripping and running into logs with his groin. There is a very low bar for comedy in the army.

The obstacles are easier than the ones on the marine course, and the only ropes in the army are for swinging, not climbing, which is reason enough to join the army over the marines. There are also other differences: We are asked what we thought about the obstacles and what we learned from them. It's a little more *Free to Be You and Me* here. "We turned down the volume of drill sergeants," Sergeant Richie tells me about some recent changes. "The marines create robots. We create thinkers."

Still, army boot camp is stressful. My fainting freak-out, while totally pathetic, wasn't that unusual for a recruit. "You have to learn how to deal with stress," Private Adam Yubre says as we sit on bleachers waiting to start the obstacle course. "The first couple weeks, a lot of people were crying. But now, not so much."

Though I am technically old enough to be most of the recruits' father, I am not technically too old to join the army. In 2006 the army increased its maximum enlistment age to forty-two—it had been thirty-five until 2005—and almost every platoon has a guy around forty. One guy in this platoon is thirty-nine, and he seems like he is having an easier time than most other guys.

The troop's sergeant splits us into groups and puts me with the strongest one, which is not the way I would have gone with a guy who fainted looking at tanks. I would have put me with the fainter-types, so that when we got killed by the enemy, our troop could stop carrying around Pedialyte. But instead I'm with the star athletes of the troop, flying through the obstacles. I am able to do things I never thought I could: jumping over logs, pulling myself under logs, balancing as I walk on logs, touching logs without getting a splinter. I push soldiers over log walls, and hoist them up log towers.

Afterward, Captain Fritz and the two sergeants take me for a four-mile hike, which includes a hill called Motherfucker, which really isn't any worse than the hike Cassandra and I do from our house that leads right up to near the HOLLYWOOD sign. Our hike is only called "Bronson Canyon," but I'm thinking of asking the LA City Council to rename it "Motherfucker." I think it will do a lot for tourism.

I feel surprisingly great. My new boots, though, are tearing my feet up; my heels have turned into bloody onion skin, peeled away in layers.

We sit outside on the grass and eat a meal the sergeants had gotten to go from the chow hall. I'm pretty sure it's spaghetti and meatballs, but they insist it's yakisoba. It seems weird that Congress calls french fries "Freedom Fries" while the army calls spaghetti and meatballs "yakisoba." I like to believe that the Japanese army calls sushi "fillet-o-raw-fish."

I put on a helmet and a bulletproof vest with two metal plate inserts. The vest is only 16.4 pounds, but it is pulling at my shoulders, making me hot and uncomfortable and, while I'm not stupid enough to say it, a little faintish. I don't know how soldiers can possibly wear this for extended periods, in the Iraqi summer. I need to get it off, but Sergeant Richie tells me that I'll get used to it. He wore his all day in the Iraqi heat.

We are waiting for it to get completely dark so we can do the Night Infiltration Course, which is called NIC at Night. They seem to really want to stress that "night" part. Recruits run this exercise one week before graduation as their last big training event. I join recruits sitting on bleachers and get briefed. Like everything I've done at Fort Knox, there is a sign with rules, which always includes: (1) Don't mess with any animals; (2) If you see any ammunition shells, don't touch them. I did not realize these were rules that need to be put on a sign since they came engraved in my genetic makeup.

We are supposed to low crawl on our stomachs through dirt

toward two towers. On the top of each tower, men will fire machine guns just over our heads. It is very important, therefore, that we don't stand up. While I have no intention of standing up, I am pretty sure that they will actually shoot blanks, and are just trying to scare us. But Captain Fritz insists they're real bullets, and promises he'll tell me more about it afterward. What he'll tell me later is that when he did the exercise during his basic training, the following happened to a guy near him due to a faultily secured machine gun, as reported by the *Orlando Sentinel*:

DECEMBER 05, 2003

FORT JACKSON, S.C.—The Army has suspended training exercises at night that use live ammunition after a soldier was shot and killed earlier this week. Pvt. Joseph Jurewic, 18, of Altamonte Springs is the first soldier to die during training at Night Infiltration Course since it was opened at Fort Jackson 20 years ago, the Army said.

Speakers blast the Muslim call to prayers into the darkness. This seems a bit racist, largely because it is. But as beautiful as the Muslim call to prayers is, even if you were a devout Shiite, it will freak you out when it is blasted right before someone shoots machine guns at you.

The deejay then mixes the call to prayers with sounds of people screaming. Captain Fritz and I stand in a ditch, at which point I realize just how counter-instinctual it is to move toward machine-gun fire.

We lie down and, with one hand on our rifles, pull ourselves forward with our elbows, dragging our cheeks through the dirt. Bullets fly above, every fifth one an orange tracer bullet allowing us—and hopefully the person shooting—to see just how close we are. We climb under barbed wire and around fences enclosing piles of TNT that explode inches from our faces. Every so often, a flare lights the sky and we have to freeze so the enemy can't see our movement, which is a nice break, since dragging your cheek through the dirt is exhausting.

I don't expect this sense of calm. It's beautiful, this sudden silence, the sky lit orange, time stopped. I feel very awake and super-clear, waiting for the feet of the recruit in front of me to proceed so I can move on. I have never been this aware of my surroundings, even though I can barely see. I tell Captain Fritz to go around the TNT fence, to which he says "Roger." It is totally, illogically fun. Part of happiness is being fully present, thinking of nothing else. That feeling is so strong right now that it trumps the unpleasantness of people shooting machine guns at me.

We reach the machine-gun towers, but I am not taking any chances and refuse to stand until many yards later, when someone pulls me up. Still, I feel pretty manly. Until a group of medics I have never met appears in the dark, kneels in front of me, and starts talking to me about my fainting. The entire U.S. Army, I'm pretty sure, knows about the guy who faints when he looks at tanks. I could rescue a camp of POWs and as I led them to safety, they would make fun of me for fainting three hours into fake boot camp.

But I still feel hyper-alert from the Night Infiltration Course. I know it's not a Disney ride, but I want to do it again. I think about what Tom, the twenty-five-year-old firefighter who decided not to be a writer, told me: "I want to stop thinking about stuff and start doing stuff." I don't know if crawling through dirt while being shot at is a form of meditation or the opposite of meditation, but it's waking my brain. I'm definitely doing stuff. And even more thrillingly, not thinking about stuff.

Instead of sleeping in the barracks with the 1980s heavy-metal murals, Captain Fritz and I go to a tent, which is part of a giant training course recruits live in for their final four days. It's a fenced-in area with guard towers and tents that mimics an overseas base, particularly, in my opinion, the *M*A*S*H* 4077th. Captain Fritz snaps a chemlight so we can get ready for cot, and I appreciate how the army gives things man names, like calling glowsticks "chemlights." This theory falls apart minutes later when Captain Fritz pulls out an official army poncho liner that he uses for a blanket, which I think he calls a woobie. It is, in fact, officially called a woobie.

We use our canteens to brush our teeth outside our tent, and then lie down on our cots and talk for a while, almost like it's a sleepover. Of all the real traditional men I've met—from which I am excluding Shawn Green and Matt Nadel—Captain Fritz is my favorite. He's calm, happy, curious, brave, has a great attitude, isn't judgmental, and enjoys life; he's exactly the kind of guy you want to be stuck with in a war. He doesn't have just that Buddhist contentment with wherever he is, but a drive to enjoy his situation no matter what it is. Not much, I think, can get Captain Fritz down. He wears his manliness lightly. It's how I'd like to be.

Captain Fritz looks like a smarter, less skinny Matthew McConaughey, and he does all the man stuff: hunting, home repair, car rebuilding, fishing. He goes to Bible study group every Saturday by the lake with some male buddies. The surprising part is that he didn't grow up around this lifestyle. He grew up in Southern California, went to college in Napa, and, while he was there, signed up for officer training school. His parents tried to talk him out of it, but he'd known joining the army was what he wanted to do since he was a kid. And, unlike nearly every other kid who feels that but doesn't grow up in a military family or town, Captain Fritz actually did it. "I was a backyard commando as a kid. From the moment I can remember, three, four years old, I wanted to join the military," he says.

Captain Fritz gives me a rifle. A real one. An M16, which is unloaded, but still makes me nervous. Like the recruits and soldiers, I am not allowed to go anywhere without my gun, even when

I go to the Porta-Potty. I can also never look sloppy, so a bathroom trip—from a tent to a Porta-Potty, with no women within miles—requires getting fully dressed, tucking my pants into my boots, and putting on my hat at the perfect army angle.

I'll feel much better tomorrow, Captain Fritz tells me, since we don't have to wake up until 0400, thereby getting a solid four hours of sleep. I laugh. Which confuses Captain Fritz. He did not mean this as a joke. It turns out we'll actually get a little less than four hours, since as soon as we get in our cots, a sergeant explodes a fake grenade right next to our tent and yells, "Welcome to the army!" It really does make me feel welcome. I finally get what Sparky at the firehouse was trying to tell me with his complaints about not being allowed to haze firefighter recruits anymore: Hazing can be more authentically warm than the way girls fake hug. These guys are busy, and yet they put some effort into scaring the crap out of me. I feel, at least a little bit, like I earned some inclusion.

At 0400 we get up, brush our teeth, and get picked up by Sergeant Feldman in a van. I cannot go out in my uniform with even the minuscule bit of stubble I grow, so I join Captain Fritz in shaving in the reflection of the van's windows. Inside the vehicle Sergeant Feldman tells me to "lean your M16 up behind the driver's seat." Leo Zamboni would totally fail Sergeant Feldman on his hunter safety test. We join a platoon of recruits exercising in the dark, doing weird little yoga drills mixed with football-like sprint drills. It is not at all like the rigorous workout you get when you sign up for one of those boot camp workouts at your gym. General Hertling—the one who wants me to shoot a tank—redid the recruit physical training schedule in 2010, mostly because all the overweight, video-game-playing recruits couldn't handle the sit-ups, push-ups, and running. This was after a bunch of retired generals and admirals wrote a report ingeniously titled "Too Fat to Fight," which showed that between 1995 and 2008, the percentage of potential recruits who failed their physicals because they were overweight rose by 70 percent.

So we do 60/120s, in which we sprint for one minute and then walk for two minutes. Then we stretch in silence under the bright stars. It's beautiful. I've had four hours of sleep, I'm in the army, and, for some reason, I'm happy.

At the Team Development Course, I join a group of recruits who just finished their first three days, all of them in classes. This is the first time they've actually been asked to do something. I get the feeling none of them has fainted yet.

Their first exercise is a series of simple tasks with tricks you have to figure out: using logs to walk over water when there aren't enough logs to get across. (You pick them up and move them as you go.) They give you ten minutes to strategize and forty minutes to do it.

As soon as the strategizing time starts, the recruits commence yelling at one another. Nobody is in charge, nobody is nice, and nobody can keep his cool. I can't believe how eager, intense, and stupid they are. I have no interest in getting involved in this kind of chaos. Captain Fritz is disappointed, saying that a thirty-nine-year-old with a Stanford degree could help them solve this puzzle. But I don't want to yell with a bunch of morons. He calls this a lack of leadership. I call it not wasting my energy. Captain Fritz calls that a lack of leadership, too.

I can't believe that in less than thirteen weeks, this troop will evolve into the great group of guys who brought me over the obstacle course yesterday. My experiences with job training teach me that thirteen weeks transforms you from a guy who isn't sure what to order in the cafeteria into a guy who knows it's better just to order lunch from a restaurant.

I don't want to let Captain Fritz down. So for our last challenge, I think about what Wiggles would do if forced to lead these misfits instead of his awesome Master Exploders: I calmly pretend to listen to their ideas, as if we had all the time in the world and no chance of failure. I show them how to crawl upside down on a rope tied between two trees, which I'd learned in the marines the hard way, by destroying my cell phone. I send the loudest guys first to get rid of them. Thanks partially to me, we almost finish that task in time.

Still, after an hour of listening to teenagers yell at one another, I'm happy to leave this troop. Sergeant Feldman takes me to the middle of a forest so we can learn land navigation. I calculate that I take sixty-seven steps to walk one hundred meters, get a compass, and then go into the woods to find a flag that I'm given coordinates for. But there are a lot of butterflies. Like more butterflies than I have seen in butterfly sanctuaries. So eventually Sergeant Feldman and I have a long talk about butterflies and how pretty they are. Instead of the army manning me up, I am de-manning the army.

What I don't notice is that, possibly because I haven't tucked my pants as tightly into my boots as I was instructed, I am getting attacked by chiggers. So a few days from now I'll wind up with these little welts all over the lower half of my body, especially my ankles and waist where they snuck into my pants. Cassandra will panic that they are bedbug bites. I will try to reassure her that they are probably shingles from the stress and lack of sleep in the army, and she will lovingly look at me and say, "I hope to God you have shingles." But she will still fear the bedbugs, and force me to go see my LA doctor, who will have no idea what they are and give me a shot of steroids in my ass for no reason. After meeting a guy from Kentucky weeks later, I will learn that the welts are from chiggers, which are the larval stage of the trombiculid mites, which jump from grass to your body, where they live for three to five days, eating your skin, before leaving. They will cause me to itch a little, but, far more annoyingly, they will cause me to constantly yell "Chigger, please!"

But right now, I am blessedly ignorant of the larvae burying themselves in my skin. Instead, as we get deep into the butterfly-less regions of the forest, I feel that same sense of boredom I felt in the woods hunting with Matt. So after failing to find the flag, I'm pretty glad to leave the forest and head to a fake Middle Eastern city the army built at Fort Knox. Though I didn't get to see it, the marines spent twenty-three million dollars building two fake cities, Khalidiyah and Wadi al Sahara, which are populated by more than 250 actors who are really from Iraq. The army's version of a fake Middle Eastern city isn't quite as good, more like visiting the Eiffel Tower at the Paris casino in Las Vegas, only the barren, Afghani-town version, which, frankly, should be easier to re-create.

Before hitting the army's fake Arab town, I get a tour of a museum of Improvised Explosive Devices (IEDs), the roadside bombs that are U.S. soldiers' greatest danger in Afghanistan. First Lieutenant Matthew Robey, a thirty-two-year-old, slightly nerdy guy in glasses, shows me all the different devices—each a techno-logical improvement to counter the army's method of discovering and dismantling the previous version. There are bombs that look just like rocks, ones that are camouflaged into guardrails, ones that look just like a brick in a wall. Lieutenant Robey seems impressed by the enemy's ingenuity, almost as if he enjoys the game of figur-ing out how not to be killed. When I ask if any part of him respects the insurgents' relentless technological one-upmanship, he says that he completely does, even though some of these IEDs have almost killed him. In fact, he says that if someone invaded his hometown, he'd be building them, too. He does not at any point say that the bomb makers "hate freedom."

I push a cartridge of blanks into my M16 and get in a Humvee. We drive in a convoy of three trucks for about four blocks, before our lead Humvee is hit by a little explosion from a fake road bomb. It takes me a surprisingly long time to figure out how the Humvee door handle works. But once I manage to get out, I go right to a fake-injured soldier and join Captain Fritz in carrying him to the back of our Humvee.

"How does it look?" the fake-injured soldier says as I tie a tourniquet on his arm. "Am I going to make it?"

"You're fine. It looks fine. It's fine," I say. "Fine. Fine." My assurances would kill a man who simply had chiggers.

Back in our tent that night, Captain Fritz gets a text about a friend at a military hospital in Texas. He just got a leg amputated after catching shrapnel in Iraq that weekend and will probably lose the other one in a few days. Captain Fritz is going to fly to Texas to visit him this weekend. It makes the military feel much more real than bullets flying over my head. I've never heard anyone talk about a tragedy without looking for sympathy, but Captain Fritz presents it plainly. He doesn't think about whether the trip to Texas will be difficult, unpleasant, or depressing. It's not something he thinks about. It's just what he's going to do.

I fall asleep at 2200. At 2300 Captain Fritz wakes me up and shows me an AK47 and a rocket-propelled grenade launcher he brought from his collection at home. This seems like a pretty weird thing to collect. I'm more of a leave-work-at-work kind of guy. I suspect I'd be even more so if my work were blowing other people up with rocket-propelled grenade launchers.

But this is not why Captain Fritz woke me. It's my shift to stand guard on one of the towers. I straighten my cap, grab my rifle and box of blanks, and climb a ladder to the top of the tower where I join two recruits. We aren't staring at the dark forest for long when I get completely convinced that I see people moving. Everyone points their weapons, and after fifteen minutes I concede that all I see is swaying leaves. I make a nervous soldier.

Half an hour later there is some movement in the woods, nowhere near where I saw it. A bunch of smoke bombs go off, and I go through my blanks in no time. Our troops leave base to run into the forest, which I think is a really dubious decision, since the forest has people with smoke bombs in it. I try to figure out how to call in a fake air strike.

Captain Fritz joins me in the tower, and we watch our troop exchange a lot of friendly fire, in which, according to the officers who decide who got fake shot, a lot of our guys kill one another, even though they've lined up correctly. It is pure fake chaos out there.

After a while Captain Fritz and I head back to the tent, agreeing that if anyone uses actual tear gas, we are taking off. Though he does not specify where, I am hoping for a charming bed-and-breakfast. We talk in our cots and I get an insane thought: I don't want to leave tomorrow. Being in boot camp is exciting, with new things all the time and a feeling of accomplishment. Time is moving slowly in a wonderful way. I like being outside. At home I sleep more and feel less awake. I can almost see why people would sign up for this. Again, except for the killing part.

In the morning Captain Fritz does a very un-Captain-Fritz thing and decides we should sleep in, skipping the hike. We stay in until 0430, racking up more than three hours of sleep. We are army slackers.

Despite sleeping late, it's still pitch-black when we head to the army's combatives training. Like the marines, the army has switched their fighting style to mixed marital arts, though, unlike the marines, their program isn't officially affiliated with the UFC. But they do have a UFC-style caged octagon where, once a year, soldiers at Fort Knox fight against one another in a tournament to decide who gets to go to a bigger mixed martial arts army tournament. Outside, on a pit of shredded car tires, under the stars, I meet Sergeant York, who makes me realize that the fake names I've had to make up for soldiers are more believable than their actual names. Sergeant York teaches me the rear naked choke hold, in which you strangle your opponent from behind. He also teaches me the standing guillotine, in which you just shove someone's head under your armpit. Then you can just walk around with your enemy's head in your armpit, presumably slamming into things and laughing.

This move, I'm told, is particularly useful in a bar fight. Because when guys in bars see a man in a military uniform, they will often start a fight with him—just like they do to UFC guys and athletes. It takes a lot of explanation for me to understand why this would be, but from what I can understand it seems like guys want to brag that they fought someone tough, even if they lose. So putting a guy's head under your armpit is a good way of ending a fight without getting cops involved and getting in trouble with your superior officer, which would not be accomplished by other forms of army fighting, all of which involve killing.

As I get thrown over and over into the cut-up rubber tires, I pay particular attention to all the jujitsu moves, so that when Randy Couture does them to me, I'll know what each one is called.

We head out to a really good breakfast at the mess hall, where Sergeant York tells me he spends his weekends competing in local drag races. He then asks what my hobbies are. I do not have hobbies. He finds this impossible; there must be something I do at home. In fact, everyone at the table has a hobby: hunting, fishing, fixing old cars, building model cars. Basically everything on my list, these guys just do in their downtime. I know from talking to Adey about cars and to the firefighters about the Boy Scouts that Sergeant York is asking this to try to connect with me, and I want to help out. I ask Sergeant York if watching TV is a hobby. It is not.

As we leave the mess hall, we stop by the side of the road to watch three huge trucks carrying enormous desert-tan tanks. Which are for me. This is how it must have felt to be the premier of the Soviet Union.

The tank simulation course is taught by two very patient civilians who used to be in the military. A surprising number of army personnel have come inside this building to watch me practice firing a tank. Like a dozen. Major Mugavero is here. I am starting to wonder if they want me to fire a tank because they're pretty sure something hilarious is going to happen. Something I might not find hilarious.

I go to an adjoining room and sit down in a simulator that looks just like a driving arcade game, while the army guys stand in the next room, watching what I'm doing on their own screen. I start turning my virtual tank to shoot virtual stuff. Because I have very little gun experience, I mix up the trigger button and the laser-sight button. A lot. Which means I shoot a lot of stuff that I'm not supposed to shoot. So much stuff that Major Mugavero walks toward my simulator, leans down into my chair, and angrily tells me that if I don't fix my laser/trigger problem, I can't fire the real tank. Which I don't believe, since I'm pretty sure that all these people aren't going to want to spend their afternoon seeing *Ramona and Beezus* instead of watching me fire a tank. I can faint five times and they'll still let me fire the tank.

After I get the laser thing under control, I'm pretty good. Because this is really just a very simple video game on a green-on-black screen. I spent my entire tween years playing simple green-on-black video games on my Apple IIe. I just move a controller, push a button, and other tanks disappear or rows of troops fall away. I do so well that they let me try "Killer Tank," the hardest simulator, used after days of training. I get a B, and only because I misunderstood some of the rules at first. Also, I got a 1480 on my SATs.

I hear cheers from the other room every time I destroy something, but I don't realize just how many soldiers have gathered to watch. After it's over, Colonel David E. Thompson, who runs the 194th Armored Brigade and is Captain Fritz's boss, gives me a commander coin, which is so heavy and spiked that I mistake it for some kind of throwing weapon. According to the coin,

it is "presented for excellence" although it doesn't say in what, so
I'm going to assume "fainting recovery." It is also decorated with
swords, lightning, eagles, axes, guns, tanks, lions, and a morning
star: It is clearly designed by a barracks muralist. On the outside
of the coin it says HARD BATTLE and on the inside it has a bunch
of man words: LOYALTY, DUTY, RESPECT, SELFLESS SERVICE, PER-
SONAL COURAGE, INTEGRITY, HONOR. After these three days, I
understand them all just a little bit more than I did before.

I walk outside to the actual tanks, perched on a ridge, pointing
out to a range of empty hills. The tank guys I fainted in front of
days ago take me into a small concrete building. I receive a combination of a safety briefing and the ranting of a bunch of guys excited
that I'm going to fire a tank for my first time. "Honestly, the things
you'll never forget are being with a beautiful woman, being in battle,
and gunnery," says Captain Fritz. When Captain Fritz was in battle
in Iraq, there were periods where they were in so much danger they
couldn't leave the tank for days, sleeping inches from one another.
When they had to defecate, which, thanks to the MREs, was rare,
they did it in a bag and threw it outside. And he still loves tanks.

The next nine paragraphs have to be vetted by the army's oper-
ations security to make sure I don't reveal any secrets about the
tank to the enemy, thereby endangering American troops. The
U.S. government feels my prose is so powerful, it could kill U.S.
soldiers. This is the manliest moment of my writing career. The
least manly moment of my writing career was when I wrote my ex-
girlfriend from college a letter about how I would never take her
back and didn't send it to her.

Not only do I now write dangerous; I also look dangerous. I
put on a fire suit, gloves, a balaclava, and a heavy bulletproof vest,
which I am indeed starting to get used to, as well as a helmet with
a microphone in it, just like the firefighters wore. I look badass.
Largely because you can see almost none of my face.

But I'm a little afraid of this tank. The M1A2 Abrams tank

costs $6.21 million and looks it. It's so big I have to use its steps and handles like a jungle gym just to get inside—totally different from my Mini Cooper, which you just kind of duck your head for. Inside, however, the M1A2 Abrams is not so much bigger than my Mini Cooper. It seats four and has no beverage holders. The driver sits alone in a tiny enclosed space in the front, while the commander, loader, and gunner sit in the main space, really close to one another. It gets hot in here fast. And yet, no beverage holders.

I climb back out and stand on top of the tank, which has two machine guns mounted to the top. This, apparently, is not a big military secret. I am supposed to grab one of these huge machine guns—an M240—and rotate it to shoot at a plywood tank on a hill in the distance, but it's so far away, I can't make it out. The sergeants help me aim my machine gun toward it, and I pull the trigger. And I laugh, just like I laughed when I felt the acceleration of the Lamborghini. Even though it's mounted to the tank and I'm not holding it like Rambo, the M240 is so incredibly violent, loudly sucking up a ribbon of bullets in seconds, that it feels preposterous. It shoots so quickly that you aim it mostly by seeing where the bullets are going and readjusting. I try to pace myself, but in one minute two hundred bullets are gone, ripping into plywood that is football fields away.

There's an even bigger machine gun attached to the tank, a .50-caliber that shoots bullets the size of my finger that can travel a mile, punch through tanks, and take down building walls. In one minute two hundred of them are gone. It is such a fast, intense spurt of violence it is jarring, like you don't know what just happened or if you really caused it.

I climb in and stand to the left of the sunken chair of the guy who fires the tank. The first task everyone in gunnery is given is loading the rounds, which are kept inside a cabinet in the tank. They are less like bullets and more like nuclear weapons, about four feet long and really heavy. I have to stand in a tiny space to keep all of my body behind a little foldout metal divider; after the round is shot, the back of the giant bullet flies out with such force that, during gunnery training, a lot of the soldiers have bandages wrapped around their hands.

I am given seven seconds to tap my knee against a lever that opens the panel door, take out a round, close the door, pack the round into a hole, close the hole's metal door, and yell "Up!" I cannot do it fast enough. I am sweating, trying to get the order right and remember to close everything and move this very heavy bullet. Before I left, my dad told me to use a fist when I shut the door, so my fingers don't get cut off, which is the one thing I can remember. It takes me six times to get it in under seven seconds, which is not very good. I am told that I do not do things with nearly enough violence and aggression. I fear for the women these guys have sex with right after firing a tank.

I finally load a round in under seven seconds and the gunner shoots it off. The tank lurches forward and the back of the shell—a long pole attached to a steel base—flies back thirteen inches, right near my face, as if it's trying to get me back for shoving it with my fist. I pick it up and throw it out the top of the tank, and even though I've got gloves on, it is so hot it hurts.

Sergeant Wise, a chipper, Opie-ish-looking guy in his thirties, takes me out of the tank to go over what's going to happen when I fire it. Sergeant Wise is about to retire from the army to enter a program that trains soldiers to be high school teachers. Which he will be great at. He calms me down, explains everything clearly. I'm concerned about the recoil from the tank, so I ask Sergeant Wise how I'll feel right after I fire. "Same as everyone, sir. You'll get a hard-on and a big old smile on your face," he says.

In the tanker's seat, I look into the small green-on-black monitor, which lets me see the opposing plywood tank on a ridge that is so far away I couldn't make it out with my bare eyes when I was outside. I tell the loader to throw the shell in, use the controls to center the tank onto my screen, yell "On the way!" then "Fire!," and pull the trigger. I wait for the tank to shake, to feel the power of launching a giant bullet across the sky, to hear the crunch of destruction, to see puffs of gouged earth pluming. I wait to feel the satisfying thud of delivering a giant punch for America.

But the seat is so stable, I don't feel the tank shake. From where I'm sitting, I can't even see the shell's recoil. The tank I blew up is so far away and I am so sheltered in this giant piece of metal, I don't hear or see an explosion. On the screen, the tank goes up in a puff of smoke, like a video game. I could do this all day, destroying village after village, not feeling a thing.

I don't have a hard-on. I don't want a beer. I don't want to have sex with a beautiful woman any more than I always want to have sex with a beautiful woman. I don't even feel the little jolt I felt when I fired the shotgun with Matt Stedina. Power and violence don't give me much of a rush. They make me sad. It's like when alcoholics talk about how much they loved being drunk, and all I can think of is nausea and spinning heads. But outside my tank, there is a small party going on. I am happy about their happiness over my non-existent happiness.

I fire the tank a second time, destroy some more Plywoodians, and feign excitement so I don't let these whooping good men down. If I have to drink a beer and get it up for my country, I am going to manufacture a patriotic rager.

I climb off the tank and say good-bye to my new tank friends. Then I go to Captain Fritz's office, which is somewhere I don't like to picture him sitting, writing memos, filling out forms, wasting all that enthusiasm and unflappability. He looks much smaller in here.

I hand back my gear: the bulletproof vest, the helmet, the neck protector, the groin protector, the dorky protective goggles, the boots that tortured me. I put my own jeans and shirt back on and they feel sloppy and juvenile. Captain Fritz expected me to have a suit and tie, since I'm a journalist. And an adult male. I'm disappointed that I don't.

Captain Fritz's wife comes by, as pretty and cheery as I could have hoped. They recently got married and are looking forward to having kids. That kid is going to have an amazing dad. I don't want Captain Fritz to be stationed overseas ever again.

Before I leave, Captain Fritz gives me a gift—an inscribed *Jane's Tank Recognition Guide*. He signed it "From one tanker to another." He shows me the page he circled with a photo and specs of the M1A2 Abrams. I think of all the time Captain Fritz has spent in that sarcophagus, and the confidence that comes from having that much power against real people really trying to kill you, and I get why they were all so excited to let me fire the tank. Because it was the only way I could really understand their lives.

I call my dad to bond about the tank, but he tells me that while he loaded them, he never got to fire one. He did fire a lot of Howitzers, though. And he never got a jolt out of it either. I am surprised to learn that, between not liking to drink and this, we have two genes in common.

At a restaurant in the Louisville airport, two marines sit at the table next to me: they came to Fort Knox for tanker training, since the marines don't have their own facility. I have never known how to talk to soldiers, or how to act around them, whether to give them my seat or if that's treating them with pity, like a pregnant woman. Do they want to avoid me and my repulsive wimpiness? Do they just want to blend in and be left alone?

Now it's easy. They just finished basic training in San Diego, and we get in a long discussion about The Crucible, and hiking The Reaper. I buy them beers and tell them about my man project. Julius Tayo, twenty-one, reassures me: "If you shot an M240, you're not a pussy." When his drill instructor gave him his eagle, globe, and anchor emblem, he said to Julius: "I remember the two times you cried. I'm proud of you for pushing that hard." Which made Julius cry a third time.

His friend, Andrew Steck, also twenty-one, tells me I would have adjusted to the stress, even getting yelled at during meals. "After a while, you're like, 'I don't care about talking to you. I just want to eat as much as I can.'" I ask if, after all he's been through, he thinks a man who hasn't served in the military is less of a man. "Not less of a man, but one with less discipline," he says. "I'm a nervous person, but after boot camp I could handle anything. Not much stresses me out."

There's a bunch of marines on my connecting flight through Milwaukee, and Nate Firestone, twenty, takes the seat next to me. Back at the desk, I noticed how much calmer he was than the other passengers when our connecting flight was canceled before this other one popped up. And unlike us, he was going to miss one of his four days of leave, the first he's gotten since he graduated boot camp. "The people behind me were whiny about their wants. If you want to be a man, you have to be thankful for what you have," he says. Which he learned in his eight months as a marine. "Not showing your emotions is just as important as controlling your emotions."

Nate is a skinny kid from Minnesota who's afraid of flying because he hasn't done it much. He thinks he sees the brightest star ever until I explain that it's the control tower. He turns down a soda and cookies until I tell him that they're free. We watch the sunset and then the lights of Louisville fade away, and Nate tells me that his girlfriend cheated on him, and I tell him that my girlfriend did the same when I was his age, and he can't believe it happened to someone else, too.

Halfway through the flight, his buddy Nick Hosto, twenty, from Vidor, Texas, comes by. Nick came from a family that watched a little more Fox News than Nate's. He thinks global warming is a hoax and that girls don't make good soldiers because "they've got too much oceanside in them." Nick thinks war is a natural, permanent state: "If there's peace in the world, it means the world is going to end. Animals fight all the time. We're just sophisticated animals."

Nate, however, thinks, despite enlisting, that the wars in Iraq and Afghanistan are over oil and shouldn't have been waged. Which Nick thinks is stupid.

"Why are we over there, then?" Nate asks.

"To help them."

"That's what we think."

I get off the plane and say good-bye to Nate. He's going off, in a little while, to Afghanistan. He says he feels ready. I have absolutely no doubt he is.

Even though I was with the army for only three days, and I got the stress-lite, post-fainting version of it, I did things I never thought I'd be able to do. But I got something more than confidence. I understood something no one—not my parents, not Hebrew school, not college—had told me: There are ideals far more valuable than personal success. Our culture might celebrate power, money, and fame, but that's not what they talk about at your funeral. Honorable conduct, even unrecognized, is its own reward. Without that code, every decision is a selfish weighing of morality versus personal gain. A code makes life easier, and more worthwhile.

I still don't know if I support what the troops do. But I know I want to be a lot more like them.

I always said if there were a draft, I'd go to jail or, if that weren't an option, move to Canada. But now I think I wouldn't. I still can't think of anything more repugnant and terrifying than shooting and being shot at, but I can see how between the awfulness, there might be a wonderful adventure. I might instinctually be a fainter, but with a little practice I can endure what everyone else can. And like Captain Fritz and my dad, I can do it without complaining. In fact, basic training and firing a tank made me think I'm a little more like my dad than I thought. I like that. I like that a lot.

11
PROTECTING MY FAMILY

Everything does feel flat, just like Sergeant Feldman told me it felt when he came back from Iraq. But it also feels fast, like whole days can pass where nothing happens. Being back feels like adjusting after a vacation, only the opposite. It's not that I wish I was sleeping in a tent with Captain Fritz instead of my bed with Cassandra, but it wouldn't be bad if Cassandra, Captain Fritz, and I could sleep in a bed in a tent. I do not think I should suggest this to either Cassandra or Captain Fritz.

I can't stop talking about all the army stuff, often starting sentences with the phrase *When I was in the military*, which is technically correct but makes it sound like I served my country instead of vice versa.

Now I just need to make sure that, without Captain Fritz spurring me along, I can still take on challenges. That my new confidence will make me actually want to confront the next guy who threatens Cassandra. Because I know that since that guy flipped her off on our block and I didn't do anything, Cassandra doesn't feel protected. She made us get an alarm system, and she turns it on every night. Which means she doesn't feel like I'm much of a man. Which means that she's attracted to other men. Men who fight.

When Cassandra sees a boyfriend go psycho on a guy who is simply looking at his girlfriend, she calls it romantic, whereas I see romance as a nice night where no one gets hurt. The closest I've ever come to physically protecting her was in New York, when three thirteen-year-old kids tripped Cassandra on purpose coming up the subway steps and I yelled at them. I said, "Hey!" They were thirteen. And I was scared.

What I need is simply to be punched in the face one time. Actually, I do not think this is something I need. My friend Jonathan Karsh, a reality show producer, does. He thinks that getting punched really hard right in the face will teach me that it's not that horrible and give me some confidence about getting in the ring with Randy Couture. Jonathan, I will learn later, has never been punched in the face. Which is especially surprising, since he's a reality show producer.

Jonathan wants me to appear in a pilot he's shooting in which Dave Salmoni teaches wimpy guys how to be men, partly, it seems, by hitting them in the face. When I look Salmoni up online, I glean that he is Canadian, hosts shows on Animal Planet, has lived alone for months with lions, has worked as a bouncer, and does not own any shirts. Dave is the kind of guy who not only carries a pocketknife everywhere he goes, but thinks it's weird that when he flicks it open, I sing songs from *West Side Story*.

We go camping together and, thanks to the Boy Scouts, I'm able to set up my tent, impressing the lion man. When I ask Dave where his tent is and if he needs help, he tells me we're sharing the tent. It is a small tent. After cooking a rabbit on a stick over a campfire and picking fur out of our teeth, we sleep in the tiny tent together. Which is nothing at all like sharing a big tent with Captain Fritz, since Captain Fritz, who has lived with humans and not lions, knows about personal space and not farting. Still, we stay up and talk, about our careers and his dating life, which involves looking at photos on his phone of naked models Dave slept with. In return, I open up and tell him about my experiences being attracted to the photos of the naked models he slept with.

The next day, Jonathan—who slept in a hotel—makes us pretend to be scared as we stand by a creek and a trained Hollywood bear walks by. Emboldened by my experience with Montana, I do something I could have never imagined doing a few months ago: I let the bear eat a cookie from my mouth. Which isn't that scary until I start to wonder if someone feeding a monkey a cookie from his mouth is how AIDS started.

Reality show producers have ways of making you do things you don't want to do. So I walk with Dave into a boxing gym and put on headgear and a mouth guard. I stand still while Dave pulls his gloved fist back and punches me in the face. I am knocked off my feet into the air, the back of my head slamming into the mat, a tear streaming down my face.

"You're such a dick," I say, as soon as I get up. "Does that make you feel like a man?"

"Yes, it does," Dave says.

I can see that. The sting goes away after a few seconds. But when I drive home, the road is moving a little, the equivalent of doing three quick shots of The Macallan. My nose will hurt for days. And I'll never, ever watch Dave Salmoni on any of his stupid Animal Planet shows.

Still, I know that getting punched, while awful, is something that's not all that big a deal. Which makes me extrapolate wildly. Is it possible that getting kneed in the face by a professional face kneer isn't so bad, either?

No, it is not. Which is why I have to do it. My marine sergeant told me he takes skydiving lessons because he's afraid of heights.

I've got to fight because I'm afraid of confrontation. There's no getting out of this.

I drive to Las Vegas with Cassandra and Laszlo so UFC president Dana White can spend a full day training me the day before my fight. We check into the Vdara Hotel, which is just like the snow cabin in *Rocky IV*, if Rocky had been training to be a European playboy instead of a fighter. In the morning I am upset that the room service menu does not offer a blender full of raw eggs. So, just as Rocky Balboa would have if presented with this obstacle, I go downstairs myself to Jean Philippe Patisserie, pick up a quiche and some chocolate croissants, and drive to the UFC headquarters, in a large building off a highway.

I walk downstairs into a gym with a boxing ring in the middle. The walls are lined with photos of men hitting other men and not feeling at all bad about it. Music I am not familiar with, but am pretty sure involves either the devil or murder or, possibly, murdering the devil, plays at what I assume and hope is full volume.

Dana White is my height but seems much bigger, with huge shoulders and a shaved head. During my quest to be a man, I have yet to meet a man with hair as long as mine usually is. I don't know if this depilation is to delineate them from women, or simply because long hair can get caught in man stuff like cars, guns, drills, and men you're fighting. Or maybe twirling your hair while trying to think of a witticism to end your paragraph isn't all that manly.

Dana is immensely likable, a storm of happy energy. He's got some of the lightness that Captain Fritz has, but it's topped with a ridiculous amount of charisma and braggadocio. He built a globally popular sports league out of an underground fight club that he's the star of. His personal brand is unapologetic honesty, which is always likable. He gives out his cell phone number online so fans can ask him questions about upcoming fights.

"You probably want to get on the treadmill if you want to last ten seconds with Randy Couture. Maybe you can outrun him," Dana says. "I think your five-minute fight with Randy Couture is going to be a five-second fight." I like his training strategy, to motivate me through insults. But a five-second fight is what I've secretly been hoping for. I'll walk into the ring, see some kind of blinding flash of pain, and then wake up, able to say I fought Randy Couture. This, I'm pretty sure, is how my high school girlfriend thought about losing her virginity to me.

Dana had his kids boxing at three years old and doing Thai kickboxing and Brazilian jujitsu at seven. "My kids can do whatever they want to. But they have to learn how to fight," he says. No matter how much you try to avoid fights, he argues, they are eventually going to happen, and he wants them to be prepared.

"If you've ever watched a YouTube fight with high school kids, it's fucking brutal," he says. Of all the scary things about Dana, the scariest is that he spends his free time searching "high school fights" on YouTube.

Dana pulls out a roll of thick white tape and tenderly crosses it over and under my fingers. He puts big red boxing gloves over my hands and big red circular pads over his. He tells me to hit them. It sounds good, the pop of leather on leather, but apparently I am doing it wrong. I need to turn my hand over as I punch, cock my shoulder way back and turn my foot so the power comes from my leg, not my shoulder. While I can do any one of those things, I can't remember to do them all at the same time.

After three minutes, my shoulder hurts. Luckily, we have to stop the boxing lesson when a woman walks in to get Dana's fingerprints for the state of Indiana, since the UFC is having a fight there, and they have to make sure he doesn't have a criminal record. I did not know you could not run a fighting organization if you have a criminal record. Running a fighting organization seems like the perfect occupation for people with criminal records. I think we should give them this and maybe take away security guards and babysitting.

Dana has, in fact, been in jail before. He was in his twenties at a bar when a guy grabbed his girlfriend's ass. Dana started to fight the guy when the bouncer threw the guy out of the bar. "I should have stayed inside," White says. Instead he went outside, hid behind a car, and waited for the guy's friends to leave. Then he beat the guy up so severely, the cops took Dana to jail and sent the other guy to the hospital. "I got my justice, but nobody wins in a fight," Dana says. "It reminds me of video games. The first time I played a video game, I played all day until I won. When I was done, I said, 'What the fuck did I just do?' It wasn't like anyone saw me. I didn't make any money. It meant nothing. That's how I feel about fighting." I wonder what else I naturally intuit that it takes jail time for other men to figure out.

While he was in jail, Dana was scared straight, though not by gang violence or rape. "You're sleeping on a metal bench with a toilet in the middle. Are you fucking kidding me? I didn't go to the bathroom the entire weekend." Between Dana and Chad, my eleven-year-old Boy Scout friend, who told me to withhold while camping, I am learning that my bathroom avoidance isn't wimpy. Although mine may be more extreme. For all four years of high school, I managed to never find out what our bathrooms looked like, by only urinating once a day, in gym class. This was largely because I heard that fights sometimes broke out in the school bathrooms.

Dana also hates camping. "I pay a mortgage so I don't have to sleep outside. There's no shower? We have to make a fire to eat stuff we don't want to eat? It makes no fucking sense." He feels even more strongly about hunting: "What is this, 1800? I don't need to kill an animal. Go to Smith & Wollensky, motherfucker." When Sheikh Khalifa bin Zayed Al Nahyan of Abu Dhabi took Dana hunting, Dana bailed on the rest of the day after killing a duck—business etiquette be damned.

"It's a horrifying experience. I killed a duck. That's not right. It was flying around and having a good time and now it's not due to me? Fuck that," he says. "Hunters are pussies. If you want to hunt, bring a knife. In fighting, there's no laser sight and scope. What's a deer going to do to you?"

Although he signed up for the military with a friend after seeing *Top Gun* several times, he got another friend's dad who was a lawyer to get him out of it, since he could never envision killing a person: "I wouldn't kill anything. But if I feel like punching you in the fucking face, I'll punch you in the fucking face." Dana can't handle home repairs or fix his car. "I pull up with a three-hundred-thousand-dollar Ferrari and can't open the gas tank," he says. And he doesn't care about sports: "Are you fucking kidding me that you can die in peace now that the Red Sox won? Get a life." Golf? "A bunch of rich dicks dressed like idiots following around a ball? I'd rather you beat me with a stick." The lesson is clear: You can ignore all the other man stuff if, every so often, you and another guy agree to spend a few minutes punching each other in the face.

One major difference between Dana and me is that he has to keep reminding himself not to fight. A few weeks earlier, Dana was in his Ferrari in an alley between Vegas hotels when a guy in a Camaro pulled up to him at a traffic light and challenged him to a fight, calling him a pussy and then a faggot—probably because Dana was in a Ferrari, which, apparently, is a pussy faggoty car. But he knew, at least in his head, that there was only downside in fighting this guy: lawsuit, jail time, injury, bad PR. "For me to sit there, to listen to this bullshit, you want to get out and punch him in the face. I don't care if you're fourteen, twenty, forty, or sixty, if you're the kind of guy I am, you have that in you," he says. But he knew the fight would end up with cops or, worse, lawyers, so he focused as hard as he could on staying in the car. "It bothered me for four days. At night it would keep me up."

The only thing that would keep me up at night is the fear that the guy would appear alongside me on some kind of dead end I couldn't drive away from. In The List, I tell Laszlo, "Truth and peace are in direct opposition. Some people will give up a lot of their truth for peace; others give up peace for truth. But everyone has their limit for both. Side toward peace whenever you can." But just like Dana sacrificed the truth that he isn't pussy faggoty for some peace, there's a point where I too will sacrifice peace for truth. As Dana put it, "If a guy was saying things about your wife and kid and not stopping, eventually he would get you to the point, because you're a human being, where you'll think about punching him in the face." An enormous number of Dana's sentences end with the phrase *punching him in the face.*

You're born at your spot in the continuum, Dana says, and I'm so far in one direction that I get pushed around. I need to slide myself as far in the other direction as I can. But the more Dana talks, the less I'm sure my wimpiness is merely genetic. I've had an incredibly easy life. Dana's father is an alcoholic who took off when Dana was in third grade. His dad is so difficult that even though the guy lives nearby in Las Vegas, Dana and his kids don't have much of a relationship with him. Back in Boston, after his dad left, Dana was responsible for protecting his mother, who was being tormented by their next-door neighbor. After one incident where the guy came over to their house and threatened his mom, Dana, newly sixteen and newly muscled out, walked over to the neighbor's house, knocked on his door, and told him that if he ever came to their house again for any reason, he would murder him.

"I just snapped at this guy who we were terrified of for years," he says. In my house, my father took care of anyone bothering us. Though I believe the worst we encountered was two Jehovah's Witnesses.

I am not simply conflict-avoidant; I am emotionally incapable of anger. When someone cuts me off on the highway, I can't help but think about all the times I've done stupid things while driving. I've been fired several times, and I've always listened politely and waited to react until I had a few days' time to figure out what would do me the most good in the long run. My brain skips anger entirely, going straight from wronged to sad. The few times I've felt really attacked, I completely shut off, going silent and distant. This is a slightly worse trait in a husband than drunken violence.

I've been anger-deficient as long as I can remember. "I could tell right away you were another Morris," Mama Ann told me. My grandfather Morris was exceedingly calm and patient, driving people insane with his long explanations. "You were more quiet. A gentleman. Your father was crash boom bam." I'd like to attribute my lack of crash boom bam to some Buddhist acceptance of the present, but I'm pretty sure it's hormonal. When I had my testosterone levels tested, they were within the normal range of 260 to 1,000. When I pressed my doctor for a number, he told me my testosterone level was 302. That's normal only in that it means I don't have ovaries.

But now that I'm getting this punch down, I feel my testosterone shooting up to the low 400s. My gloved fist is starting to make a terrific sound against the pads. Dana even waves his mitts from the sting. I can now punch. All I need is a psychological advantage that will allow me to trick Randy Couture into standing completely still while reminding me to turn my foot and pull my shoulder back at the same time.

Dana's assistant comes down to tell us that Randy Couture is in the building to sign some papers. "Tell him Joel Stein says he's going to get the beating of his life tomorrow. He's going to beat the shit out of him," Dana yells. In case it takes too long to get this message all the way upstairs, Dana publicly tweets this threat to Randy Couture. I do not know why Dana is working hype as if this fight were going to be on pay-per-view. I would like to switch managers.

Since there's a lot more to mixed martial arts than boxing, Dana has brought a bunch of instructors to teach me—basically everything except a professional eye gouger and biter. Peter Pinto, a Muay Thai fighter and trainer, is an expert at kicking and elbow-ing people. He's an incredibly calm, nice man, a couple of inches shorter than me, with a beard and thick, expressive eyebrows. The scariest thing about him is his Boston accent that is so Bostonian, I can't understand some of what he says. I'm pretty sure it is about Muay Thai, but it sounds like it's about how much the Yankees suck.

After a bunch of bowing to each other, Dana suggests we begin the lesson by having Peter kick me in the thigh really hard so I know how much it hurts. The lesson I learn is that getting kicked in the thigh really hurts. Peter gives it only 50 percent of his strength, which is good, since I don't want to have to hop over to the other side of the ring to collect my severed leg. The pain lasts for two minutes and feels a lot like getting kicked in the leg by a professional leg kicker.

After that, Peter focuses on classic Muay Thai moves. The very first move he teaches me is face kneeing. There's apparently no escaping this: There is going to be face kneeing tomorrow. And when it occurs, I'm supposed to know how to face knee right back, which seems impossible since I'll be on the floor, my hands over my eyes, yelling, "My face! My beautiful face!"

Face kneeing, to my surprise, is much more technical than its name implies. First you grab your opponent's neck, then you push his head down. Only then do you start kneeing him in the head repeatedly with both legs, like a psychotic Rockette. When the kneed individual manages to get out of your hold, you elbow him in the back of the head and kick him as he gets away. "The elbow is great because it opens them up and causes bleeding," Peter explains.

Another key part of Peter's strategy is the teep, which is a little jab of a kick at the opponent's stomach. This, Peter insists, will be the key to my fight: I fake the teep and then punch Randy Couture in the head with my right hand. It's some kind of secret strategic hole in Randy Couture's defense that Peter has detected. If I simply do it a few times, Peter says, I will win the fight. "I guarantee it.

That absolutely will work. Guaranteed," he says. I make him repeat this insane statement twice, in case he was actually saying something about how the Yankees suck.

The problem with my training is that it focuses a lot on how to hurt Randy Couture and not nearly enough on how to avoid being hurt by Randy Couture. When I ask Peter for some defensive moves, he teaches me one called "turtling up," in which I curl into a ball on the mat. I am phenomenal at this. I'm a born turtler. Peter also tells me it's acceptable to run away from him around the ring in a circle. I think he should have led with this lesson.

I'm wondering if I really need to fight at all. If maybe I should back out. If maybe the lesson I've learned is that a real man doesn't search for fights, but searches for peace instead. And if that peace cannot be had, then he fires a round from a tank that is safely a mile away.

It isn't just that a few days ago my mom freaked out and begged me not to fight Randy Couture. "I don't think you need to fight to be a man," she says. "There can be an accident. He might not realize how strong he is. You could get your eye knocked out." My mom's ideas about danger are pretty much stuck in the safety-scissors phase.

It is hard to listen to the warnings of someone who doesn't like fighting because it doesn't foster creativity. But I get more scared when my dad, who boxed in college, says the same thing. He argues that Couture is so strong he could slip and accidentally break one of my ribs, or that decades of training to go all-out in a fight might cause him to reflexively rip into me when I'm down and helpless.

Any thoughts of bailing disappear from my mind when Dana's attractive assistant offers me a towel to wipe my sweat with. Then she takes the towel back. This is the greatest man moment of my life. If my gym had this feature, I would work out every day.

After bowing to each other a lot to end our training session, Peter offers to be my corner man for the fight. While I could use the help, I fear bringing an expert will telegraph to Randy Couture that I am really serious about this fight and he should not hold back. This is the opposite of what I want to convey. Instead of Peter, I consider bringing that Harlem Globetrotter that runs into the crowd and throws confetti out of water buckets.

Dana brings me upstairs for lunch, which I am pretty sure will involve raw eggs. In the halls we pass what I think are two original, giant Jackson Pollock paintings. When I complement Dana on them, he tells me they're framed post-fight UFC mats, stained with human blood. The other side of the hall is lined with before-and-after photos of fighters from UFC championships: In one they look angry; in the other you can't discern any emotion because their eyes are blown shut, lips cracked in two, cheeks black-and-blued, ears cauliflowered. I get that same sad pity for these guys I got when I saw two guys fighting on TV at the spa gym. Only now I have it for me, too.

My sympathies, Dana says, are wasted. These guys want to fight. Chuck Liddell, who is tied with Randy Couture for the most UFC fights in history, was an accounting major with honors from Cal Poly, and started fighting for fifteen hundred dollars in prize money. "It would cost him more than that to be involved in these fights. Who the fuck does that? It's a fucking fact: There are people put on earth to fight. That's where that motherfucker wants to be," he says, pointing to a guy holding a bloody towel to his face who, to the untrained eye, does not look like he is exactly where he wants to be.

The world, Dana explains, divides neatly into nerds, jocks, and stoners, and none can truly understand the others. "But fighters are a completely different social group. They're the alpha fucking males. Most of their social skills aren't that great. I'm as much of a man's man as you get, but I'm not that guy," he says. When I ask him if alpha men do as well with women as I fear, he tells me that the morning after Chuck Liddell beat his archenemy Tito Ortiz,

Dana went to Liddell's apartment to get the boxing shorts he wore in the fight so he could frame them. "There were naked girls everywhere. Sleeping on the couch. There were three in his bed. I was literally tiptoeing through condoms," he says. "I got the trunks and got the hell out of there." Tito Ortiz was likely at home with his wife, porn star Jenna Jameson.

As fun as requiring guests to tiptoe around my used condoms sounds, I never wanted to be the alpha male. I didn't want to fight the bad guy, brood over my shortcomings, overcome obstacles, and get the popular girl: I wanted to make people laugh and get the girl who seemed like a lot less trouble. Even in the movies I watched as a kid—which were musicals—I wanted to be the funny sidekick. I would try to imitate Donald O'Connor in *Singing in the Rain* running into walls instead of Gene Kelly, who had to sing in the cold, unpleasant rain. My goal was to be a beta male. When my parents asked me what my dream job was, I picked vice president of the United States.

Lunch is not raw eggs. Two in-house chefs sous-vide veal, sauté snapper, and grill turkey burgers. The veal is accompanied by a side of barley-and-broccolini salad. This is a version of manhood I like.

After lunch, Dana takes me into his huge office, which doubles as the Art Museum of Badassery. There's a giant framed black-and-white photo of a gorilla pointing a gun at the camera, a huge photo of the back of Mike Tyson's head, and two big photographs of tarantulas. There's a glass-enclosed fossil of a saber-toothed-tiger skull. Another wall has a print of the Bruce Nauman painting that consists merely of the words, written backward, PAY ATTENTION, MOTHERFUCKERS. In an alcove he's got a desk, above which is a giant color photograph of porn-star-era Traci Lords. There are also two framed Bibles that have been carved into guns, facing each other, under which it's written, THESE BOOKS HAVE KILLED MORE PEOPLE THAN HANDGUNS. On the desk is a thick roll of hundred-dollar bills that I'm pretty sure isn't art but just a roll of hundred-dollar bills. On the bathroom wall is a black-and-white shot of Stephanie Seymour pulling up her see-through black dress to show her pubes. I do not have enough time to search the office for a cave painting of a man dragging a woman by the hair, but I'm sure it's in here.

On his desk, there's a copy of *Playboy*'s July 2010 issue, signed by centerfold Shanna Marie McLaughlin, which arrived unrequested. I do not understand how this kind of thing happens. Neither does Dana. A signed naked photo seems like a version of a business card that is not about business. I cannot let this go, so I find Shanna online and email her to find out why she sent it. She tells me she was in Vegas, met some UFC fighters at her hotel, and asked them to give Dana the gift. When I ask if she is attracted to Dana, she answers, "Sure." When I ask if this is due to his manliness, she says, "Absolutely!" Dana lives in a world entirely devoid of subtext. When people think you're attractive, they send you naked pictures of themselves. When they get mad at you, they punch you in the face.

Inside the huge bathroom, Dana pulls out a long, wide drawer that contains large plastic cases. There are guns inside. Bathroom drawers are not, from what I remember from Leo Zamboni's hunter safety class, the proper place to store guns. Dana lets me hold two Glock handguns, which are much lighter than I thought Glocks would be—something never mentioned in rap lyrics. In fact, Glocks look kind of fake and plasticky. The .50-caliber Desert Eagle handgun, however, looks a lot less fake: all shiny, heavy metal and giant barrel. Dana pulls out another case that could fit a pool cue and a guitar together. It contains an M82, which comes in pieces you have to screw together until it is more than seven feet long. It's way bigger than the barrel of any of the machine guns I shot in the army. American snipers have used them in Afghanistan to kill men a mile and a quarter away. Dana got it as a gift from Caesars Palace after staging a fight there.

"You definitely shouldn't have these," I say, looking at all the guns in front of me.

"I agree," Dana says.

After I insist upon fully digesting my lunch, Dana brings me downstairs for Brazilian jujitsu training with John Lewis, who is forty-two but looks way younger. John is exactly my size and weight, except where I have fat he has muscle, and where I have muscle he has some kind of steel. A former UFC fighter, John taught Dana jujitsu and also trained Randy Couture for his early fights. Despite the closely cropped hair, there's something soft looking about John, who grew up in Hawaii. He speaks quickly and quietly, the opposite of a tough guy. He shakes my hand very gently. Instead of bejeweled skulls, his shirt has a peace sign and wings. I am not sure this is the guy to help me.

John learned martial arts as a kid in Hawaii and got good enough so that he became popular by beating up bullies. This is a guy who took the movie *Karate Kid* really seriously. Being able to beat the crap out of people changed his whole perspective on life. "I can sit across the table from someone at a business meeting and think, *I could beat you up*. And they treat you differently because they know it. Anything confrontational, you feel like you're in control," he says. "We're primal. It comes down to who can beat who up and who has the most girlfriends." Fighting Randy Couture, he says, is a great first step in getting that kind of confidence. "Anything I'm afraid of, I do it. I'd say, 'I'll fight him,' just because he's big and I didn't know if I could. Even if I lose, I can say I did it." This does not seem like a great reason to get beaten up.

When it comes to actual street fights I might get into, John says having an exit strategy is the key. "If you have a goal, you're already ahead. You have a plan of getting out of it." He says that "We're going to talk this through and understand each other's point of view" does not count as a goal.

Dana suggests we start off by having John choke me out, so

I can know what that's like. Dana's suggestions, I am starting to think, might not have my best interests at heart. I point out that getting choked out was how both the INXS guy and David Carradine died. Dana says that they used a noose and were masturbating, whereas John Lewis is a fourth-degree black belt in Brazilian jujitsu who will let go as soon as I lose consciousness, without any distracting masturbation involved. He also assures me that being choked out doesn't actually involve any choking at all. The choker doesn't stop the chokee from breathing. No, he just blocks the chokee's blood from traveling through the carotid artery, causing the brain to lose oxygen and shut off. This explanation is meant to make me feel better.

I sit on the mat and John takes off his shirt, which I think is a little unnecessary since choking me out seems gay enough. John has huge upper-back muscles covered by a tattoo of a dragon that runs all the way down his right leg; another tattoo on his right arm looks like either Hawaiian flowers or the blood of a thousand opponents. He kneels behind me, puts my neck in the crook of his arm, and says, "Just trust me and go with it." Then he squeezes. My neck is burning, constricted, red, raw. Since my brain is 1 percent salt, 8 percent protein, 12 percent fat, and 79 percent pussy, I instinctively fake going to sleep, dropping my head against John's arm and going limp. Which is a great fighting technique, one that can outfox even a fourth-degree black belt in Brazilian jujitsu. John lets go, I open my eyes, and he looks down at me. "You might have faked it," he says. His solution is to do it again. I already have the worst sore throat I've ever had, but before I can argue, John puts his arm around my neck. All I want to do is fall asleep and dream about a man not choking me. But I can't fight my deep-rooted instinct to play dead when I'm in danger. I'm not trying to pretend I'm sleeping. I'm just trying so hard to get choked out and get this over with that I look like I'm sleeping. John lets go, and, when I open my eyes Dana is in my face.

"Were you asleep?"

"Yeah."

"Did you dream?"

"Did I dream?" That seemed like a lot to ask out of those two seconds.

"Dude, you dream. It's fucking weird."

They can't figure out what was wrong with their choking-out process. "You've never fought a total pussy before," I explain. I somehow convince them not to try again, probably by distracting them with a shiny metal object.

Despite all this choking and getting kicked in the thigh, I do not feel like I am learning much for my fight. John sits on the mat cross-legged and tells me to fight him. I do not know what he means by this. He keeps repeating that I should fight him. "Be as aggressive as you want. Come at me as hard as you can," he says.

I do not know what I'm supposed to do, but I want to make it look like I'm doing something. I push at John's shoulders, hoping to knock him to the floor and then maybe run away in a circle. But as soon as I touch his shoulders, John gets behind me, snakes his legs around my torso, gets his arm around my neck, and goes right back to the goddamn choking thing he loves so much. Luckily, I have somehow seen enough professional wrestling to know to tap the mat when you're about to die, which causes John to let go. Wrestlers cannot resist the sound of mat tapping. It's like a dog whistle.

"This is the shit I was talking about," Dana says, way too excited about the non-lesson I am getting. "I had been boxing for years. I could handle myself and I came in here and said, 'Are you shitting me? Another dude can do this to me right now?'" John signals for me to attack him again. I am hoping for some specific advice from Dana, but he says, "Go after him hard and try to take him out!"

That is not what I do. I try to get on top of John, since that is something I must have also seen in professional wrestling. Instead, John flips me over and starts choking my neck with his feet. I cannot believe he found an even more unpleasant way to choke me. He grabs my arm and pulls it toward him in a way that an arm is not supposed to go. Then he lets go and does something else horrible to me until I tap the mat. The next ten minutes go like this, over and over: John all calm and smiley and barely moving and me flailing and sweating and in great pain. At one point he does something to my Achilles tendon that hurts so bad I scream a little bit. There are all these parts of my body I had no idea are just as sensitive as my balls, and he finds them all, like an anti-lover finding anti-erogenous zones.

Dana sets a clock for five minutes so I'll know what my round with Randy Couture will feel like. Five minutes is a really long time. It's two ridiculous minutes longer than a boxing round. When the clock dings, I am woozy, dizzy, my throat sore, my neck destroyed. I have gone through the Kama Sutra of getting my ass kicked.

As I'm sitting on the mat, dazed, John tells me that when he wrestles some of the guys he trains, he'll sometimes "pinch their balls." I do not understand the purpose of this. He says it's really funny, this pinching of each other's balls. John had seemed like such a normal guy. Like a non-ball-pincher. The more I'm learning about real men, the less I want to be one. Sure, you walk around unafraid and women want to have sex with you, but the trade-off is that your friends pinch your balls.

Heading up to Dana's office, I get my first sign that I might not be all right: Dana's assistant asks me if I'm okay in a way that seems to imply that she doesn't say it that way all the time. And she sits outside an office where UFC fighters come in. I sink into a big, soft chair in Dana's office and he says a bunch of stuff to me that I don't hear because everything is foggy and slowed down. I do know that he told me to put Laszlo into a mixed martial arts class soon, and not a karate class: "You might as well put him in dance class. Try doing karate on a playground." I manage to ask if I should convince Laszlo to try martial arts if he has no interest in it. "The shit you want to teach him is the shit he wants to learn," Dana says. His argument is that Laszlo will be so eager to spend time with me, he'll just want to join me in whatever I'm into. If that's fighting, he'll like fighting. He's kind of right. Laszlo is already desperate to stir pots of risotto and smell herbs. Which is why I'm learning all this man stuff.

By the time I drive back to the hotel, I am clearly not okay. I am acting like a man for my first time. Like a quiet, 1950s man who just came home from a day in the coal mine. This is why men are sullen, quiet, and quick to anger: Because their lives are hard. I agree to go to dinner with Cassandra and Laszlo as we had planned, against my better judgment, because judgment would require thinking and thinking seems exhausting. Talking is near impossible. I sit through dinner silently, taking only a few bites of soft ravioli because it hurts too much to swallow anything else. Saliva keeps building up in my mouth and I want to spit it out, because forcing it down burns. "Even when you're really sick, you're not this unresponsive," Cassandra says. To which I do not respond. When we get back to our hotel room, I put Laszlo to sleep and, at 8:30 PM, feeling done, forever, with military time, I get in the bed in all my clothes and fall asleep. Half an hour later Cassandra wakes me up and makes me take a salt bath. When I take my shirt off, she sees the results of my training: black-and-blue marks under my biceps, on my wrists, around my ankles, on my shoulders, up and down my back. Over the bruises on my back are scratch marks and rug burns. I look like I had rough sex with two male lions who lined their den with Brillo Pads.

After the bath, Cassandra insists I call Randy Couture and reschedule our fight. "Part of being a man is knowing when to cancel," she says, handing me my phone.

She's right. I'm in no shape to walk, much less get in a ring with one of the greatest fighters in history. Besides, I've always known that fighting Randy Couture is an immature stunt, more about being able to tell a story than learning anything. It's as stupid as those guys at bars who start fights with military men. Fighting Randy Couture was the desperate plan dreamed up by a man who wanted his son to think he's a man. I've already completed my man mission. I can teach Laszlo what I learned in the army: that he can do far more than he thinks he can, that he can handle stress, that his fears can all be overcome. I know exactly what a mixed martial arts fight feels like from my time on the mat today with John Lewis. I don't have some new man itch that needs to be scratched by Randy Couture's knee. I am finally at peace with my manliness.

But as I'm looking up the number for Dana's office so I can cancel, I think about the sergeant in the army, Jewish Alex Rodriguez, and how he takes skydiving lessons because he's afraid of heights. I might barely be able to move tomorrow, I might get hurt far worse than I did today, and I might not be able to swallow my own spit for weeks, but I have to get in that ring with Randy Couture. It probably won't change me. But at least I won't always be wondering if it would have. I can't run away from yet another fight. I set the alarm on my phone and put it down next to my bed.

I wake up, miraculously, feeling better. Thrillingly better. My throat and neck still hurt badly, but that cloudy feeling has lifted like a broken fever. I am excited until I realize that, unlike in the fight I am about to have, my traumatic five minutes with John Lewis didn't involve any face kneeing. And that Randy Couture weighs forty pounds more than John Lewis.

My dad left a voicemail reminding me to buy a cup to protect my testicles. I direct all of my anxiety into the task. I drive off to Dick's Sporting Goods, figuring they cannot call themselves that and fail to sell cups. I drive by billboard after billboard for much better things to do in Las Vegas besides getting beaten up by a UFC fighter: restaurants, Cirque du Soleil shows, a Barry Manilow concert, watching other people get beaten up by a UFC fighter.

Dick's Sporting Goods is not open yet. I start to panic. If I lose a testicle, I'm going to have to endure a life of "I told you so" from my dad. I am driving way too fast, searching on my phone for sporting goods stores, punching addresses in my GPS, and calling to see if they're open. Eventually, I drive into a tiny strip mall, pre-sweating, and ask the guy where he keeps the cups. When I pay, he asks if I need it for softball. I am so focused I do not even answer him. I am starting to get why this silent-man thing happens.

I pull into a block of warehouses and enter the enormous training gym that Randy Couture owns. At the desk of the Xtreme Couture Mixed Martial Arts Gym, a woman gives me a bunch of releases to sign, each of which includes the word *death*. I ask if I can change into my cup, and she points me toward the bathroom. Halfway through urinating in the toilet, I realize I am in the women's bathroom.

Randy Couture is in his office just to the side of the waiting area with his door open, sitting at his desk and typing. I introduce myself and he just nods back. Randy Couture looks like he's made of stone, like he should play the comic book superhero The Thing. I figure we'll have some kind of friendly pre-fight chat where I charm him and let him know that I'm too great of a guy to hurt. Instead, he leads me to a steel-caged octagon ring without talking. He looks at my cutoff hospital scrub shorts and black T-shirt that says SULTAN OF SNARK and asks if that is what I am going to fight in. Randy is wearing a black T-shirt that says XTREME COUTURE. We both seem appropriately self-branded. I do not see what the issue is.

Randy asks me if there's anywhere he should avoid hitting me. I am tempted to say "everywhere," but instead try to gain some sympathy by telling him about my sore throat. Randy gets very upset about what was done to me. He is not, however, upset that those madmen tried to choke me out. That was a fine idea. He is upset that they did such a poor job of it. It should not have affected my windpipe. He shakes his head at the lack of professionalism, like a contractor looking at what the last contractor did to your house.

After Randy helps me lace on some gloves and knee guards, I ask him if he has headgear, which my dad stressed I'd need as much as the cup. Randy says we won't need headgear since he won't hit me too hard in the face. I fear Randy's idea of too hard might differ from my too hard. I also am a little insulted that he isn't worried that I will hit him too hard.

We get in the ring, and Randy suggests we do a five-minute warm-up. He starts running in circles, so I run in circles right behind him, trying not to get in his way. Then he starts doing pushups. With boxing gloves on. This looks really hard. I do some stretches. Randy Couture is terrifying.

He resets the clock and we get into fighting stances. Or at least he does, and I attempt to copy his stance. Before Randy makes his first move and ends the fight with one blow that will send me to the hospital, I go at him with my fake teep. To my shock, he backs off as my foot flicks toward his midsection. Just like my Muay Thai trainer said he would. I have fooled Randy Couture. I am some kind of stealth black belt, like those old bearded men in Bruce Lee movies. But I forget what I'm supposed to do after the fake teep. Then Randy jabs at me with a fist, and, when our gloves touch, I jump back like it's an electric shock. He's grown wise to my plan.

For nearly one minute, for which I thank Dana and Peter, I am able to use a series of jabs and teeps to stand upright. I get punched and kicked a few times, but Randy holds back the vast majority of his power, maybe about 99 percent, and his punches merely sting. My plan for this fight ending in a few seconds with one punch is ruined. Randy is going to torture me for the whole five minutes.

I want to kick Randy like Peter told me to, but I am too afraid that he'll grab my leg and throw it over his head, sending me flying outside the ring. So instead Randy knees me in the stomach, I bend over in pain, and Randy throws me down to my knees and starts punching me in the face, which I cover with my gloves. It hurts, but he's holding way back, so I don't feel anything like the sting from

Dave Salmoni's punch. Eventually, he gives me a second to stand back up. It's becoming gloriously clear that there will be no face kneeing.

There are, however, a lot of these punches. And they do not feel good. They're enough, in fact, to make me lose my footing and send me to the floor. But on my way down, I use my right arm to punch Randy in the face. Which, luckily, does not seem to make him angry. Most likely because he doesn't notice.

Lying there, I try to grab his legs in order to do something to his legs that I haven't really figured out, but he backs up and lets me get back to my feet. I jab at his face, which he pushes away. Then he pushes me against the chain-link fence, where he starts punching me in the face repeatedly. It definitely hurts. When I try to stop him, he throws me down and sits on my chest, punching me in the face repeatedly. Then he puts me in a headlock, to make it more convenient to punch me in the face.

We're just two minutes in, and I am so tired, I don't mind getting punched in the face, as long as I can rest here in this headlock. It's like when you're driving and you're so tired you don't really care if you get in an accident—you just want to shut your eyes for a second. I just want to relax and get punched.

With one minute left I corral all my energy and, drawing on the training Peter gave me, run in a circle away from Randy. Then I try to get back in the place where I am hugging him and he is punching me in the face, but he keeps pushing me away. It is the longest minute of my life, including when I lost my virginity. When the bell rings, I drop to the mat, exhausted.

I have survived. There was a fight, and I didn't run away. I mean, technically I ran away, but that was a planned, totally acceptable mixed martial arts move.

I am not bleeding. Nothing feels broken. In fact, I feel nothing like the pain I endured yesterday. I am simply more tired than I've ever been from anything. And thrilled to be done with my man tasks.

Randy looks down at me like Muhammad Ali and through his mouth guard says, "Want to go another round?" To which I say, "Fuck no!" I figure he is cleverly taunting me, like Dick Cheney asking his friends if they want to go hunting with him again.

We take off our gloves and knee braces, and sit against the fence. Randy compliments my use of the jab and teep to establish distance. He is sweating and breathing hard, and I am extremely proud that beating me up took some energy. Randy says I was exhausted before the bell rang, that I wasted all my energy on fear and anxiety. Experience calms you and focuses your energy into the fight. "It doesn't feel good to get punched. It doesn't feel good to get kicked. But you get used to it. You learn you're not going to die. You learn to push yourself. You could have gone another round," he says. "That's the point of measuring yourself in competition. You keep finding that wall and pushing it back."

I wish I had gone that second round. I could have made it. And I might have tried some of the moves I spent the day learning instead of my improvisational hugging technique. But our gloves are off, our tape is unraveled, and now it feels too late. I did not expect to feel so depressed about not fighting Randy Couture for a second round. I had ignored one of my own lessons from The List: "Say yes immediately. You can always back out later."

Sitting there, regaining my breath more quickly than I expected now that the fear is gone, I ask Randy if he's been in a lot of fights outside a ring. Never. "My dad has this philosophy where if we wrestled or roughhoused, he'd always make sure I got a little bit hurt. So I knew that someone always got hurt in a fight," he says. "My stepdad used to say, 'You never want to fight. Find a way out until you are backed in a corner and then come out with everything you got.' Even if you win a fight, there's still a downside. There are repercussions." If Randy had been at a stoplight and another guy challenged him to a fight and called him a pussy faggot, he says he would laugh it off.

Randy's dad was a welder, and he grew up in rural Washington

State, where he would hike four miles to fish. He built forts and set up ramps for his bike. Not once, in his description of his childhood, did he use the word *mall*. "I don't know if I were born in another environment if I would have gravitated toward these things," Randy says. Randy also writes poetry and paints, and he doesn't like watching sports. No one, it seems, is purely the stereotype I assumed all real men were.

Laszlo, Randy says, will be his own person, and Dana's plan to make him learn to fight is foolish. "Trying to steer or push him in any way is going to be unsuccessful. He's going to gravitate toward the things he has an affinity for," he says. His own son is about to have his first professional mixed martial arts fight, but he also has a degree in math from the University of Washington. "He could have been playing the cello and if he loved it, that would have been great with me," he says.

I change into my normal, non-cup clothing in the men's bathroom, which is almost as nice as the women's. When I get out Randy is gone. So I drive back to the hotel.

Later that night Randy Couture somehow gets my cell phone number and invites Cassandra, Laszlo, and me to dinner. I am pretty excited, since I have never had a meal with someone who beat me up. We'd reminisce about great punches he landed on my face over soup and other soft foods. I imagine us fighting over who pays the check with teeps and rear naked choke holds to the delight of our servers.

But Cassandra gets upset that I am considering accepting the invite, since we are supposed to have a celebratory dinner together. So I thank Randy for the offer, but tell him I have plans I can't cancel. I have to be with my son. And watch him become whoever it is he's going to become. He doesn't have to be at all like me to make me happy. But now, I won't be upset if he is.

CONCLUSION

Before I started this book, I was fearful, lazy, and soft. Today, I am fearful, lazy, and soft. I wasn't able to change how much I hate conflict, how I can't get angry, how bored I get fixing things, how I greatly prefer not getting punched in the face to getting punched in the face.

But I have changed how I react to those emotional responses. I am not *as* afraid of conflict, not *as* unwilling to screw in a pipe. I have transformed into the kind of guy who will merely run in a circle to get away from a guy who wants to punch me in the face instead of running in a circle while screaming and crying and begging for him to go away.

The country of manliness doesn't feel as foreign. I know its language, its customs, its cultural references. I needed to have these experiences as touchstones to remember and dispel the fear of the unknown. When I talk to men just a little about what they're into, I discover that they're not so different than I am.

I admit that I expected the conclusion of this book to be like the end of *The Wizard of Oz*, where Dorothy realizes she had the power to go home the whole time just by clicking her heels. That's how feminine my metaphors used to be. So if I'd written the ending to this book before starting, it would have gone like this:

> Being a man isn't about fighting or shooting things or throwing a football. It's about the sacrifices we make every moment by not surrendering to childishness: going to work, being faithful, telling the truth when the truth is ugly, taking care of others. That's harder than low crawling under barbed wire while machine guns shoot at you.

But that's not what I learned. I learned that fighting, shooting, and throwing a baseball does make you a man. You change not by deciding, but by doing. We fetishize epiphanies, but only experience changes you. Just like the act of smiling makes you happy, climbing a log tower makes you confident, taking punches makes you tough, repairing your own roof makes you self-reliant, showing your doctor a chigger bite on your dick makes you appreciate dignity. If I did these things every day, I could become a lot like the men I met. But even doing them once made me realize that this change is possible. These experiences made me more confident, if not much more capable. Which would be a dangerous combination as far as home repairs if it weren't for the fact that I am still very lazy.

I've never understood what people mean when they talk about spending time alone to find themselves. It sounds like something you'd say if you think you might be gay or a dentist and want to feel out how the other elves in Santa's workshop would feel about you being gay or a dentist. The idea that we're each a black box we have to unlock always baffled me. I'm the sum of my experiences and my reaction to those experiences. There are so many experiences to have and people to know that I didn't feel the need to spend a lot of time alone in a room working on me. Except for masturbating. And the only thing I found out about myself that way is that I'm not nearly as soft and gentle a lover as I'd like to be.

Because my experiences are now manlier, I'm more of a man. I thought the Boy Scouts would teach me survival skills, but at this point, I don't even remember how to tie a square knot. What I remember is the rebellious freedom of not brushing your teeth, cooking eggs the wrong way, and drinking Coca-Cola that wasn't prepared precisely the way the Coca-Cola Corporation does at its bottling plant. I thought Cassandra's father would teach me a few shortcuts about replacing fixtures or pipes, but instead he showed me that a man could just pound a hole into his own wall, hope he figures out what's wrong, and plaster it up if he doesn't. I thought drinking Scotch would make me fight and say mean things, but it really just made me hug my friend when he told me how much he likes to have sex with fat women.

The happiest single memory from all my adventures is crawling under barbed wire while soldiers shot machine guns over my head, when chaos transformed into stillness. I wasn't happy to have bullets flying over my head. Happiness is overrated. Most of the experiences that have made my life better have been hard and unpleasant. Living on my own and working for a small paper in Paradise, California, for a summer, interviewing people while bent over with stomach pain from anxiety, not only gave me my career, but made every social and professional interaction after that easier. Like every study shows, having a child didn't make me happier—taking care of Laszlo is tiring, boring, and frustrating, and twice has caused my eyes to burn in response to foreign urine. But it has given me fulfillment that I wouldn't trade for a thousand blowjobs. I believe that is the going price of a baby, according to one of those *Freakonomics* books.

I think the reason more than twice as many women than men are on antidepressants, and that women are 60 percent more likely to have an anxiety disorder, is that they're not raised with the same expectations to compete and provide. Every marine I met told me he would have dropped out of basic training at some point if he were allowed to. And not one of them said they weren't glad they finished. Nearly a year later, I still regret not fighting Randy Couture for a second round. I regret not doing that far more than I regret the things I did do. And I fainted daintily into the arms of a soldier.

I'd always been ashamed of being a man. Not without reason. I will never leave Laszlo alone with a male besides Cassandra's dad and my own father, providing he promises to keep Laszlo away from dangerous situations such as food and wine festivals. You don't see a lot of women in jail. You don't have to break up a lot of bar fights between women. And the rare times you do, they are awesome.

We're hairy, smelly, inconsiderate, violent, and will stick our penises in nearly anything. Those are not the kind of qualities listed in ads for roommates. But throughout my manventures, I saw the virtues of masculinity. Our hormones propel us toward challenges. When there are no challenges, we bet on other people's challenges. When we win those bets, we celebrate as if we met those challenges ourselves. It's a pretty fun way to look at life, this confidence and optimism, and it leads us to do all kinds of things we shouldn't be able to do, such as hiking The Reaper with a broken ankle and throwing a tennis ball to a pit bull. Along with all the terrible things men do, we do great things, too, like rescuing people from the terrible things other men try to do to them.

One night, when Laszlo was about a year old, he got sick and coughed so much that Cassandra brought him to the doctor in the morning. The doctor sent him to the closest hospital's emergency room, where they hooked a breathing mask over his face and pumped in steroids to open his lungs. I stayed with him overnight. The next morning he was diagnosed with asthma, which is probably related to his nut allergy. Cassandra looked at him the next morning and said, "We got a lemon."

But he's not. He made our hospital stay fun, laughing over the crib that raised and lowered, pushing a cart around the halls, giggling over the fact that we could order up meals. My favorite photo of him is from that night. His eyes are puffed, his skin is pale, and he's standing up in this industrial metal hospital crib, a pacifier in his mouth, smiling and waving with one hand right into the camera, like a POW trying to piss off his captors as they take his hostage photo. Whenever our little lemon gets sick now, we have to get up with him every two hours and strap this little plastic mask with a duck bill painted on it around his mouth, and sit with him for twenty minutes as the nebulizer pumps medicine into his lungs. He's cool about it, simply reminding us to turn on the TV for him. He knows one of the great joys of being a man is not making a big deal out of big things.

That's the attitude you need to be happy, whether you're in a hospital or being shot at by machine guns. In Friedrich Nietzsche's theory of eternal recurrence, he imagines a demon that tells you that you have to repeat your life over and over for all eternity exactly as you've lived it the first time, and you must get to the point where this is great news:

> My formula for greatness in a human being is amor fati: that one wants nothing to be different, not forward, not backward, not in all eternity. Not merely bear what is necessary, still less conceal it—all idealism is mendaciousness in the face of what is necessary—but love it.

I needed more loving what I have to do, and less avoiding it. I regret that it's taken me until I was almost forty to pursue these man experiences. And my instinct is to make sure Laszlo tries all of this stuff as soon as possible.

I feel bad that my own dad had to watch me avoid all this manliness. All my father ever wants for his birthday is a letter. For this last one, his seventieth birthday, I wrote: "It must have been frustrating that I didn't know how to fight, or stick up for myself, or be aggressive." Nearly every time I've talked to him since, he has brought that sentence up, flummoxed that he could be so misunderstood. He didn't care if I was like him. He was proud of me for all the ways I'm not like him. He calls me the more polished version of him. Though it's not all that hard to seem polished when the original version challenges people to fisticuffs at food and wine shows.

When I asked my dad why he never taught me any man stuff, he mentioned my mom, the 1970s, feminism, and my mom again. "I should have been more assertive on this, and many more things. It was not her fault, but my lack of courage," he said. But while he wishes he introduced me to a few more manly activities, he doesn't regret not pushing them on me: "Trying to get your son interested in what you're interested in might be good for your ego, but it's not good for the child. You see what he likes and what he doesn't like. You can certainly tell with Laszlo by now. You pay more attention to him than anything in your life. You see what lights up his face, and what he wants to do."

When my mom decided to leave my dad, she went to a therapist and told a story about being impressed with my father when they first met. "I was seventeen years old and I was a little spacey, as I still am," she said. "I'll never forget being at his apartment and seeing that he had a file cabinet. I said, 'What do you put in there?' He asked, 'Where do you put your papers?' I said, 'My purses.' " My mom told her therapist that what she loved about my dad was that he made her feel safe in the world. And the therapist made her realize that he didn't. She took care of lots of things herself. She made herself feel safe.

The therapist was wrong, though. My dad does make people feel safe. It's the very best thing about him. My dad still pays for every meal we have together. Sure, he could make me feel successful by letting me pay, which would be generous, too, but instead he's created this unshakable relationship where he is the provider. It makes me know that if I ever need help, he will be the first one there.

My dad gave me the very manliest gift: feeling safe. Because once you feel safe, you can take risks. I want to make Laszlo feel that way. And now I think I might be capable of doing that. Just like my dad did.

I finished that list of life advice for Laszlo that I started when Cassandra got pregnant. It's three pages long and took me two years to finish. It's as smart a piece as I've ever written. And I'm never going to show it to him.

In fact, I don't know why I told you any of this stuff. A man needs to learn for himself.

ACKNOWLEDGMENTS

I could not have written this book without Thomas Pynchon. Thank you, Tom, for making this possible. The wise counsel of Philip Roth has proven invaluable, even if I only read that counsel in his essays and never spoke to him. Likewise, I am grateful for the support of Jonathan Franzen, Nelson Mandela, Oprah Winfrey, and whoever the Pope is right now. That guy gave me the courage I needed to finish the book, if he's into courage. If not, then love or faith or whatever he's into. Or she. Books take a shockingly long time to come out after you write them.

Like most of my ideas, this one wasn't mine. It came from Josh Tyrangiel, who was my editor at *Time* and is my editor at *Businessweek*, and unofficially edited this book. As did Neil Strauss, the guy who wrote *The Game*; Scott Brown, who wrote, among many things, *Gutenberg! The Musical!*; Dan Snierson, who writes for *Entertainment Weekly*; A. J. Jacobs, who writes books like this, only better; Martha Brockenbrough, who edited my column in college and wrote a young-adult novel called *Devine Intervention*; Romesh Ratnesar, who wrote *Tear Down This Wall*, a book about Ronald Reagan; the screenwriter Adam Tobin; Chris Noxon, the author of *Rejuvenile*; my wife @CassandraBarry who writes on Twitter; Walter Isaacson, author of *Steve Jobs*, who not only gave me my career by hiring me at *Time* but read this book the day after I sent it to him to give me comments; my mother, who also edited all my papers in high school; and my father, who, to my great shock, gave amazing advice. I had no idea you could learn so much about character development and structure just from reading Civil War books.

It was also edited by my editor, Editor Ben Greenberg, who is shockingly smart except for the part where he convinced his company to pay me a bunch of money for this book. He also used his expense account to buy me a really nice lunch. Thanks to those *Twilight* books, apparently Ben's bosses don't pay close attention to what he's doing with their money.

Along with Josh, the idea for this book was shaped by Suzanne Gluck, my book agent, who also suckered Grand Central into paying a lot of money for it. David Matthews, the author of *Ace of Spades*, came up with the title. My Facebook friends voted on the first paragraph of this book. I ran spell check.

The army not only let me train with them; they took great photos and videos of it. Dana White and Randy Couture helped me shoot my ass whooping. If you're a cruel, sadistic person, you can see video of all of this at thejoelstein.com.

I am deeply grateful for all the people in this book who let me write about their lives and the things they value, especially because they knew I'd make fun of them. And all the people who let me, but got cut from the final version of this book: Patrón CEO Ed Brown and the Patrón racing team, who let me work in their pit crew; Robert Sloan and the guys at S3 Partners in New York, who taught me how much more badass Wall Street was in the 1980s. And my son, Laszlo, who didn't exactly agree to let me write about him and may have been misled into thinking I was paying attention to him because I'm his father. It would only be right for me to share the vast fortune that Ben Greenberg stupidly gave me for this book with all of them, but that's not going to happen. But I bet if you email Ben, he will give you a good chunk of Grand Central's money.

AUTHOR'S NOTE

The order of some events has been changed in a way that I would characterize as journalistically unethical. And I've got a pretty low bar for journalistic ethics.